T0155638

AGILE PRODUCT AND PROJECT MANAGEMENT

A STEP-BY-STEP GUIDE TO BUILDING THE RIGHT PRODUCTS RIGHT

Mariya Breyter

Apress®

Agile Product and Project Management: A Step-by-Step Guide to Building the Right Products Right

Mariya Breyter
New York, NY, USA

ISBN-13 (pbk): 978-1-4842-8199-4   ISBN-13 (electronic): 978-1-4842-8200-7
https://doi.org/10.1007/978-1-4842-8200-7

Managing Director, Apress Media LLC: Welmoed Spahr
Acquisitions Editor: Susan McDermott
Development Editor: Laura Berendson
Coordinating Editor: Jessica Vakili

Distributed to the book trade worldwide by Springer Science+Business Media New York, 233 Spring Street, 6th Floor, New York, NY 10013. Phone 1-800-SPRINGER, fax (201) 348-4505, e-mail orders-ny@springer-sbm.com, or visit www.springeronline.com. Apress Media, LLC is a California LLC and the sole member (owner) is Springer Science + Business Media Finance Inc (SSBM Finance Inc). SSBM Finance Inc is a **Delaware** corporation.

For information on translations, please e-mail booktranslations@springernature.com; for reprint, paperback, or audio rights, please e-mail bookpermissions@springernature.com.

Apress titles may be purchased in bulk for academic, corporate, or promotional use. eBook versions and licenses are also available for most titles. For more information, reference our Print and eBook Bulk Sales web page at http://www.apress.com/bulk-sales.

Any source code or other supplementary material referenced by the author in this book is available to readers on the Github repository: https://github.com/Apress/Agile-Product-and-Project-Management. For more detailed information, please visit http://www.apress.com/source-code.

Printed on acid-free paper

Contents

About the Author

Dr. Mariya Breyter is an educator and a practitioner who brings 20 years of leadership experience to the Agile and Lean community. Her passion for managing complex business initiatives and delivering superior products to clients through efficient Agile, and Lean processes has produced success after success in companies ranging from Big 4 consulting and Fortune 100 technology, insurance, and financial services firms to startups.

Dr. Breyter has a PhD in computational linguistics from Moscow State University followed by a postdoctorate scholarship at Stanford University. She has built her career optimizing and improving software delivery and instilling Agile and Lean values at multitudes of companies while keeping the primary focus on the people within those processes. The list of her certifications includes CSP, SPC, CSM, PMP, PMI-ACP, ITIL 3.0, Agile Facilitation, and Agile Coaching from ACI. She teaches Agile Project Management and other related courses at New York University.

Dr. Breyter is an Agile project management thought leader and an established speaker at Agile conferences, from the keynote at Product World and a presentation at Lean IT conference in Paris to the Agile Conference in San Diego, CA, and a popular blogger. Her article was included in the Best Agile Articles publication. Dr. Breyter's free educational and coaching websites are popular among the Agile and Lean communities. Dr. Breyter is passionate about diversity, equity, and inclusion, and is a mentor and presenter at the Grace Hopper conference and a co-organizer of the Women in Agile chapter.

About the Technical Reviewer

Moshe Rasis has extensive experience in business and technology leadership, with interest in talent development, coaching, mentoring, and teaching. He has held senior leadership roles with multiple large corporations including Merck, Dun & Bradstreet, the Washington Post, the Federal Reserve Bank, and Dentsu Aegis Network. Primary industries he has worked with include healthcare, financial services, and media. He has expertise in PMO-related disciplines (e.g., PMO leadership, Portfolio/Program/Project delivery, Agile, and traditional methodologies), process and performance improvement frameworks including Six Sigma, and management consulting. He is a lecturer and speaker at national conferences.

Moshe has an MBA from Case Western Reserve University (Operations Management and Information Systems) and a Six Sigma certification; he is a Certified Organizational Coach from New York University, member of ICF (International Coach Federation), Project Management Professional (PMP), and an Agile/SAFe practitioner.

Acknowledgments

I want to thank many thought leaders and supportive friends and colleagues who encouraged me and shared their feedback on the book: Johanna Rothman, my mentor and the author of many groundbreaking books on Agile project management and product delivery; Moshe Rasis, a program management leader and executive coach; Dana Pylayeva, an Agile and Leadership coach; Leila Rao, a Business Agility and Diversity expert; Steven Pae, an NYU Professor and Technology Leader; Andrey Bykov, a product management practitioner who exemplifies customer obsession; my NYU mentors, Professors Edward Kleinert and Larry Mantrone, my NYU students in Agile project management and IT Management Principles; and many other Agile and Lean professionals and colleagues who shaped my experience and extended my horizons. I am grateful to my editor Susan McDermott and to my longtime friend and colleague, and the author of an inspirational book on high-performance teams Alberto Silveira who made this introduction. And most importantly, I am grateful to my husband, Greg, and our sons, Max and Anthony, who tolerated my hours of writing and inspired me throughout my personal and professional journey – without all of you, this book would not be possible.

Preface

The goal of this book is to share my real-life experience in leading and supporting Agile transformations — from both a product and a project perspective. While it was written with my graduate-level course in Agile project management in mind and is well suited as a textbook, I can see the audience as anyone involved in delivering products that delight customers. These products may range from software products in any industry to any deliverable that accomplishes its purpose in sales, marketing, recruiting, service industry — virtually anywhere. Understanding how Agile works in practice is equally important for a student entering the workforce and for an experienced IT, marketing, sales — you name it! — professional who wants to make a difference and build the right products right for their customers.

This idea originated as a means to fill the void in higher education. With over 20 years of industry experience, I was able to evidence multiple examples of how higher education is disconnected from the actual experience of building software products or delivering services. In many instances, students complete their education with advanced technical knowledge and yet without a clear understanding that they are building products for their customers — whether it is a human capital management system for internal customers within their company, data center migration to the cloud to support company's product offerings, or an innovative financial services solution for external customers.

This book is full of IT examples but is not limited to IT. Everything that we deliver day-to-day is a product or a service. The goal of this book is to enable readers (students at the graduate or advanced undergraduate level as well as professionals who want to be equipped with modern knowledge) to succeed in the real world, the world where everything and anything they do professionally leads to the delivery of a product or a service to their customers.

Why This Book?

When I started my professional career in software development in the year 2000, my life was easy: every few weeks, my manager would give me an assignment, and I would be working on it while providing status updates until it was done. Once I had completed it, I would let my manager know, inform the quality assurance team, and have it tested by one of my colleagues on the test team. If everything was fine, I would get a new assignment; in case of any defects, I would proceed to fix them. My job was clear and simple, and I enjoyed providing good quality work on time to my manager. I never thought too much about who was using it and how; I was doing my job diligently day-to-day and taking pride in growing my mastery.

Then, on a bright morning of September 11, 2001, my husband and I were driving to our jobs toward Manhattan from Brooklyn where we lived with our one-year-old son, and we saw papers flying in the air, just regular office papers; then we saw heavy fog over downtown Manhattan – and we turned on the radio to find out whether there is a strong wind or a hurricane coming over. This is how we learned the news. I miraculously made it to my office in Brooklyn right in front of the Brooklyn Bridge, where my colleague and I watched the tragedy. One of the senior managers at the NYC Agency for Child Development, where I was working at that time, was worried whether her son, who worked for New York City Fire Department (FDNY), was safe. Later, we found out he was among the first responders to the September 11 events and never made it back. I felt that my personal duty was to support these people and families of those who suffered in this tragedy, and I applied for a software development position at FDNY.

After an extensive interviewing process, I joined FDNY, and shortly after that, I was promoted to a Java team lead. In parallel, I was assigned as an Oracle Forms and Reports developer (at that time, it was a powerful tool new to the market) to the division that was responsible for pensions and retirement support to the FDNY workforce. Soon, I found out that I was not comfortable working the same way I did before. I was not motivated by designing systems, giving assignments to my staff, and ensuring that those were delivered with high quality. I cared about the people we served. Even though I was responsible for the software delivery team, I no longer found satisfaction in just writing code and building systems; it was important to me what kind of customer experience those systems provided to the people they served. I did not see my job as writing code anymore; I saw it as delivering service to our customers, FDNY employees, the people who made me join FDNY, and whose experience I cared about.

When my team got an assignment to build a Telemetry system for FDNY establishing a workflow of prescribing, approving, and distributing controlled substances by NYC paramedics, I did not call my team to the office for a long kick-off meeting to discuss phases and deliverables, their own roles, or the new technology stack. Instead, I called the paramedic running this team and asked if we could shadow them in the work they are doing every day in the Telemetry office in Queens, NY. And this is how it started. My team and I would take our trips to the telemetry station, observe, then go back to the office to design and build, go back the next day to validate screens and sample workflows with paramedics, get their feedback, and go back to the office to make changes based on what we learned. Their existing system was slow and unreliable; it was based on email and had a heavy paper trail to maintain. We learned about their challenges and decided that it had to be a streamlined workflow with proper tracking, and most importantly, the cycle time from when the request from the field comes in till the decision is made by a qualified medical professional and approved via the required channels had to be limited to seconds because it was literally a matter of life and death. We were not motivated by writing clean code; we were motivated by saving people's lives, by thinking of those whose lives depend on us. We delivered the minimum viable product, or MVP (at that time, we were not familiar with this term), Telemetry system in three months to the highest satisfaction of our stakeholders and got the FDNY award for this application.

Frankly, at that time, we were not aware that the world was already open to these principles. The Agile Manifesto was already created in 2001. The understanding of customer interaction, the value of incremental delivery, the concept of MVP, and the benefit of developers working with the business and their customers were already known to the software world. However, my personal journey to Agile software development taught me these values through my own life experience, and it became my life goal to share them with others.

In over 20 subsequent years of my professional career, having led organizations in their digital transformations and changing the ways thousands of people deliver IT products to the customers, I have not been more proud of the work that my team has done. Nowadays, when I interview software developers and ask them what their biggest professional passion is, I hear a lot that they enjoy learning about new technologies, writing elegant code, implementing cutting-edge IT solutions, or designing new cloud infrastructure, but frequently, they are missing the most important part of software delivery – the product we are building and the customers we are building it for. This is the passion I pass to my students of Agile Project Management and Principles of IT Project Management at New York University – passion for Building the Right Product along with Building the Product Right – and now I am passing it to you.

Why Today?

Despite Agile software delivery becoming a mainstream way of delivering IT products and services to customers, our higher education institutions are still significantly behind in the way we educate our students. I am proud to be part of a team that makes an effort to build education around customer-centricity and product-based thinking. The concepts of design thinking, validated learning, user research, and incremental delivery are now included in college curricula around the world.

However, this process is still slow, and many higher education organizations are still teaching their IT students based on traditional concepts of phased software delivery (also referred to as "Waterfall" because of the sequential nature of IT delivery – Conception, Initiation, Analysis, Design, Construction, Testing, Production/Implementation, and Maintenance) and ignoring that modern technology supports rapid delivery. There is no need to wait until the analysis is completed to design the system and no need to wait until the system is fully designed to start building functionality for users to test and provide their feedback about.

Frequently, college graduates come to job interviews with high grades but without a clear understanding of how customer needs impact the software delivery process. They are well prepared to answer questions about multitenant databases, architectural design principles, microservices architecture, cybersecurity, authentication, and machine learning, but they are not aware of the nature of a cross-functional team or the value of collaboration in IT delivery. Instead of thinking end to end from envisioning their system to the experience their customers have and the value these systems provide to the customers, they think code, testing, security, automation – all the right topics, but definitely not sufficient for IT professionals nowadays.

We are not designing systems for the sake of building them. We do it to provide value to our customers in order to empower them in solving their regular challenges – whether it is to buy food from a store, build a house, give education to their children, or manage their life's savings. We build systems for people, and the goal of this book is to facilitate and expedite the transition from an execution-focused approach to a customer-centric one.

This ability proves to be career changing nowadays. In my experience, IT professionals who employ product-based thinking, who care about their customer experience, and who understand the need for incremental delivery and risk management have a significantly higher chance to advance in their fundamental knowledge as well as in their career progression. While there are thousands of IT professionals who have advanced technical skills, the understanding of customer value and team-based delivery proves to be a career-changing differentiator in getting job interviews and landing the best job opportunities. Those IT professionals who understand both how to build the right product and how to build it right have a career advantage over those who are only focused on the technical aspects of IT delivery.

Who Is This Book For?

This book is meant for graduate students and early career professionals who want to advance their careers to the next level. While the primary audience is graduate students in computer science and engineering, every professional will benefit from getting themselves familiar with the concepts described in this book. The examples used in this book are primarily related (though not exclusively) to computer science and IT, including software products and services, IT operations, computer hardware, and telecommunications. It touches multiple industries and provides real-world examples in IT and beyond.

There are two ways to read this book. First, it is a textbook. The concepts provided here cover product envisioning (building the right product) and delivery (building the product right), intertwined in the concept of incremental and iterative delivery. Each chapter is built on previous ones and is equipped with learning materials, tips, references, and case studies. If you are a college professor, you can take this as a textbook for your IT project management, Agile delivery, or software delivery life cycle (SDLC) course – it has questions, quizzes, and a list of material for extra studies. There is a project throughout this course where each assignment builds on the concept learned in class. If you are a student, there are templates, concepts, and techniques that will prepare you for the real world of IT delivery. This book will also prepare you for a job interview and establish foundations for your success in the workplace.

Second, this book can be used for self-learning, whether sequentially or as a reference book. In the Glossary, we provide references to major concepts related to modern software delivery. For project managers, IT managers, or HR professionals, this book provides an interactive and powerful guide to mastering complex concepts of IT delivery in a simple, concise, and logical way. If you are an Agile practitioner, this is a way to get a comprehensive overview of this important area of study as well as get helpful tips on common challenges, such as getting leadership buy-in for Agile transformation or which framework to pick for your enterprise. If you are a new Scrum Master or a development lead on a newly created Agile team, this book will provide a solid foundation for your Agile thinking.

It is not a replacement for your software delivery or IT project management textbook, even though it can be successfully used for either course – it is a new book for a modern generation of software engineers, IT professionals, and forward-thinking and customer-centric leaders.

The Legend

Throughout the book, we use different ways of designating sections that will help you with navigation. The following legend will help you with navigating those:

Image	Description
	Key quote
	Group discussion topic (for group studies) or analysis item (for other readers)
	Tips for practitioners reflecting experience or real-life situations
	Free online materials to watch from multiple recommended sources not related to this book
Simulation Project	The Simulation Project is an ongoing assignment throughout the book that builds on the content of each chapter
Self-Review Quiz	Self-review quizzes provided in Appendix B are recommended for self-learners and students. The answers are provided at the end of each quiz
References [ ]	The sources referenced in the chapter
Videos, books, and online sources for in-depth learning ( )	The sources recommended for in-depth learning to those who want to know more about the topic described in each chapter

Disclaimer

None of the content of this book directly reflects on my employment experience, past or current. Any company-specific examples and case studies referenced in this book are either fictional or based on public sources.

Building the Right IT Product

The Role of Project and Product Management in Software Delivery and IT Services

This chapter covers the history of project management as a profession and provides an overview of the primary delivery frameworks.

What Does It Mean to "Deliver" Software and IT Services?

A product is not possible without its customers. Not only are they expected to purchase and use it once it has been built, but they can also provide input and even inspiration during the design process. This applies equally to software

© Mariya Breyter 2022
M. Breyter, *Agile Product and Project Management*,
https://doi.org/10.1007/978-1-4842-8200-7_1

products and IT services. Nowadays, engineers and IT professionals are not simply handed a hundred-page requirements document followed by many days of individual coding. They must instead define their products and services in full collaboration with their customers and business stakeholders.

However, these collaborations are not "ad hoc" interactions. They have to be planned, managed, and delivered to mutual satisfaction. This is achieved through product and project management, which covers end-to-end delivery (in software, this is referred to specifically as SDLC – software delivery life cycle) – from envisioning the products through execution, customer delivery, and ongoing support and maintenance. IT professionals must be full participants in this process. They engage in customer interactions, provide their input into features that are being delivered, use customer feedback to fine-tune their deliverables, and continuously improve both the products and the way they are being built.

Yet according to a 2019 Product Management survey from Gartner, only 55% of all product launches take place on schedule [1], and the Product Development and Management Association (PDMA) points out that the product failure rate in software and IT services is 39% [2]. It is up to future software engineers and IT professionals to improve this success rate and more effectively manage expectations with their stakeholders. The purpose of this book is to equip them with the means to do so.

First, some definitions: By "delivering software products and IT services," we mean the *ability* of IT professionals to properly understand, interpret, and address customer needs by providing high-quality, adequately priced products and services. We also refer to this process as "delivering customer value."

When we use the term "building products," we refer to the *features and functionality* of the software that is being built or the service being provided. This also includes peripheral areas such as marketing and pricing the product, and the professionals who specialize in this particular area of delivery are called product managers. When we refer to *how* these products are being built or how the services are being provided, we call this project management. However, you do not need to be a product manager or project manager to take an active role in ensuring customer success. IT professionals too have a role to play in delivering solutions to customers.

The History of Project Management as a Profession

The first recorded project in the history of project management goes back to 2570 BC, when the Great Pyramid of Giza was completed. Ancient records show that there were managers for each of the four faces of the pyramid. Each of them covered planning, execution, and control in managing their part of the project. Similarly, there are records confirming that the project managers of the Great Wall of China, constructed over 2500 years, starting in the 7th century BC and completed in the mid-1800s, used soldiers, common people, and criminals and organized them by their deliverables to complete the project [5].

It was only in the 20th century that traditional project management became a profession and a formalized school of study. In the 1910s, Henry Laurence Gantt, an American mechanical engineer and management consultant, produced a concept of a graphic representation of tasks across time. His chart – now known as a Gantt chart – clearly illustrated a project's individual activities and deliverables and allowed visual indications of how well the work was progressing, who was responsible for it, and when and where action would be necessary to keep the project on schedule (see Figure 1-1).

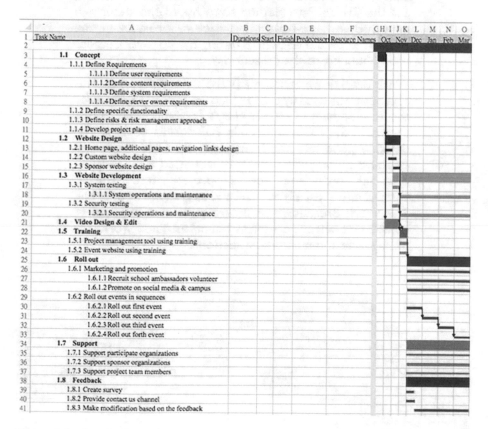

Figure 1-1. Sample Gantt chart

A significant leap forward in professional project management happened in the 1960s when a number of new techniques were introduced by industry leaders. These included the following:

1. Critical Path Method (CPM): This technique, developed by the DuPont Corporation, was used to define a project's duration by sequencing all of its activities and identifying which sequences had the least amount of scheduling flexibility. The intent was to keep this sequence of activities (referred to as "the critical path") on track. This technique allowed DuPont to manage the process of shutting down its many large chemical plants for maintenance and restarting them on time once the maintenance was complete. This technique allowed the company to save millions of dollars per shutdown project, and the Critical Path Method contributed enormously to many other large-scale infrastructure projects in the United States and elsewhere during the postwar decades and continuing to the present day.

2. Work Breakdown Structure (WBS): See Figure 1-2. This approach was used by the US Department of Defense for the development of the US Navy's Polaris nuclear missile project in the 1950s and 1960s. Polaris was a submarine-based weapon that helped usher in the Cold War. In an era before computers, WBS represented a deliverable-oriented breakdown of a project into smaller components – usually as small and as granular as possible. The Work Breakdown Structure remains a key project component since it organizes teams' assigned work into manageable and measurable sections.

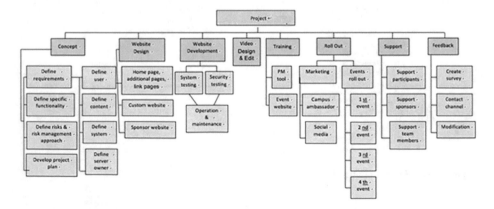

Figure 1-2. Sample Work Breakdown Structure

3. Program Evaluation and Review Technique (PERT analysis): This method for planning or coordinating large-scale projects is used as a management planning control chart. These charts list all major elements and their corresponding interrelations. The goal is to identify critical dependencies between these elements. In its implementation, PERT analysis uses CPM to define schedules for deliverables and related dependencies.

Throughout the decades of the 20th century, project management allowed for significant savings and greater efficiency and was highly regarded by major industry players. In the 1960s, project management was launched as an official profession, with responsibilities for organizing, planning, executing, and delivering products and services. In 1969, the Project Management Institute (PMI), a nonprofit professional organization dedicated to advancing the practice, science, and profession of project management, was launched in the United States.

Almost immediately, project management practices were applied to the emerging software engineering profession, and industry-agnostic standards were developed. In the 1980s, the PMI created a guidebook known as the Project Management Body of Knowledge (PMBOK). In Europe, a parallel project management approach was developed called the PRINCE Methodology, and this became the standard for all government and information system projects in the UK from 1989. In essence, the difference between the two is that PMI focuses on tasks (activities) first while PRINCE focuses on roles (people). However, both adhere to a discipline of effective and thorough planning and communication to ensure on-time, on-budget, and on-scope delivery. These naturally became important concepts for IT professionals in all specializations.

The seminal book on software engineering and project management, *The Mythical Man-Month: Essays on Software Engineering* by Fred Brooks (1), discussed the insights for managing complex software projects based on the importance of meeting timelines in software delivery. The book presented thought-provoking concepts, which are well understood nowadays, such as the notion that adding people to a delayed project only makes it slower. This statement is now known as the Brooks' law.

As Brooks put it, "while it takes one woman nine months to make a baby, nine women can't make a baby in one month." This was one of the first attempts to show that IT project management is in no way similar to many other industries that require repeatable work delivered with minimum variation and maximum efficiency. Software project management is an art as much as a science and needs to be managed with a full understanding of its unique complexities and challenges.

"Adding manpower to a late software project makes it later."

— Frederick P. Brooks Jr., The Mythical Man-Month: Essays on Software Engineering (1)

Lean

In parallel to project management, the concept called *Lean manufacturing* was becoming increasingly popular in heavy industry, and it too was to become a staple of IT and influential in the development of SDLC, DevOps, and continuous testing. Lean manufacturing is based on rigorous *process thinking* in manufacturing, and as such, it has its roots in the construction of the Arsenal in Venice in the 1450s, where the first highly efficient production line was implemented for shipbuilding. The Arsenal employed over 1,600 people, and the production was divided into three main stages: (a) framing, (b) planking and cabins, and (c) final assembly. The Arsenal used standardized, interchangeable parts, streamlined the assembly line, and enabled minimal handling of materials during each stage of production.

In the early 20th century, Henry Ford implemented a similar streamlined and highly efficient process in car building. He modernized the car assembly line and grouped assembly activities by steps while making an inventory of parts available by each process group. This process of increasing efficiency and minimizing "waste" during production was adopted by Toyota manufacturing and allowed for the efficient mass production of high-quality cars after World War II (2). The Toyota Production System was brought to the attention of the global community by American writer and management consultant Peter Drucker. It included five important concepts (see Figure 1-3):

1. Define value: Value is defined by the customer's needs for a specific product. All activities that do not add value are defined as "waste" and should be avoided.

2. Map value stream: A value stream is a set of processes involved in taking a specific product from raw materials to customer delivery. The process of identifying the value stream, referred to as Value Stream Mapping (VSM), is an important first step in the approach to any delivery or optimization effort.

3. Optimize flow: The flow defines the sequence of processes and their efficiency in order to ensure that the work being done to deliver the product or service will flow smoothly from one step to another without

interruptions or delays. As a result, time to market improves, and efficiency increases. This is a simple but extremely hard-to-implement concept. In his novel about transformative management style using the concept of flow and the flow-based theory of constraints, Eliyahu M. Goldratt (3) tells a story of a plant manager who is using the flow-based theory of constraints to improve performance and save the plant in 90 days, or it will be closed by corporate headquarters with hundreds of jobs lost. The *theory of constraints* is a methodology that takes a scientific approach to improvement. It is based on identifying the most important limiting factor (i.e., constraint, referred to as a "bottleneck" in manufacturing) that stands in the way of achieving a goal and then systematically improving that constraint (the "weakest link in the chain") until it is no longer the limiting factor. This approach is based on a hypothesis that every complex system consists of multiple linked activities, one of which (the bottleneck) acts as a constraint for the entire system.

4. Establish pull: There are multiple manifestations of "waste" in the delivery life cycle, and overproduction is a major root of inefficiency. Work is pulled step by step based on capacity rather than pushed to the next step in the value stream upon completion of the prior step. This ensures that spare parts, as well as manufactured items, are "pulled" by the next step in the value chain by the customer for the finished product when they need those. This is known as "just-in-time" manufacturing or delivery vs. creating expensive inventory that needs to be managed.

5. Pursue perfection: Despite all the significant gains that Lean thinking brought to manufacturing, it is important to understand that Lean is not a static system. The concept of continuous improvement was at the center of Lean. Continuous reflection and retrospection are the foundation of Lean thinking. There is a well-known quote from one of Toyota's top managers who was asked why they are keeping their production facilities open for tours and whether they are concerned that their competitors will copy their practices. The response was that the competitors would copy today's practices, and tomorrow, Toyota will be already doing things differently. The concepts of personal accountability, respect for people, lightweight leadership, continuous improvement, and delivery of value to customers made Lean more than a project management method. It became a mindset.

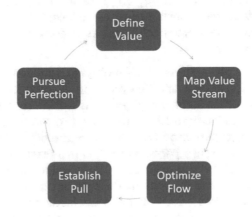

Figure 1-3. Toyota Production System Summary

Despite its apparent simplicity, Lean thinking was a revolutionary method of delivering products. In his book *Smarter Faster Better: The Transformative Power of Real Productivity* [3], New York Times bestselling author Charles Duhigg describes the transformation that was brought by Lean practices to a GM production plant in Fremont, CA, in 1982. At that time, the plant earned a reputation as the worst auto factory in the world – the employees were continuously absent from work due primarily to drinking issues, and the quality was so low that one out of every two finished cars had major problems. Two years later, the plant was reopened in partnership with Toyota and adopted Toyota's Lean manufacturing framework, the Toyota Production System (TPS). The author describes multiple mindset changes that were adopted:

- Decisions were pushed to the lower level: Workers on the assembly line took ownership over identifying and addressing any mistakes – quality gaps, efficiency opportunities, assembly issues, etc.

- Individual accountability: There were "Andon cords" (signaling pull cords) installed along production lines, which every worker was encouraged to pull to halt the production line whenever they saw a defective product. Stoppages of this sort cost the factory $15,000 a minute (over $43,000 a minute in 2022 dollars), but it trusted employees with making the right decision to address quality issues and avoid waste.

As a result of TPS adoption, by 1986, productivity had doubled, and absenteeism was down from 25% to 3%.

Topic for Group Discussion   Split into five groups and have each group discuss one of the concepts described before. How does it apply to IT services and software delivery? Does it resonate with you? Can you think of any real-world examples?

"As workers were empowered to make more choices, their motivation skyrocketed."

— Charles Duhigg, Smarter Faster Better: The Secrets of Being Productive in Life and Business [3]

Even though Lean as a concept originated in manufacturing, it is equally applicable to information technologies. In their book *Lean Software Development*, Mary and Tom Poppendieck have shown IT professionals how to achieve breakthrough quality, savings, speed, and business value by adopting Lean principles that have already revolutionized manufacturing [4]. These principles include the following:

1. Eliminate waste.

2. Amplify learning.

3. Decide as late as possible.

4. Deliver as fast as possible.

5. Empower the team.

6. Build quality in.

7. See the whole.

Based on these principles, they created a concept of Lean software development, which focuses on the following areas:

1. Build the right thing: Understand and deliver real value to real customers.

2. Build it fast: Dramatically reduce the lead time from customer need to delivered solution.

3. Build the thing right: Guarantee quality and speed with automated testing, integration, and deployment.

4. Learn through feedback: Evolve the product design based on early and frequent end-to-end feedback [4].

The concept of optimizing software development and IT service delivery over the entire value stream became the foundation of Lean software delivery. Companies applied classic Lean tools such as value stream mapping and flow-based tools to increase flow efficiency. Specifically, these included the theory of constraints (TOC), building quality "in" (test automation) to increase the efficiency of software delivery and IT services. Even more importantly, Mary and Tom Poppendieck focused on the importance of building the right products vs. building the product right. This distinction allowed for the emergence of a profession that was parallel to project management, called product management. While the project manager was responsible for "how" to deliver the project, the product manager was responsible for "what" needs to be built.

"In a three-year period, we had 78 projects, and 77 of them were delivered on time, on budget, and in scope. Then I surveyed the customers and found out that none of them was happy!"

— Mary and Tom Poppendieck, Lean Software
Development [4]

Topic for a Group Discussion   How do you distinguish between building the right product and building the product right? Think of specific examples: defining budget for a new project, deciding on the features that address customer needs, automating testing to improve the quality of the software, moving systems to the cloud to improve reliability – which ones are examples of building the right product and which ones are examples of building the product right? Why are both concepts important? Which one do you find more important and why?

Agile

The advancement of traditional project management and the power of Lean thinking made the emergence of Agile software delivery only a matter of time. Like many great ideas, Agile was born out of frustration. In February 2001, 17 software practitioners met at the Snowbird ski resort in Utah. They were all thought leaders in software delivery. They were also all frustrated about the inefficiency of software delivery management.

In the 1990s, software projects were managed the same way as construction projects, which is to say sequentially. For example, to build a house, you first need to create and finalize designs and blueprints, prepare the construction site, pour the foundation and complete framing, then install plumbing and electrical and complete drywall, install interior trim, and so forth. You cannot start plumbing until your foundation is complete. The same project management principles were applied to software delivery – phase by phase. It took weeks to write requirements. After those were signed off, the software design phase started, which took several more weeks. Then, the development would start. It would go on for a few months, followed by testing.

During testing, bugs were found, which would require a significant amount of rework by developers and sometimes would even necessitate a redesign. When testing was completed, users would get engaged in user acceptance testing, and frequently, they would say "this is not what we envisioned" or "this is what we wanted a year ago when we started this project, but it is no longer valid," and the whole project would have to start from scratch or just get canceled.

The 17 people in Utah challenged the most fundamental concept in this traditional, so-called "Waterfall" delivery method. Their reasoning was that in software delivery, it should take only hours, if not minutes, to alter code, and if the users were able to review the result right away, the amount of rework would significantly decrease. Software delivery is different from house construction, so why should construction rules apply to software delivery?

Meanwhile, an average project was measured in years rather than months or weeks. In some industries, such as aerospace and defense, sometimes, it took 10, 15, or even 20 years to develop a complex system before it went into production. For example, the Space Shuttle program launched in 1982 used information and processing technologies from the 1960s.

While the Waterfall model was widely adopted, alternatives were already emerging. The 17 signatories of the *Agile Manifesto* had already been experimenting with different frameworks that are now united under the Agile umbrella. Jeff Sutherland and Ken Schwaber invented the Scrum process in the early 1990s. The term came from the British game of rugby and referred to a team working toward a common goal. Kent Beck developed extreme programming during his work at Chrysler and published his findings in 1999.

The group of 17 practitioners did not challenge tools or techniques; they came together to solve a fundamental problem, which had a root cause in obsolete thinking. To do so, they suggested a new set of values and principles, which they called the *Agile Manifesto*.

They spoke about valuing individuals and interactions over processes and tools and valuing working software over comprehensive documentation. For example, why should negotiation over hundreds of pages of a requirements specification take 30–50% of project delivery time if it would just take hours to build the feature, show it to the customer, and receive direct and immediate feedback? Why would it take weeks to approve project plans, which became obsolete the moment a new requirement came in, which happened in 89–93% of all software projects? As intuitive as it seems now, this was a major breakthrough in thinking about software delivery.

In writing the *Agile Manifesto* (4), the authors came up with four values and 12 principles of software delivery:

Manifesto for Agile Software Development

"We are uncovering better ways of developing software by doing it and helping others do it. Through this work, we have come to value:

- Individuals and interactions over processes and tools

- Working software over comprehensive documentation

- Customer collaboration over contract negotiation

- Responding to change over following a plan

That is, while there is value in the items onthe right, we value the items on the left more.''

The *Agile Manifesto* did not materialize out of thin air. One of the major sources of Agile is Lean thinking. If we consider the Lean framework based on customer value, value stream, continuous improvement, and collaboration, these principles will sound familiar:

- "Working software is the primary measure of progress."
- "Deliver working software frequently, from a couple of weeks to a couple of months, with reference to the shorter timescale."
- "Welcome changing requirements, even late in development. Agile processes harness change for the customer's competitive advantage."
- "Maintain simplicity – the art of maximizing the amount of work not done."

The Agile Manifesto took Lean thinking to the next level. It added or emphasized several important components such as teamwork and self-organizing teams focused on end-to-end value delivery

- "The best architectures, requirements, and designs emerge from self-organizing teams."

They took the quality-in concept well known from Lean to a new level:

- "Continuous attention to technical excellence and good design enhances agility."

They put the customer in the center of software delivery, rather than as a recipient of the end result:

- "Our highest priority is to satisfy the customer through early and continuous delivery of valuable software."
- "Businesspeople and developers must work together daily throughout the project."

They paid a lot of attention to people vs. process and face-to-face communication vs. documentation:

- "Build projects around motivated individuals. Give them the environment and support they need, and trust them to get the job done."
- "The most efficient and effective method of conveying information to and within a team is face-to-face conversation."

They also addressed major challenges of the Waterfall software delivery, such as inconsistent utilization. In Waterfall, people were allocated to projects rather than working together continuously as a long-standing team. Allocation usually happened at the beginning of the project, meaning that testers sat idle for weeks until the coding was completed. Even worse, capacity management was done by project, so people were working on multiple projects at a time, lacking predictable work management and losing time at context switching. They were overloaded toward the end of the project while not being utilized at the beginning of it.

The Agile Manifesto addressed these challenges by the following principles:

- "Promoting sustainable development, meaning the sponsors, developers, and users should be able to maintain a constant pace indefinitely."

- "Allowing teams to reflect, at regular intervals, on how to become more effective and then encouraging them to adjust their activities accordingly." (4)

🔅 **Tip**   Agile Manifesto is the foundation of Agile thinking. Many practitioners refer to Agile as a mindset or culture because it fundamentally changed the way that software delivery was approached. By thinking of a customer as an end point of value delivery, Agile introduced a concept of customer-centricity and enabled IT professionals to interact with the customer throughout the delivery process. From a project management perspective, Agile is a framework (a structured approach defined by values and principles) that is different from the way a traditional project is defined by the Project Management Institute (PMI) and documented in the Body of Knowledge (PMBOK). To embrace this difference, the PMI also published a Software Extension to PMBOK (5), and now the latest editions of PMBOK cover Agile delivery as well.

Nowadays, Agile is no longer specific to software delivery or IT management. Customer-centricity, self-organizing teams, and iterative delivery with a short feedback loop are equally essential in delivering value to any customer in any industry. Agile has been adopted by airlines, financial services companies, human capital divisions, leadership teams of major companies, and many others. When we talk about Agile, we think about iterative delivery of value to customers; we think about the collaboration between business, engineering, and the customer; we think about a short feedback loop to learn directly from the customer and to continuously improve the products that we build or the services we deliver. We think about teamwork based on optimizing end-to-end delivery flow while empowering people and teams. It is important to realize that Agile is not just project management – it's a different mindset. Agile brings in a mindset of collaboration, value delivery, and continuous improvement via short feedback loops.

From this point of view, Agile is being used as an "umbrella" term for a number of different frameworks used in software delivery and IT management. (See Figure 1-4.) Some of these frameworks are listed as follows:

1. Scrum: The most popular Agile framework. It is designed for small cross-functional software delivery teams who break their work into goals, which can be completed within timeboxed iterations. These one-to-four-week iterations are called Sprints. As mentioned earlier, Scrum takes its name from the sport of rugby, emphasizing the team-based nature of work performed.

2. Extreme programming (XP): An Agile software development framework that has the goal of delivering high-quality software with high responsiveness to changing customer requirements. XP is focused on engineering practices for software development. The term "extreme programming" is based on the concept of taking the most beneficial aspects of traditional software practices, such as code review and refactoring, to extreme levels. For example, code refactoring is a beneficial software development practice, and when taken to the extreme, code is continuously being refactored. Peer reviews are beneficial practices, and when taken to the extreme, it results in the practice of "pair programming," which is a situation in which two developers collaborate in code delivery.

3. Kanban — literally translated from Japanese as "visual board" — is a Lean method of highly visual workflow management. Most teams practicing Lean use Kanban to visualize and manage their work. Kanban promotes continuous collaboration and encourages ongoing learning and improvement through workflow optimization.

4. OSAM (Optum Scaled Agile Model), DSDM (Dynamic Systems Development Method), FDD (Feature-Driven Development), Crystal, and RUP (Rational Unified Process) are proprietary Agile frameworks focusing on different aspects of Agile software delivery with a lower rate of adoption.

5. There are a number of competing Agile frameworks related to the adoption of Agile within large organizations with multiple software delivery teams, frequently with hundreds of people working on the same product. These frameworks include SAFe (Scaled Agile Framework), LeSS (Large-Scale Scrum), DAD (Disciplined Agile Delivery), and Scrum@Scale. We will discuss these in Chapter 10.

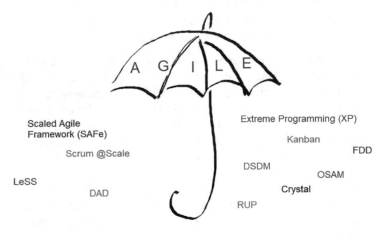

Figure 1-4. Agile Frameworks

💡 **Tip** In the traditional project management, a project is defined as a temporary endeavor undertaken to create a unique product, service, or result. A project is temporary in that it has a defined beginning and end in time and therefore defined scope and resources. Contrary to the traditional project management, in the Agile framework, we are talking about a product or a service. Products have their own life cycle from envisioning to sunsetting, but there are no predefined timelines since this is determined by customer demand.

While Lean works traditionally well in manufacturing where similar products are being delivered (e.g., car manufacturing), it was a common opinion that Waterfall is best for large projects such as airplane assembly and software delivery, while Agile works best for smaller, less risky projects. However, this opinion has been recently invalidated. Companies like Boeing, SpaceX, and Tesla use Agile successfully for complex projects with elevated risk levels, such as space shuttles, cars, and airplanes. Nokia Network adopted Large-Scale Scrum (LeSS), while UnitedHealth Group and developed its own Optum

Scaled Agile Model (OSAM) based on the Scaled Agile Framework (SAFe). Other examples of successful SAFe adoption include Porshe, CVS, Deutsche Telekom, Kaiser Permanente, and US Airforce [6].

In this textbook, we will discuss Agile frameworks through the prism of software delivery and IT services from two points of view:

1. Building the RIGHT product: Software product engineering principles and IT service delivery. We will discuss the concept of a product in IT, review examples, and discuss how design thinking applies to IT product delivery. In this part, we will cover Lean startup principles and the use of personas, validated learning, and experimentation when prioritizing product features and building product roadmaps. We will discuss modern principles of requirements management based on customer journeys, scenarios, and user stories. Finally, we will discuss feature prioritization and user research principles to define the priority of feature delivery.

2. Building the product RIGHT: Agile principles of software delivery, including Scrum, Kanban, and extreme programming. We will discuss the importance of planning in Agile and how teams achieve accuracy in their planning efforts by using estimation techniques. We will cover Sprint-based planning as well as continuous flow and limiting work in progress using Kanban. In conclusion, we will review scaled Agile practices for large organizations and discuss your professional growth through certifications and further learning. We will review IT operations, including DevOps and customer support function, as well as software architecture, cloud software, system security, test automation and behavior-driven test principles, and best practices of code management and review.

With that, let's start the journey, but just prior to that, let's review the topics we covered.

Key Points

1. Nowadays, software engineers and IT professionals are fully engaged in defining the products and services they create in full collaboration with their customers and business stakeholders. This is done via product and project management, covering end-to-end delivery — from envisioning the products through execution, customer delivery, and ongoing support and maintenance.

2. Project management is an important competency for IT professionals. The first records of the history of project management go back to 2570 BC, when the Great Pyramid of Giza was completed. In the 20th century, traditional project management became a profession responsible for defining key deliverables, timelines, and costs. Important methods and techniques in traditional project management include the Gantt chart, Critical Path Method (CPM), Work Breakdown Structure (WBS), and Program Evaluation and Review Technique (PERT analysis).

3. Since the 1960s, project management practices were applied to the emerging software engineering profession, and industry-agnostic standards were developed. In the 1980s, the PMI created the first Guide to the Project Management Body of Knowledge (PMBOK Guide), followed by PRINCE Methodology, which became the standard for all government and information system projects in the UK from 1989 onward. The idea of on-time, on-budget, and on-scope delivery became an important concept for IT professionals of all specializations.

4. Traditional project management applied to software delivery is informally referred to as "Waterfall" due to the visual representation of the sequential phases in software delivery, that is, requirement analysis, system design, implementation, system testing, deployment, and maintenance.

5. Parallel to the traditional project management, software delivery forward thinkers started adopting concepts introduced by Lean manufacturing that were implemented and enhanced by the Toyota Production System (TPS). The concept of optimizing software development and IT service delivery over the entire value stream became the foundation of Lean software delivery. Multiple companies applied classic Lean tools – value stream mapping, flow-based tools to increase flow efficiency, such as the theory of constraints (TOC), and building quality "in" (test automation) to increase the efficiency of software delivery and IT services.

6. The advancement of traditional project management and the power of Lean thinking made the emergence of Agile software delivery only a matter of time. The Agile approach challenged the most fundamental concept of the "Waterfall" delivery method. Their reasoning was that in software delivery, it would take only hours, if not minutes, to alter code, and if the user would be able to review the result right away, the amount of rework would significantly decrease.

7. The *Agile Manifesto*, created in 2001, defined four values and 12 principles of software delivery. It specified the importance of individuals and interactions over processes and tools, working software over comprehensive documentation, customer collaboration over contract negotiation, and responding to change over following a plan (4).

8. Agile is an iterative and incremental (feature by feature) delivery framework for IT services and software products. Once a releasable functionality is developed, it can be released to the customer for immediate feedback, which informs subsequent deliverables. In Agile, there is no need to wait for each of the phases to be completed to start a new one. To achieve this, Agile underlines the value of self-organizing cross-functional delivery teams where team members collaborate with each other, their business stakeholders, and their customers in creating high-quality outcomes and establishing a continuous feedback loop with the customers. By doing so, it puts the customer in the center of software delivery rather than as a recipient of the end result.

9. Agile is a framework that provides values and principles rather than a methodology. Within the Agile framework, there are multiple methodologies, techniques, and approaches to managing software delivery, including Scrum, extreme programming (XP), and Kanban. Agile is not just applicable to software delivery – it applies to other areas of value delivery (e.g., marketing, sales, human capital) and to whole organizations with thousands of people involved in value delivery. These frameworks are referred to as scaled Agile, and some examples include SAFe (Scaled Agile Framework), LeSS (Large-Scale Scrum), DAD (Disciplined Agile Delivery), and Scrum@Scale.

10. The two most important topics of IT services and software delivery include the definition of the product that addresses customer need ("building the RIGHT product") and managing software deliverables with complete transparency, high quality, and maximum predictability ("building the product RIGHT").

Starting with Why

This chapter covers the first and most important aspect of building the RIGHT products and introduces the OKRs (Objectives and Key Results) framework as a part of project management. It outlines why every project has to align with organizational objectives and shows how these objectives are used to measure project success.

Introduction

In Chapter 1, we covered the history of project management and discussed the concept of project management as it relates to IT services and software delivery. Since the 20th century, project management has been a competency and an area of knowledge that is widely adopted in IT. Whether teams deliver software or provide ongoing IT support, they need to manage their time according to the deliverables – software products enabling specific functionality or software products that allow them to manage all aspects of their business (for organizations) or their life (for individual clients).

Frequently, people think of the IT industry when they think about computer science and software delivery; however, in fact, software development and IT services cover absolutely all aspects of our life – from designing spaceships to performing complex surgery or managing activities on our calendars. Each of

© Mariya Breyter 2022
M. Breyter, *Agile Product and Project Management*,
https://doi.org/10.1007/978-1-4842-8200-7_2

these activities requires products – software for aircraft design, calculations for fuel, and user interface for calendar management. In the real world, we are surrounded by software products. Each product enables us to perform specific functions, and this is why we refer to the product life cycle – from envisioning to adoption and then sunsetting once it is replaced by higher functional and more modern products with similar or higher capabilities.

A project, on the other hand, is a specific effort with the deliverables outlined in the beginning. For example, a compliance project could be created as a result of an audit check to implement the changes outlined in the audit and resolve all the issues listed there by a specific date. Projects have a defined start and a finish date, while product life cycle is dependent on the market and provides flexibility to address customer and market demands on a rolling basis. In modern project management, project-based thinking (specific deliverables done one by one) is replaced by long-term thinking based on the flexible understanding of customer needs within a constantly changing landscape.

Chapter 2 covers the most important starting point of any initiative – whether it is a new project of a specific scope or a brand-new product being launched via a startup or in a corporate setting – establishing a shared understanding of why this is being done and what are the measures of success.

In traditional project management, this is being done by establishing a Project Charter. PMBOK defines a project charter as a document issued by the project initiator or sponsor that formally authorizes the existence of a project and identifies key resources and deliverables. Project Charter usually is a one-pager providing the project name, one-line description, listing sponsor(s), key stakeholders, and team members, stating business objectives and key milestones, and managing risks and constraints. In Agile, charters are not frequently used since flexibility is implied from the beginning. However, for larger product initiatives, team charters or product charters are sometimes used to establish a baseline understanding and connection between the team and stakeholders. Instead of defining timelines and deliverables, Agile Charter establishes a vision and a mission, outlines the minimum viable product (MVP), describes major resources and repositories, and summarizes stakeholder expectations.

The goal of this chapter is to start with the vision and mission for your product and discuss mechanisms of establishing clear and unambiguous success criteria along with the ways of measuring progress against those. This allows to align deliverables with the vision and mission as well as establish clear ways of measuring progress toward achieving those.

"All organizations start with WHY, but only the great ones keep their WHY clear year after year."

— Simon Sinek, Start with Why: How Great Leaders Inspire Everyone to Take Action (1)

Simon Sinek is a bestselling author who understands the power of starting with why. He shares an example of TiVo, a great product that did not address the why. It was launched in 1999 and marketed as a digital video recorder that was able to pause live TV, skip commercials, rewind live TV, and memorize an individual's viewing habits. It was a high-quality product, and it was well funded. However, commercially, it was not successful. Some analysts thought it was a few years ahead of its time. This is not so. The major reason for that is that instead of a vision, they had a list of features. If they said: we want to give you full control over what you watch and how, and this tool provides you with the ability to be in control. After this "why," they could have listed the same features: pausing live TV, skipping commercials, and others, but they failed to do so. Establishing "why" is the first step in positioning your product or project for success – it inspires the Scrum team and the customers alike. This concept lies at the start of any software product or service delivery.

The following are the concepts we will cover in this chapter:

- Organizational mission and vision
- Product vision
- Objectives and Key Results (OKRs)

Organizational Mission and Vision

Each organization, from a startup to a corporation, has its mission. The mission statement is a formal summary of the aims and values of the organization, an explanation of why it exists. It shapes the products that the company creates and the behaviors of its employees. Customers take their perception of the mission statement in making purchasing decisions related to the company's products vs. their competitors as much as the features of the products themselves. Companies that have compelling mission statements that resonate with their customers create products that achieve success in the market.

A mission statement is closely connected to its vision. Vision is focused on tomorrow and describes the desired future position of the company and what it wants to become. According to multiple studies, organizations that align their mission and vision statements with their strategic planning perform significantly better than those that do not take their mission and vision statements that seriously. As stated by John Kotter, a Harvard University professor and a thought leader in organizational change management, "a vision always goes beyond the numbers that are typically found in five-year plans. A vision says something that helps clarify the direction in which an organization needs to move" [1].

"If you can't communicate the vision to someone in five minutes or less and get a reaction that signified both understanding and interest, you are not done."

— John Kotter. Leading Change: Why Transformation Efforts Fail [1]

When creating corporate mission statements, it is important to share a compelling outcome with current or future customers. For example, Southwest Airlines' mission statement emphasizes customer service linked to employee behavior and corporate image. It states: "Connect people to what's important in their lives through friendly, reliable, and low-cost air travel." Southwest Airlines' corporate vision is "to be the world's most loved, most efficient, and most profitable airline." It reflects the company's long-term strategy to expand its operations globally and to achieve significant growth while continuing to be people oriented and service focused [2].

Topic for a Group Discussion   In groups, review two to three vision and mission statements of well-known companies and reflect whether they resonate with you or not. Suggest ways to rewrite those that need improvement. Some of the examples:

InVision is the digital product design platform used to make the world's best customer experiences. We provide design tools and educational resources for teams to navigate every stage of the product design process, from ideation to development.

Apple mission statement is "to bring the best user experience to its customers through its innovative hardware, software, and services."

Google company mission is to organize the world's information and make it universally accessible and useful.

In the 20th century, the company's mission and vision would not be directly relevant to IT professionals who saw their role in developing, testing, and delivering high-quality code, no matter which industry and which mission they supported. Nowadays, IT professionals are direct drivers of business success, and their contribution to and support of the company's mission and vision are paramount to business success.

Frequently, even for technology companies, their mission and vision are not driven by technology; it's driven by people and positive change to the society. Microsoft's mission statement is "to enable people and businesses throughout the world to realize their full potential." Vision statements change over time, though not frequently, to reflect rapidly changing reality. For example, Microsoft's original vision was "A computer on every desk and in every home."

 Exercise   Match mission statements to the company name in the following examples:

1. We believe in a world where everyone can contribute. Our mission is to change all creative work from read-only to read-write. When everyone can contribute, consumers become contributors and we greatly increase the rate of human progress.

   Samsung Electronics, Oracle, Intel, Alphabet, GitLab

2. We foster an inclusive environment that leverages the diverse backgrounds and perspectives of all our employees, suppliers, customers, and partners to drive a sustainable global competitive advantage.

3. Delight our customers, employees, and shareholders by relentlessly delivering the platform and technology advancements that become essential to the way we work and live.

4. Mission is to make the world around us universally accessible and useful.

5. We will devote our human resources and technology to create superior products and services, thereby contributing to a better global society.

Answer Key: 1 – GitLab, 2 – Oracle, 3 – Intel, 4 – Alphabet, 5 – Samsung Electronics

---

Product Vision

Within each organization, there are multiple products and services. For example, Atlassian products include Jira Software, Jira Service Desk, Jira Core, Confluence, Bitbucket, Trello, and Jira Align. Each of the products has its own vision that drives its delivery.

A product vision statement describes the overarching long-term mission of a product. Vision statements are aspirational in nature. They concisely communicate what the product will achieve in the long term. Product definition will be reviewed in detail in Chapter 3, but for the purposes of defining organizational strategy, it is important to understand how product vision is derived from the organizational mission and vision.

To formulate the product statement, use the following "elevator pitch" template introduced by Geoffrey Moore in his book *Crossing the Chasm* (2). An elevator pitch is a short description of a product that explains the concept of this product in such a way that any listener can understand it in a short period of time. The goal is to convey the overall product concept in an exciting, clear, and concise way. The name – elevator pitch – reflects the idea that if an employee gets into an elevator with a business executive, it should be possible to deliver the summary in the time span of an elevator ride. The template for the product vision suggested by Geoffrey Moore is provided below.

This template reflects the product's value proposition by summarizing the customer segment, competitor targets, and the core differentiation of the product from the competitor offerings.

FOR (target customer)

WHO (statement of need or opportunity)

THE (product name) IS A (product category)

THAT (key benefit, reason to buy).

UNLIKE (primary competitive alternative)

OUR PRODUCT (statement of primary differentiation)

It is important that the elevator pitch is compelling and reflects customer value rather than technical implementation. For example, for Intuit tax software, TurboTax, the product statement would emphasize the value of saving time and money for individuals to dedicate to their families rather than providing spreadsheets to calculate annual taxes. A compelling product vision statement would sound like "For the family members responsible for the annual tax return, who spend a lot of time and effort to prepare their taxes and frequently make mistakes that need to be corrected afterward, TurboTax provides a fast and worry-free way of preparing their annual tax return. Unlike other tax preparation software, TurboTax is inexpensive, intuitive, and easy to use."

Topic for a Group Discussion   In groups, create a product statement for one of the products you all know – use any electronic or software product that all team members are aware of. Read your statement to other teams without naming the product and see whether they can get what the product is. If it is easier to guess, your product statement is adequate. If not, discuss how to change it in order to represent the product in a clear, concise, and non-ambiguous way.

Objectives and Key Results (OKRs)

Throughout this chapter, we started with the company's mission and vision, then moved to the product-level "elevator pitch," and now arrived at defining strategic objectives.

Every product should have a set of well-defined quantifiable objectives shared across all the stakeholders so that everyone has a shared understanding of the "true north" – how success will look like. As with everything in Agile product management, OKRs may change if the market situation changes or any major enterprise-level decisions are made; however, those are usually quite stable for the period they are set up, with any change being discussed, aligned, and communicated to a broad group of stakeholders.

OKRs are a popular concept nowadays. There are opinions that OKR is a buzzword for "key performance indicators" (KPIs) or even for "management by objective" (or MBO), described by Peter Drucker in his 1954 book *The Practice of Management* [3]. Management by objective refers to a process of defining specific goals within an organization that management can convey to organization members, followed by the decision about who will be responsible for achieving each objective in sequence and how. An integral part of MBO is the measurement of an employee's performance and comparing it with the previously established management expectations.

In fact, OKRs are as far from MBO as the Agile mindset from Waterfall project management. MBO is about top-down management, and OKRs are about self-organization; MBO is about individuals, and OKRs are about high-performing teams; MBO is about performance, and OKRs are about outcomes. MBOs were a tool that worked over 50 years ago; OKRs work today.

The reason why OKRs work is because they are about motivation (people are setting objectives that they are passionate about); they are about collaboration (people who have similar passion collaborate to achieve results); they are about innovation (no one tells them how to do things and achieve the results they chose), and furthermore, they are measurable (3). OKRs are aligned across the organization so that everyone has a chance to contribute.

OKRs have been around since the 1970s. The concept was invented by Andy Grove at Intel. Andy Grove used to say "Leaders have to act more quickly today. The pressure comes much faster." OKRs fueled Intel's ability to respond fast to market needs by aligning on jointly set objectives. This concept was made popular by John Doerr, who was one of the earliest investors in Google. OKRs quickly became an important focus for Google, and companies such as LinkedIn, Twitter, Dropbox, Spotify, Airbnb, and Uber have since followed suit.

> "Contributors are most engaged when they can actually see how their work contributes to the company's success. Quarter to quarter, day to day, they look for tangible measures of their achievement. Extrinsic rewards—the year-end bonus check—merely validate what they already know. OKRs speak to something more powerful, the intrinsic value of the work itself."
>
> — John Doerr. Measure What Matters (3)

John Doerr suggests the following template to use while setting OKRs: I will (Objective) as measured by (this set of Key Results). As the name implies, there are two components, objectives and key results. As Marissa Mayer, former Google Vice President, said, "if it does not have a number, it is not a key result." The objective should be simple, aspirational, and easy to relate to and memorize. Key results should be no less than two and no more than five, specific, and measurable. Felipe Castro, one of the leading consultants in the OKR field, makes a great observation that if you have to stop breathing while reading your Objective, you are doing it wrong.

 Topic for a Group Discussion   Review the following OKR from GitLab:

OBJECTIVE – We will achieve market leadership for GitLab by

KEY RESULT 1 – The growing use of GitLab for all stages of the DevOps life cycle by 10% via establishing three proven case studies (Product)

KEY RESULT 2 – Ensuring appropriate transactional business pricing (Sales)

KEY RESULT 3 – Launching advertising for the customer base for Manage, Plan, Create and increase overall pipeline coverage by 8% (Marketing)

What do you think about this OKR? Does it follow best practices in terms of the number of key results, ability to quantify progress against each of those, clear ownership, and other best practices discussed before?

In sum, objectives are ambitious and qualitative. They are almost impossible to achieve fully. On the other hand, key results are specific and measurable. They can be quantified in one of the multiple ways:

1. Volume outcomes: Achieve $5 million annual profit.

2. Relative outcomes: Increase paying customer base by 5%.

3. Volume events: Conduct product roadshow in ten states with at least 30 successful engagement events.

4. Binary: Launch a new online product within the load business.

5. Nonfunctional: Achieve 99.9 availability.

6. Subjective (based on surveys and other feedback mechanisms): Improve net promotion score by 10%.

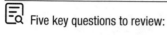 Five key questions to review:

1. What is the goal of OKRs?

2. What format is used for defining OKRs?

3. Who makes decisions about key results to achieve?

4. Which companies implement OKRs?

5. Why the number of key results within each objective should be limited to five?

OKRs are "cascading" throughout the organization – from company level to divisional, product, and team. Some companies introduce individual OKRs related to the professional growth of their employees. (See Figure 2-1.) It is important that OKRs are set and assessed by individuals who do the work rather than being imposed by the managers.

4. ORGANIZATIONAL ALIGNMENT

OKRs help companies set goals at enterprise level and then focus on achieving the outcomes quarter after quarter. OKRs are a powerful investment and budget allocation tool, as well as a dependency management mechanism.

It is important to establish OKRs by value stream, e.g. there could be an objective to establish a market share, attract specific target audience, or achieve revenue objectives.

3. PROGRAM-LEVEL DELIVERY

I. INDIVIDUAL MOTIVATION

Professional development OKRs align individual professional growth objectives with enterprise goals by creating transparency into value delivery.

OKR framework promotes team collaboration and alignment in day-to-day execution.

2. TEAM-LEVEL GOAL SETTING

Figure 2-1. Overview of the OKR framework

Once OKRs are established (usually annually), they are reviewed, self-graded, and adjusted (if needed) at least on a quarterly basis. OKRs have to be realistic but aspirational, almost impossible to achieve. They reflect outcomes (actual product or business deliverables, such as features delivered, number of users, or profitability data) vs. outputs (how many meetings the team had, how many hours they spent building the functionality, or how many bugs were fixed).

 Topic for a Group Discussion   Review the following OKR:

OBJECTIVE – Increase the efficiency of QA process*es*

KEY RESULT 1 – Test cases for all P1, P2 stories are completed and handed over to dev before development starts (compliance to be measured every Sprint)

KEY RESULT 2 – One week before the release date, no blockers and critical bugs should be open. Bug leakage to production for critical issues is less than 1%

KEY RESULT 3 – Less than three bugs reported by end users per release

What do you think about this OKR? How would you rewrite it to make it more meaningful?

Most companies use Google's self-grading scale from 0 (no progress has been made) to 1 (objective and all key results are fully achieved). They specify that since OKRs are highly aspirational, a grade of 0.6–0.7 or higher is considered a success. It is important to use OKRs as a visibility and alignment mechanism, rather than using this data for blaming teams and team members for not meeting the OKRs they have set for themselves. OKRs review sessions are a prompt to have a meaningful conversation about challenges, learnings, and continuous improvement opportunities.

In large organizations, cascading OKRs are frequently visualized from company level to product and team level. An example is provided in Figure 2-2.

Objective: Improve Application
Quality, Stability and Reliability

Key Result 1: Reduce number of production defects by 50%		Key Result 2: Improve quality of delivery within a sprint		Key Result 3: Increase System Stability and Reliability by 30%	
QA: Reduce the number of missed defects to no more than 1 per 3 releases	Release Mgmt: Guide the process via reviews, reporting, and strategy definition	Dev: Ensure 100% compliance with code quality standards	Dev: Establish 100% coverage for peer reviews	Data: 99.9% data stability	Architecture: Proactive architecture definition and communication
Dev: Ensure 100% knowledge transfer and SME on core systems	Chief of Staff: Hire/Establish a Production Support Team & define the objectives/processes	Release Mgmt: Ensure that no stories with bugs open against them are deployed into production (or the exception process is enforced)	QA: 100% regression automation; 80% test automation	Data: 99.9% data accuracy	Security: Secure solutions defined, established and monthly communicated
Agile Practice: Ensure that 15% + of sprint capacity is allocated to defect fixing	Architecture: 100% architecture reviews completed within a sprint	DevOps: Environment setup allows for integration testing	QA&Dev: Pilot TDD practices for 2+ teams	Agile Practice: ensure that each backlog is balanced between functional user stories and non-functional technical tasks	
		DevOps: Logging and Monitoring established with clear highly automated processes	QA: 100% regression automation; 80% test automation		

Figure 2-2. Organizational OKR alignment

Case Study: DevOps OKRs. DevOps is a set of practices that combines software development and IT operations. These practices aim to shorten the systems development life cycle (SDLC) and provide continuous delivery with high software quality.

The roots of DevOps are in Agile and Lean frameworks. A key concept about enterprise DevOps to remember is that DevOps at the enterprise level are not optimized for cost; they should be optimized for speed. This is achieved by moving to outcome-based team structures, understanding value streams, defining cycle time, and optimizing for fast and high-quality delivery. In their groundbreaking book, *Accelerate. The Science of Lean Software and DevOps: Building and Scaling High Performing Technology Organizations* [4], Gene Kim, Jez Humble, and Nicole Forsgren discuss the research they have done in enabling organizations to deliver business value via DevOps. Their goal was to find relevant key results for DevOps and answer the following question: how to measure IT performance, technology performance, and software delivery performance?

In this book, the authors did extensive research to find out the difference between high-performing and low-performing organizations, and they found that when compared to low performers, high performers have

- 46% more frequent code deployment
- 440 times faster lead time from commit to deploy
- 170 times faster mean time to recover from downtime
- Five times lower change failure rate

They advocate against using traditional metrics, such as lines of code, hours of work, and employee utilization. As a result, the metrics that drive results include the software delivery performance metrics (lead time, deployment frequency, mean time to restore, change fail percentage – in the context of Lean, the latter is the percentage of changes that result in degraded service or subsequently require remediation, such as an outage, or require a hotfix, a rollback, a fix-forward, or a patch). These are all meaningful key results for DevOps [4].

They made an interesting conclusion about Lean product development that it drives software delivery performance as well as organizational performance directly. This correlation shows the importance of DevOps and other advanced technical practices at an enterprise level.

The authors suggested that each organization answers five key architecture questions:

- Can my team make large-scale changes to the design of a system without the permission of someone outside the team or depending on other teams?

- Can my team complete its work without needing fine-grained communication and coordination with people outside the team?

- Can my team deploy and release its product or service on demand, independently of other services the product or service depends upon?

- Can my team do most of its testing on demand without requiring an integrated test environment?

- Can my team perform deployments during normal business hours with negligible downtime?

Finally, they came up with a list of 24 capabilities that drive improvements in software delivery performance and divided them into five categories:

1. Continuous delivery (this includes version control, deployment automation, continuous integration, trunk-based development, test automation, test data management, shift left on security, and overall continuous delivery practices)

2. Architecture (loosely coupled architecture, such as the use of microservices. Another great example is containerization. Containers offer a logical packaging mechanism in which applications can be abstracted from the environment in which they actually run. This decoupling allows container-based applications to be deployed easily and consistently, regardless of whether the target environment is a private data center, the public cloud, or even a developer's personal laptop.)

3. Product and process (value stream optimization, working in small batches, short feedback loops, limiting work in progress (WIP))

4. Lean management and monitoring (application monitoring, proactive notifications)

5. Culture (team empowerment, learning organizations, collaboration, and job satisfaction)

These capabilities provide a set of meaningful key results in defining DevOps OKRs.

Source: Gene Kim, Jez Humble, and Nicole Forsgren. The Science of Lean Software and DevOps: Building and Scaling High Performing Technology Organizations [4].

 Five key questions to review:

1. What is meant by DevOps?

2. Why DevOps OKRs are important for business?

3. What are the five architecture questions for each organization to address?

4. What are DevOps competencies that may be measured via OKRs?

5. Come up with a DevOps OKR for a well-known company and explain the value of this OKR to the business.

Case Study: OKRs at Google. Google has used OKR processes since 1999 because it helps them align toward a shared set of business objectives. They set ambitious objectives and self-grade their key results by the end of each quarter.

In his book *Measure What Matters* (3), John Doerr describes how he introduced Google founders Larry Page and Sergey Brin to the OKR concept that he brought over from Intel. He describes how this concept helped make Google what it is today by focusing on collaboration and helping set measurable goals at every level in order to unify aspirations and keep everyone on track toward the same objectives.

According to Rick Klau, a partner at Google Ventures, annual OKRs are long-term goals that might change as the year evolves. Key results against these objectives are assessed on a quarterly basis. Having OKRs at a company and team level allows Google teams to work together and keep the company aligned against shared outcomes. OKRs are open to everyone at Google, including Larry Page, so that everyone has full transparency of what others are working on.

Every Google employee has 4-6 OKRs every quarter, with each key result measured at the end of the quarter on a scale from 0 to 1, with an acceptable outcome of 0.6–0.7. If OKR is achieved at 1, it means that it was not ambitious enough. Since the grading process is quite simple, employees and teams focus on achieving results rather than providing complex status reporting. OKRs are not used to define compensation and promotions – the goal is to increase focus and productivity.

From Google, OKRs spread to many other tech companies, such as Twitter, LinkedIn, and Zinga. Today, organizations from startups to Fortune 100 companies have embraced the OKR framework.

Tip OKRs cascade across the enterprise, thus aligning all functions and creating transparent outcomes. In order to provide full transparency at enterprise level, it is usually not sufficient to use spreadsheets, a collection of basic templates, or a common repository, such as SharePoint or Confluence. Large organizations are using online cloud-based tools to record, align, and grade their OKRs. Popular tools include Betterworks, Workboard, 7Geese, Perdoo, Weekdone, and many others. In addition, Agile management tools, such as Jira Align and Rally Software, provide cascading OKR functionality.

Four Steps in the Annual OKR-Setting and Alignment Process

There are four steps in the OKR process:

1. OKR setting: This is done at the beginning of every year when organizational-level OKRs aligned with the company's mission and vision are communicated, and the product teams and individuals engage in setting their OKRs, taking organizational-level OKRs into account. At this time, basic information is provided, as shown in Figure 2-3.

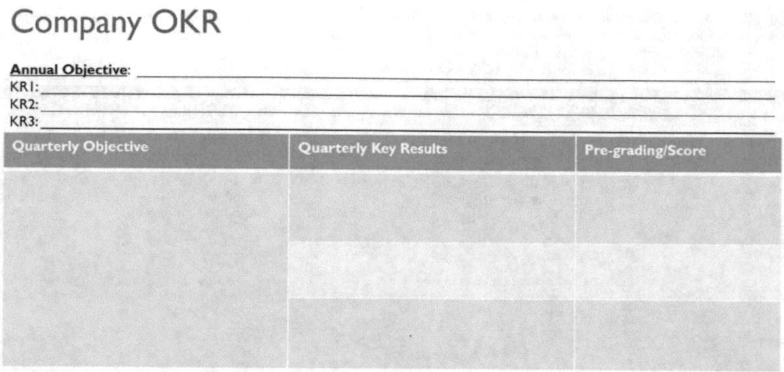

Company OKR

Annual Objective: _____
KR1: _____
KR2: _____
KR3: _____

Quarterly Objective	Quarterly Key Results	Pre-grading/Score

Figure 2-3. OKR setting

2. OKR alignment: The goal of this process is to identify any dependencies and resource constraints and have the teams engage in a meaningful dialog to resolve any resourcing, budgeting, or prioritization conflict. This step takes care of external dependencies and other related risks.

3. OKR refinement: Based on the alignment conversations and related prioritization decisions, product teams further refine and update their OKRs to ensure that those are realistic and aspirational at the same time. They ensure that their key results are outcomes (business-facing results) rather than activities (meetings, deployment activities, personnel events such as hiring new team members, and other day-to-day execution activities that are not directly driving the outcomes). At that time, OKRs are pregraded by those who set them up to avoid future confusion about whether the results have been met and at which level.

As a result of this process, the information is more detailed and validated within the organization, as shown in Figure 2-4.

DevOps Objective: We will enable daily production deployments to global customers with high quality at no additional expense by
KR1: Performing 80% of application testing without requiring an integrated environment.
KR2: Enabling daily deployments with full regression testing.
KR3: Reducing high priority and critical production defects to no more than one per 20 deployments.

Objective	Key Results	Score
Q1: Improve application architecture to decouple solutions for testing and deployment purposes	Perform 80% of application testing without requiring an integrated environment	0-integrated environment is required in 100% of testing; 0.5 – 50%; 1- integrated environment is required in 20% of testing
	Deploy the application independently from other services/applications it depends on	0 – deployments are tightly coupled; 0.5 – deployments are loosely coupled; 1 – components can be deployed independently on demand
Q2: Ensure that all delivery teams are cross-functional	All delivery teams have skills necessary to design, develop, test, deploy, and operate the system on the same team	0 – none of the teams are cross-functional; 0.5 – 50% of teams, 1- 100% of teams are cross-functional
	Each team has access to manage relevant lower environments with a dedicated team member authorized to perform production deployments	0 – no access, all done by a dedicated team; 0.5 – lower environments only, 1 – all environments including production within agreed upon process
Q3: Ensure proper deployment tools and related skills	Optimize deployment tools and frameworks to enable daily deployments with full regression testing	0 – no changes; 0.5 – implement daily deployments with some manual testing; 1- full regression automation
	Ensure necessary skills are in place on each team	0 – no training; 1- train everyone
	Ensure all technologies are correctly licensed	0 – no audit; 1- internal audit, 100% confirmed
Q4: Build quality in by implementing BDD for 100% of regression testing	Reduce high priority and critical production defects to no more than one per 20 deployments	0 – more than 5 defects per 20 deployments (current data), 0.5 – no more than 3 defects, 1 – no more than 1 defect

Figure 2-4. OKR refinement

4. OKR iteration: Once OKRs are set, aligned, and refined, a review cadence is established, which allows the whole organization to review progress against OKRs with full transparency and traceability at the organizational level (see Figure 2-5).

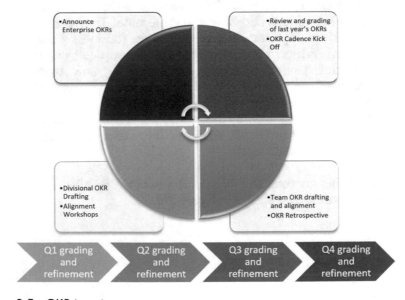

Figure 2-5. OKR iteration

I refer to this sequence as the SARI framework based on the first letters of each step – setting, alignment, refinement, and iteration. It is important that the SARI framework for OKRs is not sequential; it is cyclical – all steps repeat on a regular basis allowing for continuous alignment and ongoing value delivery as shown in Figure 2-6.

Figure 2-6. SARI framework for OKR setting, aligning, refining, and iterating

---

💡 **Tip**   Remember that OKRs are about outcomes, not about processes or activities. Setting up a process is not a good key result; we want to measure the objective why this process has been set up. Grading is seen here as a prompt to a conversation, not a punishment or a measure of performance. The worst OKRs are the ones that are ambiguous, for example, "achieve significant increase in performance," "empower the teams to deliver applications to customers," or "implement a new pricing strategy."

Different organizations create their own practices of OKR adoption. One fact is absolutely clear: OKRs need to be managed. If OKRs are set once and reviewed at the end of the year, this framework becomes just another bureaucratic overhead for companies.

There are multiple examples of Agile rituals adopted by companies, but all successful OKR adopters view it as a framework rather than a concept and establish a process, tooling, ownership, and clear expectations around the OKR setting. Some successful practices include the following:

1. Annual cadence with quarterly progress reviews.

2. Role of OKR Champions who spearhead and drive OKR adoption and execution.

3. Some companies build OKR-level cadence around their ongoing execution, for example, weekly Commit, monthly Retro and Reboot, and Friday Wins. Other companies align OKR implementation with their Agile cadence. Whichever way it is done, establishing repeatable OKR rituals allows driving delivery with visibility and transparency into OKR implementation.

4. There are OKR roles (not titles) that usually allow for professional growth for high-performance individuals. Whether these are OKR Champions or OKR Sponsors, many organizations define expectations and empower people in their roles. Some successful implementations include three levels of these roles: OKR Champions responsible for divisional implementations, OKR Sponsors driving success, and OKR Removers (usually Business Heads responsible for unblocking progress against OKRs.)

5. Finally, there are tools and techniques for OKR adoption, as well as artifacts – repositories, online systems, and related processes. Examples of creative approaches include OKR Appreciation Badges, OKR Onboarding process, and shared OKR repositories. Many Human Capital Divisions rely on OKRs in motivating and empowering their employees, though the use of OKRs for promotions and compensation decisions is strongly discouraged.

Overall, many companies see OKRs as a mechanism for setting their business and implementation objectives and aligning business, technology, and other organizational structures with the needs of their customers. OKRs are a way for IT professionals to erase the division between business and technology since this framework empowers developers, testers, and other engineers to deliver products and services that delight the customers.

While OKRs are a popular and powerful framework, many companies do not use OKRs and still deliver high-quality products and services that delight their customers. OKR framework is not a pre-requisite for success. However, a clear mission and vision, well-defined goals that drive prioritization, and quantified progress against these goals is a must for any successful company.

Key Points

1. Each organization, from a startup to a corporation, has its mission. The mission statement is a formal summary of the aims and values of the organization, an explanation of why it exists. It shapes the products that the company creates and the behaviors of its employees.

2. A mission statement is closely connected to its vision. Vision is focused on tomorrow and describes the desired future position of the company and what it wants to become.

3. Thirty or more years ago, the company's mission and vision would not be directly relevant to IT professionals who saw their role in developing, testing, and delivering high-quality code, no matter which industry and which mission they supported. Nowadays, IT professionals are direct drivers of business success, and their contribution to and support of the company's mission and vision are paramount to business success.

4. A product vision, or product vision statement, is different from the company's vision statement. It describes the overarching long-term mission of your product. Product vision statements are aspirational. They contain information about the objectives of the product (customers and problems it will solve for them) and its future.

5. An elevator pitch is a short description of a product that explains the concept in such a way that any recipient can understand it without additional context. The goal is to convey the overall product concept in an exciting, clear, and concise way.

6. It is important that the elevator pitch is compelling and reflects customer value rather than technical implementation.

7. OKRs are a goal-setting "framework for thinking big." OKRs help to establish high-level, measurable goals for a business by establishing ambitious goals and outcomes that can be tracked for the long term (usually aspirational annual objectives with measurable quarterly key results for each function).

8. OKR concept was invented by Andy Grove at Intel in the 1970s. OKRs fueled Intel's ability to respond fast to market needs by aligning on meaningful and audacious goals, thus enabling successful execution. This concept was made popular by John Doerr, who was one of the earliest investors in Google. OKRs quickly became an important focus for Google, and companies such as LinkedIn, Twitter, Dropbox, Spotify, Airbnb, and Uber have since followed suit.

9. Once OKRs are established (usually annually), they are reviewed, self-graded, and adjusted (if needed) at least on a quarterly basis. OKRs have to be realistic but aspirational, almost impossible to achieve. They reflect outcomes (actual product or business deliverables) vs. day-to-day activities.

10. In large organizations, cascading OKRs are frequently visualized from company level to product and team level. There are four steps in the annual OKR-setting and alignment process: setting, alignment, refinement, and iteration. This is referred to as the SARI framework for managing OKRs.

Getting to Know Your Customer

This chapter covers Agile, Waterfall, and hybrid product management practices based on a customer-centric approach to IT delivery. It builds on the knowledge of business objectives to focus on customer needs. It explains the concept of a persona type and provides tools and templates to identify the customer, empathize with the customer's problem, and define the product while "working backward" from customer needs.

Introduction

In Chapter 2, we discussed how modern companies develop their products and services and how the role of IT professionals changed over the last 20–30 years. Writing code, building networks, and providing IT hosting or security services are no longer sufficient for IT professionals. Working jointly with the business to provide products and services to their customers, internal or external, IT professionals are defining and executing toward the mission and vision of the company they work for and are inspired and contribute toward the product vision. They set up aspirational objectives and measurable key results and hold themselves accountable for product delivery to their customers' satisfaction.

© Mariya Breyter 2022
M. Breyter, *Agile Product and Project Management*,
https://doi.org/10.1007/978-1-4842-8200-7_3

In order to achieve these objectives by focusing on customer needs, it is important to understand who the customer is and what problem this product solves for the customer. This approach to building products is referred to as "customer-centricity," a.k.a. "working backward" from customer needs. In this chapter, we will discuss different techniques of identifying customers, understanding their needs (referred to as "Job-to-Be-Done"), and using this information in defining IT products and services. Without this fundamental step, we are in danger of building products or offering services that no one is interested in using.

The following are the concepts and techniques we will cover in this chapter:

- Product definition
- Persona analysis
- User segmentation
- Customer journey
- Empathy map
- Product canvas
- Technology adoption curve
- Product life cycle
- Lean UX concepts

Product Definition

What is a product or service from an IT perspective and how much should IT professionals be involved in defining those? This is one of the most important questions nowadays since the concept of a "technology product" has changed drastically in the last 20–30 years. The range of consumer technology products spreads from smartphones or personal computers to automatic lights for our homes and health monitors. Overall, in information technology, a product is something that is created and made available to customers.

Products do not need to have a physical shape or form. For example, digital products are created in a digital form to be used on computers and other electronic devices. As opposed to physical products, they are created once, incrementally enhanced, and used by any number of adopters. The distinction between a technology product and service has blurred, and a good example of it is the concept of the "Internet of things" – a system of interrelated computing devices transferring data over a network without requiring human-to-human or human-to-computer interaction. Internet of things became possible due to the multiple interconnected technologies that are common in our lives nowadays.

Internet of things enabled the productization of modern technology by using these advancements to establish healthcare services, run our home and business, provide education, and manage communications in an interconnected world. For example, home automation includes lighting, heating, air-conditioning, media systems, security systems, and so forth. Wearable software includes a wide range of smart electronic devices that allow to detect, analyze, and transmit information concerning vital signs, body signals, and biodata and track activity. Many of those solutions are now incorporated into smartphones, smartwatches, and activity trackers.

IT teams are not focused on software, hardware, or networks from a value delivery perspective. IT teams are focused on what experience their products or services need to provide and why. They create the strategies and blueprints for other teams and enable the customer to achieve their needs via their deliverables. The role of IT professionals today is not to write code, establish a computer network, develop computer hardware, or test software – their role is to provide capabilities to their customers. Many technology companies, such as Google, implemented a role of a Technical Product Manager who is focused on user needs and product positioning, and encourages innovation in the delivery team.

🔅 **Tip**   If we adopt a wide definition of technological products as material or nontangible objects or services that have been designed by people and developed through technology to service customer needs, almost everything is a product, and almost every company is a technology company. There are two things that actually make it into a product: the first one is a customer, that is, a person, a system, an organization, or a service that consumes (i.e., uses) this product to address a specific need, and the second one is the value – the benefit that this customer gets by using the product or service to satisfy their needs.

From the product value perspective, an important concept is the "Job-to-Be-Done" (JTBD), which reflects underlying user needs. This theory was popularized by Clayton Christensen, a Harvard University professor, in relation to using innovation to meet user needs [1]. "Jobs" are foundational for understanding what motivates the customers and why customers behave the way they do. JTBD framework focuses on the "why" behind customer behavior. In his famous lecture on the topic of Jobs-to-Be-Done (1), Prof. Christensen described research to improve milkshake consumption in McDonald's. When the visitors were asked to taste new milkshake flavors and share their preferences, the improvements did not influence the product consumption in any way.

Then, the research was done in a different way. The researchers were observing the reasons why the customers were "hiring" the milkshake and found out that most milkshakes were consumed in the morning when people were going to work, and the reason was a long and boring drive to work. Their respondents revealed that they tried to "hire" bananas and donuts as competitors to milkshakes, but neither was a good competitor to milkshakes because the banana was gone in three minutes and the donut was too messy to eat in the car. The milkshake was taking over 20 minutes to consume; it fits well in a car cupholder and was filling enough. In sum, they found out that competitors to the milkshake were not milkshakes of different flavors, but rather bananas, donuts, and snacks. As a result, they improved the checkout system and established a drive-through for faster delivery so that people do not lose any time on their way to work and put tiny pieces of fruit and berries in a milkshake to allow reengagement with the product, but not too thick to stuck in the straw. They also made the drink thicker so that it lasted longer. All of this significantly improved consumption.

As a simple way of presenting JTBD theory, if a consumer goes to a store to buy an electric bulb, their goal is not to buy a bulb – their ultimate goal is to make their house well-lit at night. The value of a computer is not to provide a keyboard to type commands – it is to process and retrieve information. The invention of the single-button smartphone addressed this in a brilliant way. The concept of "Job-to-Be-Done" is the next step in product adoption because it extends the concept of a product to the value it provides to the customer.

Topic for a Group Discussion   In groups, discuss what are Jobs-to-Be-Done for the companies you all know. You can start with consumer goods companies, for example, IKEA. IKEA's JTBD is not selling furniture to its customers. There are multiple famous furniture brands that do much better job in selling high-quality elegant furniture to their customers. IKEA's JTBD is to enable you to make your apartment livable at low price in no time, which is a completely different outcome from that of traditional furniture stores. OpenTable online platform did not simply address restaurant reservation needs – it addressed the problem of needing to find a suitable place to dine in a new location, which it extended to the reservation service, upon connecting restaurants with their customers. As the next step, move to technology companies and online platforms. What is Twitter's JTBD? LinkedIn? Intel? Microsoft? Share your own examples and compare JTBD definitions you came up with.

"The customer rarely buys what the business thinks it sells him. One reason for this is, of course, that nobody pays for a 'product.' What is paid for is satisfaction. But nobody can make or supply satisfaction as such — at best, only the means to attaining them can be sold and delivered."

— Peter Drucker. Managing for Results [2]

Case Study: Global Medical Diagnostic Software Company. GMDS, a leader in medical diagnostic software, experienced a steady decline in demand for their software. They were continuously collecting feedback from their power customers – specialists in the field that were the most advanced. The company worked hard to understand the needs of these lead users and made them part of their customer advisory board. They also depended on this group for new product ideas and to evaluate ideas they had for product and service offerings.

The lead users had become an integral part of the company's innovation and development practices. They provided feedback, which was used to deliver new features that were immediately delivered, but despite all of that, the company's position in the marketplace was continuously declining.

In order to address the challenge, the company decided to use JTBD analysis along with customer segmentation, including highly experienced as well as less experienced physicians in their analysis. To do so, they captured desired outcome statements from approximately 170 users. What they found out was that lead physicians did not represent the customer market – they represented only 21% of the physician population. On top of it, the company found out that physicians in this overserved segment were not at all dependent on the diagnostic software to make an accurate patient diagnosis. As lead users, they had the experience, knowledge, and skills to make an accurate diagnosis on their own – and they only used the software to verify that they were correct.

In contrast, 79% of the physicians were highly dependent on the diagnostic software to gather the needed information and process it to make an accurate diagnosis. Their needs were vastly different from those of the lead users – they needed to see the details and understand the reasoning and wanted the system to generate a detailed script they would be able to share with their patients.

Because the company was focused on its lead users without understanding the outcomes desired by 79% of their target market, they failed to understand the needs of the underserved customers, putting themselves in a position of declining market share. The discovery of these outcome-based segments and the outcomes they expected from this software changed the focus of the organization. They chose to decouple from the lead user and target the underserved physicians with a new portfolio of products and services that addressed their most underserved desired outcomes.

The lesson learned is the importance of tying the product strategy to understanding unmet customer needs. By using the JTBD approach, GMDS management was able to deliver products that met the needs of their target audience and get their business back on track.

Source: Tony Ulwick. Jobs-to-Be-Done Case Study: Beware of Lead Users [3]

In the preceding case study, we saw how important it is to identify the right customer. While the diagnostic software was targeted at physicians, the understanding of the difference in JTBD between experienced physicians and the majority of the target market almost cost the company its business. This brings us to the most important concept of product definition, persona analysis.

Persona Analysis

Persona analysis is a method of representing the target audience for a product. In product analysis, the user persona is a customer type represented as a fictional character – with a made-up biography, demographics, characteristics, and a clear representation of their need.

It is important to differentiate between the customer and the client. The client is the end user that uses the product or consumes the services.

Case Study: Test Prep Company.   In early 2010, TPC, a leader in college exam prep, was experiencing a major decline in its profits. Despite the high quality of education, their brick-and-mortar business was not popular with the students who were looking for flexible and asynchronous education. They found in-person and predominantly one-way online classes equally boring and ineffective. TPC CEO Jack Paulson called his leadership team to discuss what needs to be done.

The leadership team suggested going mobile – since the release of the first iPhone in 2007 and the support of third-party applications, this seemed like the right way to go. However, it was not clear which functionality would be most important to the users. The customer base included high school students preparing for college admissions with ACT, SAT, and PSAT and graduate students working on their GRE and GMAT, bar review prep, medical and licensing exams, such as USMLE, NAPLEX, NBDE, and other specialized exams.

TPC was one of the early adopters of Agile delivery for its IT organization and the Director of Agile PMO. Marsha Taylor was part of the TCP leadership team. She suggested defining personas or customer types and researching their needs before creating mobile apps and releasing those to the students. As a result, TPC invited one of the well-known consultants in IT product delivery to help them organize the product discovery workshop and assess customer needs.

During this week-long workshop, over a hundred of TPC's Agile team members (developers, testers, IT engineers, system administrators, and network administrators), along with their business stakeholders, engaged in prototyping and analyzing user needs. Each of the research teams focused on one of the customer types – high school students taking admission exams, legal professionals preparing for a bar exam, medical professionals, or college graduates taking graduate school examinations. Throughout the week, they engaged in active dialog through observation, prototyping, and research and made three major discoveries:

1. Students are bored with study cards and their electronic equivalent and want a more interactive, more engaging experience.

2. Students want their experience to be heavily customized with the ability to create their avatars, specify the number of questions in test assignments, and compete with others.

3. Students prefer the questions to be grouped by topic so that their learning is better structured and logically organized.

Once the results were collected, Agile teams started rapid delivery, and in three months, the first TPC test prep app was completed. It was gamified – students were able to earn badges and keep scores for correct questions, the app was heavily customized, and all the questions were structured by topics. It was competitively priced at $4.99 per month, and TCP expected it to be a huge success on the market. However, it was not selling well. They decreased the price to $2.99 and then $1.99 before starting to offer it for free as an add-on to their in-person and live online classes. After two releases – one featuring additional gamification and competition functionality and the other focusing on additional customization with avatars and notifications – Jack Paulson called his leadership team into his office to brainstorm on the reason for the failure of their product strategy.

Jack was concerned that this product was a major waste of time and budget for the company and blamed persona analysis for the misinformation. He asked Marsha to speak about the analysis that had been completed. The first question that Marsha asked the leadership team was

- Who is the user of this app?

- Of course, these are the students.

- Who is the customer?

- The audience was confused: What is the difference between your user persona and the customer? So Marsha had to ask this question in a different way:

- Who is paying for it?

This was an eye-opening question. Even though students were the users of this app, they were not paying customers. Their parents were. The next steps became clear.

At this point, smaller-scope research was done with the parents of undergraduate students. They did not find the app comparable with in-person and even online study experience. With in-person or online, they could supervise their children; they were clear how much time they were spending studying and what scores they were receiving. On the other hand, they did not care about customization or gamification – all they cared about was the outcome: what was their child's test score and how it was improving over time.

With that, Agile teams at TPC prioritized different functionality for delivery. They created parent dashboards showing how much time their children were spending on the app, how many questions they attempted to answer, and how many of these answers were correct; they randomized questions rather than organizing them by topics in order to mimic the real test and dialed down on gamification because the goal was to educate rather than entertain. Within a short period of time, their app became super successful and earned a number of prestigious IT awards.

Meanwhile, Agile teams continued dialog with their customers. For example, they found that for nursing and medical exams, their customers preferred simple flashcards because everything else they saw was a distraction. Their graduate students preferred detailed explanations, while parents remained the primary persona for the undergraduate students. All the information allowed the company to enhance its position in the market, and its Bar Review prep app is still considered a market leader in this area.

From this perspective, how do we define persona analysis? It is a fundamental aspect of product research that will define the success or failure of your products before you engage in building those. User personas, also referred to as "proto-personas" (alternatively, you can also use plural "personae" based on the Latin origin of this term), provide a starting point for evaluating ideas and early design hypotheses. They help reinforce corporate awareness of the customer's point of view to ensure it's included in strategic planning.

Tip While doing persona analysis, always understand the difference between a customer and a consumer. A customer buys product from businesses, while a consumer uses the business products. You can actually be both a customer and a consumer in a business transaction. There is also a subtle difference between a client and a customer. Professional services organizations like consultancies, IT service companies, or advisory practices all have clients. Usually, they are supplying intangible services. Retailers and organizations supplying physical goods in general have customers. On top of it, clients have an interest in what you do or what you can do to help them acquire products or services, and customers are the ones who are purchasing these products or services.

We will review the five primary aspects of persona analysis:

- Format for describing personas
- The process to create personas
- Validation of the personas created
- Sharing persona analysis
- Ongoing refinement

1. The format to describe personas varies, with multiple excellent templates available online. The information that is usually captured is the following:

    - Name, potentially a Picture
    - Demographics and general characteristics (age, status, location, occupation, education)
    - Bio
    - Goals
    - Motivations
    - Problems/needs/frustrations
    - Personality type
    - Brand preference
    - Other (such as the level of adoption of new technology)

There are two important points to keep in mind: (1) this is a typical fictional person, not a real customer, and (2) it is not described as a type; it is described as a specific person. One of the possible formats is described in Figure 3-1.

Figure 3-1. Persona example from financial services perspective

2. In order to create personas, we need to answer the key questions:

    - Who is the customer?

    - What is the customer's problem?

    - What is the most important customer benefit?

"Any persona description should be based on knowledge gained from direct interaction with the target customers and users. This is necessary to build a connection with the beneficiaries of your product, develop empathy, and understand their current wants, needs, and circumstances."

— Roman Pichler. 10 Tips for creating Agile Personas https://www.romanpichler.com/blog/10-tips-Agile-personas

There are multiple ways of obtaining and analyzing this information, but for the initial persona analysis, it is possible to use a set of assumptions based on our understanding of the customer, their problems, and the research we are able to conduct. For the purpose of the original persona creation, it is important to involve the Scrum team along with product managers and user researchers in observation and brainstorming sessions so that developers, testers, and engineers are able to get to know their customers, internal and external, and empathize with them.

3. One initial set of personas was created (usually, more than one); this is further validated via in-depth user research – the details will be discussed in Chapter 4.

4. Once the initial persona analysis is completed and personas are created, it is important to make those personas visible to everyone so that software engineers would be able to put themselves in customer shoes while working on solutions and making ongoing implementation decisions. Persona descriptions are distributed, discussed, and placed in repositories or on the walls in physical offices. Frequently, developers would ask themselves questions: Would Eleanor appreciate this type of user experience? What user interface would she prefer? How would she like to receive notifications, and which options she'd like to choose from? What level of personalization would she like? These questions indicate a customer-centric mentality coming from the Scrum team.

5. Finally, personas change over time based on market changes, new product demands, or new information that becomes available to the product teams. This does not happen frequently, but it is important to stay open to validating, updating, and fine-tuning personas in order to create viable products.

Even though we are talking about "user personas" and "customer personas," the term "proto-personas" is used to refer to a typical person that is heave researched and validated via user research and analysis, as covered in Chapter 4.

🔆 **Tip**   The term "persona" was introduced in software development by Alan Cooper as part of his method, called Goal-Directed Design, since 1992 and described in his 2004 book *The Inmates Are Running the Asylum: Why High-Tech Products Drive Us Crazy and How to Restore the Sanity* [4]. The idea is that if you want to design effective software, it needs to be designed for a specific person. It is described as follows:

> "Develop a precise description of our user and what he wishes to accomplish... The actual method that works sounds trivial, but it is tremendously powerful and effective in every case: We make up present users and design for them. We call these pretend users personas, and they are the necessary foundation of good interaction design. Personas are not real people, but they represent them throughout the design process. They are hypothetical archetypes of actuals users. Although they are imaginary, they are defined with significant right and prevision."

—Alan Cooper. "The Inmates Are Running the Asylum" [4]

User Segmentation

User segmentation is the other side of persona analysis. This term refers to the practice of dividing all customers into segments based on characteristics – by age, region, language, goals, behaviors, status, and so forth – as relevant to the product being built. The term came from marketing because dividing potential markets or consumers into groups allows targeting marketing efforts in the most efficient way. For example, suburban living is marketed to families, while city apartments are marketed to business executives. The Job-to-Be-Done framework applied this concept to defining personas and targeting product features to their needs. However, for technology, the product persona-based approach was not sufficient. Technology products are not as consistent as milkshakes or traditional consumer products; they have a different life cycle and adoption curve based on the evolution of their customers, whose needs change frequently.

It was becoming clear that persona analysis based on user segmentation was not sufficient to identify customer needs for technology products. IT professionals realized that they needed a new way to understand their customers in a structured and evolving way. Like many technology product-related concepts, user segmentation came from business operations. The concept was to group customers based on their natural characteristics to identify the target audience and build customer loyalty through empathy.

Some segmentation categories include

- Demographic segmentation (customers of the same age, origin, or culture)

- Geographic segmentation (customers from the same geographic area or country)

- Segmentation by interests or hobbies (customers who enjoy art, music, theater, history, etc.)

- Behavioral segmentation (customer loyalty, purchase behavior, attitude toward the product)

- Psychographic segmentation (ready to purchase, open to buying but not to look, not being interested in buying)

- Brand segmentation based on brand preference or loyalty (e.g., luxury brands or preference for a specific brand for each product type)

- Customer journey segmentation (newbie, returning visitor, interested visitor, purchaser)

This information is used in designing marketing campaigns, but it is equally applicable and frequently used in designing IT products. Based on customer segmentation, their needs and goals, comfort with technology, and the industry of their choice, product managers prioritize features and refine personas to reflect their preferences and biases in technology adoption.

Five key questions to review:

1. What is a persona? Why are personas important in building software and designing IT services?

2. Are personas relevant to consumer online products or as relevant for institutions and large organizations?

3. Why is segmentation important in building software products?

4. What is the difference between a persona and a customer segment?

5. What are the key questions to answer in persona analysis?

Customer Journey

In the prior section, we mentioned the customer journey technique. Customer journey is an important technique in user analysis in software-oriented product development. A customer journey map is a visual representation of the process a customer or prospect goes through to achieve a goal with a specific product. It's a diagram that illustrates step-by-step customer interaction with a specific product based on their need, referred to as the "customer problem." This technique extends the persona concepts to show the interaction between a customer and the product and to prioritize customer needs.

> "You've got to start with the customer experience and work back toward the technology – not the other way around."
>
> — Steve Jobs

Figure 3-2 provides an example of a customer journey that describes customer experience and outlines the needs throughout the customer's experience. The persona for this customer map, Greg Hunter, has two sons, Max and Anthony, 5 and 11 years old, respectively. Greg likes taking one-day trips with his kids in New Jersey, where they live. They've already explored a lot of interesting destinations. In March, they visited a spot in Bridgewater, NJ, where American involvement in World War I officially ended in 1921. They saw a historical plague that marks the site where President Harding signed the Joint Congressional Resolution ending WWI on July 2, 1921. In April, they traveled to Asbury Park, a seaside community located on New Jersey's central coast, a historic town founded in 1871 and revived as a cultural destination in the early 2000s with a beautiful boardwalk and a vibrant community of artists and food connoisseurs.

They are trying now to find out their destination for the May trip, and each time, it takes a lot of time and effort for two reasons: there is no centralized source of this information, and there is no platform for them to collaborate, vote for the places each of them finds, and select the option that would all agree on. And when they finally agree, sometimes, each of them has their own understanding of what they have agreed on between all the phone calls, text messages, and dinnertime discussions. As the second step in their journey, they need to prepare for it: pack their belongings, purchase train or bus tickets, or decide to drive to the destination.

Each time they have to research multiple websites, and when they decide to drive, they have no trouble finding the closest way to the destination while they prefer a scenic drive with interesting places to visit on their way there. The travel itself is a highlight of their journey; however, once in a while, it happens that the destination is closed, and in this case, there is no easy way of finding a not-so-far-located alternative to their original destination. Finally, they all want to remember and share this experience with their mom and grandparents, but there are not aware of a way to personalize this trip in a digital way and share it with their relatives and friends. For now, they are ok with Instagram, while Greg uses Google photo albums, so there is no centralized repository for this experience.

The following customer journey map describes all the four phases of this experience while depicting the quality of customer experience and providing customer quotes describing their needs, as well as relevant parameters to assess their experience. Each column shows activities, the importance of those activities to customers, and the color-coded customer experience. It lists needs and expectations as well as provides the "voice of the customer" via quotes and relevant metrics. When the primary flow is not supported (e.g., their destination is closed or not available), it shows an alternative experience. It is a clear visual representation of the customer experience. If we look at the red circles in the bottom portion of the customer map, we can clearly assess customer needs to have

1. A single repository of New Jersey travel destinations by interest

2. An ability to enter new destinations

3. An ability to vote for those that the team would like to visit

4. A stored packing list that allows for modification based on destinations

5. An easy way to find the mode of transportation, make the decision, and purchase tickets or rent a car, whichever is applicable

6. A way to find a comparable alternative if the destination is not available upon arrival

7. A repository for trip information that is shareable, personalized, and persistent

We can also clearly see which areas are a major challenge and need to be addressed first. Those steps that are important to the customer (larger circles) and shown in red (the needs are not met) are the features of the products that need to be prioritized based on the customer journey.

The customer journey map describes the needs based on the persona identified at the top of the form (in this case, from the view of Greg Hunter, a New Jersey resident who likes to perform one-day local travel) and identifies parameters that influence customer choice, and priority of each of them. As we can see from the example, the most important parameter for Greg is safety. It is also important for him that he takes his sons to an interesting place, and it is also important, though it is not mandatory, that this is a historical place where kids can gather new information about their local history.

For larger systems, red circles identify business opportunities for new products to be built or the legacy products to be replatformed. "Voice of the customer" (VoC) in each column provides customer quotes that are representative of the need and allow the Scrum team to empathize with their customers, and establish a feedback loop for future product "demos" and customer interactions. There are many possible templates that describe customer journey, including customer interaction with a specific product, and each of them can be used to shape the product features and find business opportunities by identifying customer needs.

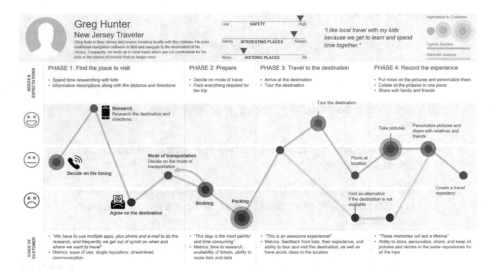

Figure 3-2. Customer journey map

Topic for a Group Discussion   In groups, discuss Aamazon Web Services (AWS) customer personas – subject matter experts within a large professional services organization who are dedicated to AWS. These groups would include (a) specialist team with a significant AWS subject matter expertise, a.k.a. AWS Partners, who are laser focused on AWS offers; (b) AWS Alliance Executive Sponsor, the person who has the override in all business and technical matters for the company, the one who knows what the organization is doing, where it is going from AWS perspective, the opportunities for growth, and how the company intends to overcome key challenges; and (c) AWS Customer IT or FinOps Persona who is well versed in AWS and aligned with AWS as part of one of specific work practices: solution architecture, sales, marketing, relationship management, or product engineering. How would AWS customer journey differ for each of these groups? Why?

Empathy Map

A customer journey map is not the only technique that allows one to visualize user experience and empathize with potential customers. Another effective technique is the empathy map.

It is essential to have a good understanding of the people who will be using the product being built. Empathy maps provide a straightforward and effective way of identifying user needs through empathy with potential customers. It is one of the customer-centric techniques. In terms of the template, it is literally customer-centric since the visual representation of the customer is placed in the middle of the one-page "map" while the areas around it represent the following topics:

- Whom are we empathizing with?
- What do they need to do?
- What do they see?
- What do they say?
- What do they do?
- What do they hear?
- What do they think and feel?
- What are their worries, aspirations, and challenges?

It is a collaborative technique used by Agile teams as a means of putting developers and testers in customer shoes in order to gain deeper insights into their customers. Similar to user personas, the empathy map represents a group of users, their needs, influencing factors, challenges, and perceptions.

Developed by Dave Gray, an Agile strategy consultant, in 2017, this technique proved to be highly effective in anticipating customer needs and providing valuable solutions to meeting those. Its goal is to gather insights into the customer segment's thoughts, feelings, motivations, and needs. The template (Empathy Map Canvas) [5] combines observation, surveying, interviewing, and understanding the Job-to-Be-Done from a customer perspective. We offer our own version of the empathy map inspired by Dave Gray's canvas in Figure 3-3.

Figure 3-3. Empathy map template (an updated version of Dave Gray's Empathy Map Canvas)

:bulb: **Tip**   Empathy Map Canvas can be downloaded at https://gamestorming.com/
wp-content/uploads/2017/07/Empathy-Map-Canvas-006.pdf.

Product Canvas

Empathy Map Canvas was not developed as a stand-alone solution. According to its author, Dave Gray, it was refined based on the comprehensive product solution — Business Model Canvas, developed by a Swiss business strategist and entrepreneur, Alex Osterwalder [6]. Business Model Canvas is a strategic product management template. It helps visualize what is important in the existing or a proposed business model and forces users to address key areas and achieve alignment — internal and with their customer personas.

:busts_in_silhouette: **Topic for a Group Discussion**   In groups, create an empathy map for a well-known online collaboration platform, for example, Facebook, LinkedIn, or Twitter. Discuss customer needs, pains, and gains. Based on this knowledge, discuss customer-centric priorities that would be reasonable to include in upcoming releases.

A business model is a business concept that has been put into practice. A model is always a simplification of the complex reality. It helps to understand the fundamentals of a business or to plan what a future business should look like. It's a visual representation of the key areas of product definition, such as

- Core strategy
- Strategic resources
- Customer interface
- Value network

These areas are translated into eight components:

- Customer segments (Who are the most important customers?)
- Value proposition (What value does the product deliver to customers, and which problems does it solve for them?)
- Revenue streams (For what value are the customers willing to pay and how?)
- Distribution channels (Through which channels do the customer segments want to be reached?)
- Customer relationships (What type of relationship does each of the customer segments expect us to establish and maintain with them?)
- Key activities (What key activities are required by value propositions, distribution channels, or customer relationships?)
- Key resources (What key resources are required, for example, physical, IP, financial, etc.?)
- Key partners (Who are the key partners – suppliers, vendors, collaborators?)
- Cost structure (What are the most important costs inherent to this business model?)

Tip   Business Value Model Canvas can be downloaded at `www.strategyzer.com/canvas/business-model-canvas`.

The ownership of the Business Model Canvas belongs to the business stakeholders; however, the team is using this single-page document to align on the product, customers, marketing, distribution, and revenue. Everyone on the product team, including Scrum team members, has to share this understanding of their business.

Technology Adoption Curve

IT products do not get adopted by users upon their introduction, as most consumer products do. They need to cross the chasm from early to mainstream adoption in order to grow their customer base. This concept was first introduced by Geoffrey Moore in his book, *Crossing the Chasm: Marketing and Selling Technology Projects*, in 1991 (3).

According to Geoffrey Moore, technology products differ by their level of customer adoption. He shows that in the Technology Adoption Life Cycle – which begins with innovators and moves to early adopters, early majority, late majority, and laggards – there is a vast chasm between the early adopters and the early majority. While early adopters are willing to sacrifice for the advantage of being first, the early majority waits until they know that the technology actually offers improvements in productivity. Early adopters (visionaries) are looking for breakthrough technology, and they are willing to pay well to be first with the new technology. The marketing strategies that win this group, however, won't work so well for the up-and-coming early majority (3). These are pragmatists and risk-averse, so they expect high quality and usability of the technology product. The details of this distribution curve are described by Geoffrey Moore in the model shown in Figure 3-4.

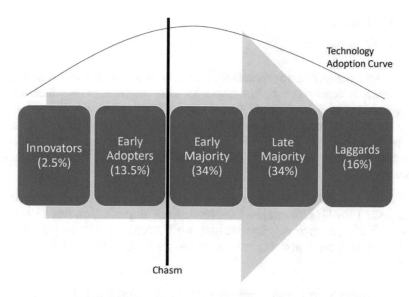

Figure 3-4. Technology Adoption Life Cycle as described by Geoffrey Moore in Crossing the Chasm: Marketing and Selling Technology Projects (3)

Building on Clayton Christensen's innovation concepts, Geoffrey Moore brings up an important concept: technology products have their own life cycle, and customer adoption is an important part of this life cycle.

> "Chasm crossing is not the end, but rather the beginning, of mainstream market development."
>
> — Geoffrey A. Moore, Crossing the Chasm (3)

Product Life Cycle

While the adoption curve is an important part of the IT product's or service life cycle, it is not the only parameter that defines its longevity and adoption. Each product passes through the following five stages:

- Development (including customer research and product design)
- Introduction
- Growth

- Maturity
- Decline

Usually, Agile teams are not directly involved in product life cycle management. However, it is important to be aware of the concept of Product Lifecycle Management (PLM) in IT. PLM has a significant potential to scale given its ability to help structure and organize independent development strategies, information, and capabilities. PLM is visualizing how the product is performing and how it's being used in real time, without waiting for customers to report on it.

PLM lowers the cost and speeds the time to market for new product development for IT products and services. Each organization has a process to manage PLM, sometimes lightweight and sometimes very prescriptive, whether it is a new product or an enhancement. This process has three elements:

- Information and communication technology (platform and systems, including architecture, tools, and standards)
- Processes, including people, skills, or organizational structures involved
- Methods (procedures, rules, practices, and tools)

Tip   For disruptive products and innovative implementations within existing products (e.g., camera in smartphones), it is important to understand which process is being assessed and where in the life cycle the product is. For example, it is unreasonable to add new features to a declining product, unless there is a regulatory requirement. Similarly, if a product is in the introductory phase, it is important to release MVP (minimum viable product) and collect and assess customer feedback before building new functionality.

Lean UX Concepts

Product innovation, personas, empathy maps, customer journeys, and other product discovery techniques form the foundation of customer research, which will be described in detail in Chapter 4. These user research and user experience (UX) practices have been referred to as Lean UX. Together, they represent the application of Lean principles to user experience in an attempt to build products and services that delight their customers.

In his foreword to the seminal book *Lean UX* by Jeff Gothelf and Josh Seiden (4), Eric Ries describes a situation from his personal practice: a company decided that it has to innovate in order to survive and hired a design team to investigate the future of its industry and recommend innovative new products. This team interviewed, observed, and analyzed customer behavior. They used surveys, focus groups, observations, prototypes, and smoke tests to create, test, and refine their concepts. At the end of the study, the team provided a set of recommendations based on the research they had done. Then, they wrote a specification document and handed it over to their engineers to implement. After years of implementation, the products that were created did not resonate with customers. Company executives went back to review the interviews, feedback, and customer analysis, and it was largely accurate, so the executives blamed their engineers and development teams for the lack of success.

In fact, the reason was the opposite: the reason why the products did not resonate with the customers despite the original research that was well conducted was that development teams – software engineers, testers, and IT professionals – were not included in the customer research, neither they had access to customers during implementation. If product discovery is separated from execution, the product will not succeed – in reality, there is a continuous interaction between the two, with IT professionals being at the center of this interaction (see Figure 3-5).

Figure 3-5. Interdependence between discovery and execution

"We are still building linear organizations in a world that demands constant change. We are still building silos in a world that demands thorough collaboration. And we are still investing in analysis, arguing over specifications, and efficiently producing deliverables in a world that demands continuous experimentation in order to achieve continuous innovation."

— Eric Ries, Foreword to "Lean UX" (4)

For IT professionals, the topic of building the right product is as important as building the product right. They are the ones that contribute to product definition and design decisions, they learn based on customer experience, and empathize with customers while building products that solve customer needs. In Chapter 4, we will discuss customer research principles and review the application of Lean UX thinking to building modern IT products.

Five key questions to review:

1. What is a customer journey? When do you use this technique?

2. How do customer journey and empathy map differ?

3. What is the business product canvas and what are the questions it answers?

4. Why is it important to understand a product life cycle when developing an IT product?

5. Why the relationship between IT professionals and product managers described as collaborative? What are the examples of this collaboration?

Key Points

1. The role of IT professionals today is not to write code, deliver IT services, or test software – their role is to provide capabilities to their customers.

2. From the product value perspective, an important concept is the "Job-to-Be-Done" (JTBD), which reflects underlying user needs. This theory was popularized by Clayton Christensen, a Harvard University professor. This concept is the next step in product adoption because it extends the concept of a product to the value it provides to the customer.

3. Persona analysis is a method of representing the target audience for a product. In product analysis, the user persona is a customer type represented as a fictional character – with a made-up biography, demographics, characteristics, and a clear representation of their need. There are multiple ways of obtaining and analyzing this

information, but for the initial persona analysis, it is possible to use a set of assumptions based on our understanding of the customer, their problems, and the user research we are able to conduct.

4. User segmentation is the other side of persona analysis. This term refers to the practice of dividing all customers into segments based on characteristics – by age, region, language, goals, behaviors, status, and so forth – as relevant to the product being built. The term came from marketing because dividing potential markets or consumers into groups allows to target marketing efforts in the most efficient way.

5. Customer journey is an important technique in user analysis in software-oriented product development. A customer journey map is a visual representation of the process a customer or prospect goes through to achieve a goal with a specific product.

6. Empathy maps are a customer-centric technique that provides a straightforward and effective way of identifying user needs through empathy with potential customers. Its goal is to gather insights into the customer segment's thoughts, feelings, motivations, and needs. The template combines observation, surveying, interviewing, and understanding the Job-to-Be-Done from a customer perspective.

7. Business Model Canvas is a strategic product management template for developing new or documenting existing business models. It helps visualize what is important and forces users to address key areas and achieve alignment – internal and with their customer personas.

8. IT products do not get adopted by users upon their introduction, as most consumer products do. They need to cross the chasm from early to mainstream adoption in order to grow their customer base. This concept was first introduced by Geoffrey Moore in his book, *Crossing the Chasm*.

9. While the adoption curve is an important part of the IT product's or service life cycle, it is not the only parameter that defines its longevity and adoption. Each product passes through the following five stages: development, introduction, growth, maturity, and decline.

10. Product innovation, personas, empathy maps, customer journeys, and other product discovery techniques form the foundation of customer research. These user research and user experience (UX) practices are referred to as Lean UX. Together, they represent the application of Lean principles to user experience in an attempt to build products and services that delight their customers.

Validating the Product Hypothesis

This chapter covers the Lean startup framework of Agile product design, based on the "build-measure-learn" feedback loop. Once the customer is identified, it is important to validate whether our understanding of customer needs is accurate. In addition, this chapter introduces the concepts of customer hypothesis, validation, minimum viable product (MVP), and the principles of making the decision to pivot or persevere. It describes the nonlinear nature of Lean startup validation, which is equally relevant for startups and large enterprises.

Introduction

In Chapter 3, we discussed different techniques for identifying your customer. Whether you are delivering a fixed- scope project or iteratively building a new product, your business will not be possible without having customer needs at the center of your delivery model. Customers define which businesses

© Mariya Breyter 2022
M. Breyter, *Agile Product and Project Management*,
https://doi.org/10.1007/978-1-4842-8200-7_4

succeed and which businesses fail. In Lesson 3, we discussed Lean UX techniques for identifying proto-personas and understanding their needs. We also covered multiple techniques for user segmentation and analysis, including empathy maps and customer journeys.

However, in many instances, our understanding of what the customers need (or even who the customers are) is not accurate. No matter how well we know those customers, our understanding of what they need is just an assumption, a hypothesis that needs to be validated. As Henry Ford is said to have stated, "If I had asked people what they wanted, they'd have said 'a faster horse'." A true product visionary frequently comes up with ideas that others have not yet suggested or tested, and yet there is a need to validate those ideas before implementing them commercially.

This need is described by Eric Ries in his book *Lean Startup* [1]. In his opinion, the ability to validate a customer hypothesis before building new products or delivering complex business solutions is as applicable to Fortune 500 companies as it is to startups. Business success can be engineered by following the right process, which means it can be learned and applied as part of the Agile framework.

This chapter covers the Lean startup method and other techniques that allow you to validate customer needs before the product is built. This approach saves time and money and helps shape and prioritize deliverables based on customer needs. It fits within Agile, flexible delivery and ensures that the organization is delivering the product that will be of value to customers. We will review multiple frameworks for conducting this research, such as Google Ventures' design Sprints, and use templates, such as Validation Canvas, to record all the steps in defining whether to "pivot" or "persevere" with product delivery.

We will review multiple techniques for conducting this research, such as "concierge MVP" or "exploration," and we will discuss user research techniques. We will also discuss innovation and disruptive solutions, which may redefine our product concepts. As a result of all these activities, we will define MVP (minimum viable product) based on customer needs and identify all the necessary details to build a prioritized list of features and start execution.

🔅 **Tip**   Even though the concepts of customer identification, hypothesis validation, product definition, and delivery are introduced in a logical sequential order in this textbook, it does not mean that they are always linear. Lean startup is built on the Lean concepts of the PDCA (plan–do–check–act) cycle, which is an iterative four-step management method used in business for the control and continuous improvement of processes and products. This cycle, proposed by Walter Stewart and later developed by William Deming, establishes a continuous feedback loop from the customers. Lean startup rebrands it as a "build–measure–learn" cycle. This means that throughout Agile delivery, we repeatedly go back to validating the customer hypothesis and redefining the product and its features.

The following are the concepts we will cover in this chapter:

- Lean startup
- Customer hypothesis
- Pivot or persevere
- User research
- Validation Canvas
- Design Sprints
- MVP (minimum viable product)

Lean Startup: Fail Fast, Succeed Faster

In May 2013, Steve Blank, a Silicon Valley entrepreneur and a professor at Stanford, UC Berkeley, and Columbia University, published an article entitled "Why the Lean Start-Up Changes Everything." In this article, he stated: "Launching a new enterprise—whether it's a tech start-up, a small business, or an initiative within a large corporation—has always been a hit-or-miss proposition. According to the decades-old formula, you write a business plan, pitch it to investors, assemble a team, introduce a product, and start selling as hard as you can. And somewhere in this sequence of events, you'll probably suffer a fatal setback. The odds are not with you: As new research by Harvard Business School's Shikhar Ghosh shows, 75% of all start-ups fail" [2].

Imagine that there is a way to predict which product, initiative, or undertaking is going to be successful before building it rather than after it is delivered to customers. How can we learn from the customers what they need before we deliver anything to them? The worst way is to ask customers what they need. They would tell you that they want a faster horse, according to the quote by Henry Ford at the beginning of this chapter.

Case Study: Iphone VS. Blackberry.   If anyone had told BlackBerry users in 2005–2007 that in ten years, a mobile phone would have one primary button, they would have never believed it. In the early 2000s, the more buttons on a mobile phone, the more complicated and hence, the more sophisticated it was considered. If anyone had asked users at this time how they would like to see the new mobile phone model, they would have wanted more buttons, not fewer.

So what happened? Did users ask for a simplistic design? No, they wanted additional functionality. Was it the smartphone market and intense competition from cheaper brands? Again, this was not the case. What happened then?

When Apple released the iPhone in 2007, Microsoft's CEO Steve Ballmer laughed at its chances. Very soon, however, the apps, their ease of creation, ease of use, unlimited functionality, and extensibility, along with simplistic user experience, killed BlackBerry. The only way to predict this was to come up with a new solution and validate it with the customer via early prototyping and customer feedback.

In one of the most groundbreaking announcements of the 21st century, Steve Jobs introduced the iPhone as a combination of three separate devices which had never before been imagined as a single device, and customers loved it. Even though the 2007 version of the iPhone had a 3.5-inch diagonal screen with subpar resolution and was not the most reliable device to use, it stood out as a truly revolutionary product. How did Steve Jobs know that customers would love it? You may think that he knew it because he was a product visionary and a genius. However, besides his vision and his ability to put himself in his customer's shoes, Steve Jobs conducted intense validation through prototyping and early user research, which allowed him to shape the model in such a way that it met customer needs.

It may be hard to believe now that the touchscreen device that blew everyone's minds didn't come about so easily. The iPhone was the result of years of hard work by Apple's industrial designers. They built a large number of prototypes and CAD designs in their quest to produce the ultimate smartphone. Multiple prototypes were created, and multiple prototypes failed as a result of customer research over three years of an intense discovery process [3].

"... today, we're introducing three revolutionary products... The first one: is a widescreen iPod with touch controls. The second: is a revolutionary mobile phone. And the third is a breakthrough Internet communications device... An iPod, a phone, and an Internet communicator. An iPod, a phone ... Are you getting it?

These are not three separate devices, this is one device, and we are calling it iPhone."

— Keynote address by Steve Jobs at the Macworld Conference & Expo held in Moscone West in San Francisco, California, on January 9, 2007

According to 2002 research conducted by The Standish Group [4], 45% of the features in the software products they surveyed were never used, and 19% were rarely used. In Lean terminology, these instances are referred to as "waste." Besides creating those unneeded features, companies need to maintain this code, upgrade it, and include it in subsequent releases of the software (Figure 4-1). Over a period of time, this level of waste can be quantified as 30–45% of the total product cost.

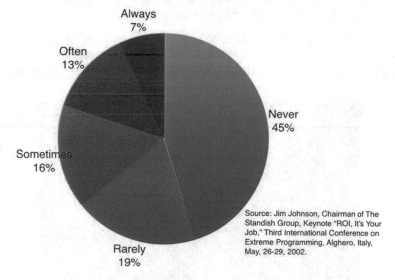

Feature Use in Four Internal-Use Products

Always 7%

Often 13%

Never 45%

Sometimes 16%

Rarely 19%

Source: Jim Johnson, Chairman of The Standish Group, Keynote "ROI, It's Your Job," Third International Conference on Extreme Programming, Alghero, Italy, May, 26-29, 2002.

Figure 4-1. Feature use data by The Standish Group

Topic for a Group Discussion   In groups, identify a software or hardware product or service that you all know and are using on a regular basis. Talk about its features. Are you aware of all the features that your group members are actively using? Are there any you have not been using? Conduct a quick online research to identify the features you may not be aware of or the ones you are aware of but are not using. Discuss why this is happening. Are you and your groupmates using the same features and ignoring the others or are the rarely used or never-used features different for each of you? Share the findings between the groups.

Incremental delivery proves to be the best way of minimizing risk over a period of time. By delivering a product incrementally, we learn from the customer and adjust the deliverables for the next iteration, depending on customer feedback. As an example, for a 12-month initiative in the case of incremental value delivery every month: if we deliver a product to the customer after month one and find out that the customer is not interested in the product or not satisfied with its pricing or quality, we have one month's work to redo and 11 months to course-correct. If we wait until month 12 to deliver and find out that the product is not viable, we have lost the work of 12 months and have no time to produce a viable alternative. Figure 4-2 clearly shows that the risk is progressively increasing month after month unless interim deliverables are validated by the customer.

What if we do not need to wait until the first deliverable? While there is no crystal ball, there is a proven way to find out what the customer needs before building the actual product. This framework is referred to as "Lean startup."

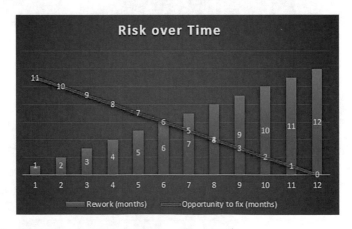

Figure 4-2. Risk advantages provided by incremental delivery

Lean startup defines a way to come up with a hypothesis about customer needs and validate it, similar to the way the Apple team of researchers validated early iPhone prototypes. According to Eric Ries, "Every business plan begins with a set of assumptions. It lays out a strategy that takes those assumptions as a given and proceeds to show how to achieve the company's vision. Because the assumptions haven't been proved to be true (they are assumptions, after all) and in fact are often erroneous, the goal of a startup's early efforts should be to test them as quickly as possible" [1].

The Lean startup approach relies on the concept of "validated learning." This principle describes learning generated by prototyping or implementing an initial idea and then measuring it against customer feedback to validate its effect. Typical steps in validated learning include the following: (1) specify the goal, (2) specify the metrics that represent the goal, (3) act to achieve the goal, (4) analyze the metrics if there is progress in achieving the goal, and (5) improve and try again. Each test of an idea is a single iteration in the value delivery process. While the term "validated learning" was introduced by Eric Ries as part of Lean startup principles, it can be applied universally.

Validated learning is applicable to almost any product or service. For example, for web products, we can use web analytics using tools such as Google Analytics and Amplitude. These tools provide capabilities to track the number of sessions (visits), the number of new sessions vs. returning visitors (this helps to determine if the website is attracting new visitors and whether it offers enough value to warrant return visits), channels (e.g., direct, organic search, referral, email, paid search, other advertising, social and display), bounce rate to define its "stickiness" (percentage of single-page website visits), conversion rate (purchases and other steps in the engagement cycle, such as email subscriptions, contact form submissions, content downloads, engaging in a live chat, and watching videos), and other relevant data.

The validated learning cycle in a Lean startup is described in Figure 4-3.

Lean Startup: Validated Learning

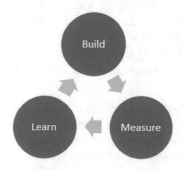

Figure 4-3. Validated learning in Lean startup

> "... the biggest waste that product development faces today is not building things inefficiently, but building things very efficiently that nobody wants."
>
> — Eric Ries "The Lean Startup." Talks at Google, April 2011

Besides validated learning, Lean startup includes experimentation to validate a hypothesis and iterative product releases to shorten the feedback loop depicted before. The Lean startup has been adopted by large corporations and smaller startups around the world due to its ability to minimize risk by shortening the feedback loop and its ability to bring the customer into the center of the development cycle.

 Five key questions to review:

1. What is Lean startup?

2. Why is Lean startup so popular?

3. Is Lean startup an approach that is relevant for startups only? Why?

4. Why was the first iPhone so successful in the market?

5. What does it mean to "fail fast, succeed faster?"

Customer Hypothesis: Fall in Love with the Problem, not with the Solution

The biggest mistake that may happen while identifying the product or service, or defining the scope for an internal deliverable, is to focus on the solution. It frequently seems that innovators come up with new disruptive ideas, implement them, and start looking for customers. In fact, this is the way to create products and services that no one is interested in, except for their creators. Lean startup provides a mechanism to validate assumptions before building the product by checking if the problem exists and, if it does, whether customers are passionate enough about solving it so that they prioritize it above others.

As an example, when selecting customers to validate a weight loss program, it is not sufficient to ask respondents if they would like to lose weight. Most of them would most likely respond that they would. Instead, the question to ask is the following: "Have you tried before, and if yes, what did you do?" This way, you would be able to select those who willingly invested their time and effort into a weight loss program before; hence, they have demonstrated that they take it seriously and are willing to invest their time in the research.

This approach is implemented by startup incubators, which provide mentorship and support to startups for the first three to six months and then allow the graduating teams to build their businesses. They start by helping startup teams empathize with their customers – observe them (for this technique, we use the term "Gemba" from Japanese, translated as "the real place") or interview them to understand whether the problem that the businesses are solving is a real problem for their prospective customers. The startups that begin with the opposite rarely survive. For example, I mentored one of the education startups, which was teaching children who had dyslexia to read by using newspaper articles as an example. They created a collection of newspaper articles of different complexity and questions related to them. However, they found that the children were not interested in reading outdated articles because the content was not relevant to them. This is one of the examples where a solution came before the actual problem. Once they found this out, they were able to focus on relevant context rather than the complexity.

There are five steps to validate a hypothesis:

1. State the hypothesis

2. Come up with a list of assumptions

3. Decide on the metrics to validate these assumptions

4. Run the experiment and compare metrics against expectations

5. Based on the results, "pivot" or "persevere" (these two concepts will be discussed later in this chapter)

When stating the hypothesis, work from your customer or persona. (Persona analysis was described in detail in Chapter 2.) Persona types have to be as narrow as feasible in order to make this process accurate. For example, for a face-to-face educational company providing test preparation services, the hypothesis is that students need support in their studies, and the assumption is that children of a certain age are still open to classroom learning for their test prep. It is important to define the right metrics. If 50% of the students are interested in the face-to-face test prep, is it enough? For that, we need to quantify the market and make assumptions about the number of students in the area where we have our physical office. To make this type of a major strategic decision, we take a lot of concepts into consideration before coming up with relevant metrics.

Eric Ries talks about two types of metrics: actionable metrics and vanity metrics. While both types may seem informative, vanity metrics are misleading, while actionable metrics help validate hypotheses. As an example, he uses a test prep company called Grockit, which changed its strategy based on moving from vanity metrics based on the number of users to actionable metrics based on customer trends for each newly released feature.

Case Study: Grockit. When this company was launched by Farbood Nivi, a test prep professional who was teaching test prep via a popular online conferencing tool, they were looking at the total number of customers and the total number of questions answered. That was causing his team to spin its wheels, and the company was making no progress. The company was not improving, and Farbood was not able to draw clear cause-and-effect inferences. As a result, he decided to concentrate on a different type of metrics: When we shipped a specific feature, did it affect customer behavior? He started launching each feature as a true split-test experiment.

A split-test experiment is one in which different versions of a product are offered to customers at the same time, and each version is provided to its own group. By observing the changes in behavior between the two groups, one can make inferences about the impact of different variations. For Farbood, split testing uncovered interesting learnings. For example, many features that made the product better in the eyes of engineers and designers had no impact on customer behavior. When they found out that social features did not change customer behavior, they measured the trends and concentrated on an intensive solo-studying model, which proved to be successful [1].

As we can see from Grockit's experience, vanity metrics are misleading, while actionable metrics provide an accurate picture of a company's performance. For Grockit, the number of users did not mean that the business was successful while shifting their business strategy based on the information obtained about measuring feature performance proved to be highly beneficial. It is important that actionable metrics are directly tied to OKRs (as discussed in Chapter 1) and are aligned with the business objectives. While concentrating on a solo-studying model, Grockit maintained its integrity by remaining one of the first social learning platforms that built its business around students, teachers, and tutors answering each other's questions online. In 2011, it passed its ten million questions, and the number of chat messages going across the site was approaching 100 million. Out of its 1 million total registered users, about 25,000 to 50,000 were active in any given month, which suggested that most students used it to prepare for a test and then move on [6].

In July 2013, Farbood Nivi sold Grockit to Kaplan Test Prep and pivoted to develop a new (now defunct) EdTech company called Learnist. Learnist was an iPhone app that allowed individuals to read content, review how-to guides, and watch educational videos on virtually any subject. The content was written and curated by experts on each topic. Farbood pivoted, but he stayed true to his mission of making education available to everyone.

As the fifth step, upon review of the metrics and all relevant data, the organization or the team implementing the initiative, building the product, or providing the service needs to make a decision: "pivot" or "persevere."

The Grockit example shows the importance of "falling in love with the problem, not with the solution." Whether with Grockit or with Learnist, Farbood stayed true to his passion for solving the problem of the availability to high-quality education for anyone; however, he pivoted in selecting the ways to make learning accessible, based on the "build-measure-learn" feedback loop. The most important part of using actionable metrics for a company is to be prepared to listen to the voice of the customer and empathize with their needs, not with the solution the company already has in mind.

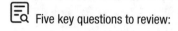 Five key questions to review:

1. Why is it important to validate the customer hypothesis before building a product?

2. What are the five steps to validate the hypothesis?

3. How do companies decide between actionable metrics and vanity metrics? Why are vanity metrics harmful?

4. In the Grockit example, how did the company's strategy change based on switching to actionable metrics?

5. Why is it important to "fall in love with the problem, not with the solution"?

Pivot or Persevere

In order to validate or invalidate a customer hypothesis, it is not sufficient just to measure the outcomes. It is important to structure multiple "build-measure-learn" feedback loops to stage experiments, measure results, and "pivot" (switch to another product definition) or "persevere" (continue with the chosen product strategy). With each pivot, there is a new set of assumptions that comes up, and a new experiment is created based on these assumptions. However, there is no need to validate all the assumptions: the right way is to start with the most fundamental and least obvious assumption, referred to as the "most risky" assumption. The experiment is based on validating this riskiest assumption, and if it is confirmed, the next step is to "persevere" and develop the idea further, and if not, the next step is to "pivot" and suggest another solution, based on the learnings from this research. This continues until the hypothesis is confirmed and the solution that addresses the customer's problem is found.

A pivot is a substantive change to one or more components of the business model. The decision to pivot is not easy. It requires an ability to look at the problem objectively. Many companies fail to do so and build products that customers are not interested in. It includes selecting the right actionable metrics, setting up success criteria, and staging their experiments in a thoughtful and methodical way to validate their assumptions. The companies that are able to take an objective look at customer feedback succeed, and those who ignore the needs of the changing market and the feedback from their customers, such as Kodak, Blockbuster, and Xerox, fail to pivot.

Kodak's failure is not about the failure to embrace disruptive innovation. It has nothing to do with technology either. Here's an example from my own experience. In 1994, when I was a visiting scholar at Stanford University, I was invited to a live demo of digital photography. Kodak researchers came over to the campus to show us pictures printed without a film. And yet Kodak suffered strategic failure because it failed to recognize the emerging customer need and tried to protect its film business. It was the wrong choice not "pivoting" the traditional model that set Kodak on the path to bankruptcy. You can read about it in the book by a former Kodak executive, Vincent Barabba, *The Decision Loom: A Design for Interactive Decision-Making in Organizations* [7]. Kodak's failure was not caused by their inability to see digital photography as a disruptive technology – they invented it. The failure was caused by their inability to understand customer needs and the resulting desire to ignore the invention in order to protect their existing business, that is, their inability to pivot.

This ability has a lot to do with the "working backward" model discussed in Chapter 2, which is the ability to work backward from the customer, empathize with customer needs, and pivot based on what we learn from customers. And frequently, this learning will be different from what we hear from customers, so we need to be prepared to think long term, based on customer problems, not based on what they tell us they need.

In the digital photography demo that I attended back at Stanford in 1994, there were about 20 or so faculty and students in the room, and while all of us were genuinely amused, no one could envision that this would become the technology of the future. The digital camera was large and ugly, the quality of the printed picture was off, and the file size was huge. None of the participants' responses showed any indication of commercial success. When I asked the researchers whether they felt this was a successful demo, they surprised me by saying that it was. I questioned this, and they explained that they were not looking for product approval – this would be vanity metrics for them in today's terminology. They were looking for ease of use: each of us was able to take a picture, save it, and send it to print. In order to decide whether to pivot or persevere, they validated their "riskiest assumption" that people would be able to navigate the digital photography process easily and seamlessly – a great example of a well-structured validation experiment, which, unfortunately, was not carried forward by company management.

Let's review some examples of the companies that were able to pivot successfully and then built their business based on the ideas they pivoted toward. You may not even be aware of the first iterations of well-known companies. For example, have you heard about an app called Burbn? In 2010, Burbn was created as a location-based HTML-5 app. The app allowed users to check into locations, make plans (future check-ins), earn points for hanging out with friends, post pictures, and much more.

It took a year to build a complete native iPhone app, but the customers were not pleased with its early version. It felt cluttered and overrun with features. Based on customer feedback, the team cut everything in the Burbn app except for its photo, comment, and "like" capabilities. What remained was Instagram. A week after its launch in 2010, they had 100,000 users, and the rest is history.

Was Burbn a bad application? Definitely not. One of the early customers shared that he found Burbn interesting because it was showing relevant locations and because this was an HTML-5 approach that was slick at that time. However, based on customer feedback, the team was able to pivot successfully, which resulted in creating one of the most successful businesses of the 21st century. It is important to understand the bold decision that was made: after a year of hard work, the team cut most of its functionality in favor of phone capabilities, and by doing that, they were able to listen to their customers, who defined their needs as social photo exchange rather than interactive location mapping [10].

Topic for a Group Discussion   In groups, review other well-known examples of well-known companies that pivoted from lesser-known predecessors. Have you heard of a podcasting platform Odeo, predecessor of Twitter? A PDA payments product for Palm Pilots? Only incidentally did they build a web interface to allow users to make payments to each other without their Palms, which pivoted into PayPal. Other examples include Tune In, Hook Up, a video dating site, which became YouTube, and an online video game entitled "Game Neverending," which became Flickr.

Tip   The "pivot or persevere" approach is equally applicable to large corporations and fixed-scope initiatives. It helps identify "how" to validate a customer problem and come up with the right solution that addresses this need.

Case Study: A Fortune 100 Health Insurance Company.   In 2015, a Fortune 100 health insurance company initiated a major tooling acquisition for its internal use. The assumption made by the executives was that users needed a robust, easy-to-use collaboration tool to align to the work that different groups within this multithousand employee organization were doing. For their teams, they wanted to come up with a robust, easy-to-navigate tool that could record everyone's work, manage dependencies at any level, and visualize progress.

The project team conducted a "build vs. buy" analysis based on these assumptions and suggested that they procure a well-known Agile project management tool. Luckily for the project team, they initiated a Proof of Concept (POC) iteration to pilot the tool with one division only. As they found out, the users did not find the tool helpful. If the project team had validated their assumptions from the very beginning, they would have found out that the issue was not coordination and not even transparency of the management or team-level reporting. The major issue was the long-term vision and accuracy of long-term planning, and the tool did not provide those capabilities. As a result, no matter the company size or type of initiative, it is important to start with the customer problem and pivot based on customer feedback.

Five key questions to review:

1.   What does it mean to pivot? For example, if a company is rebranding its website, is it pivoting? If an insurance company is expanding globally, is this an example of pivoting?

2.   Why is it important for any company or for any project leader to make a decision to pivot or persevere?

3.   What are some examples of well-known companies that were able to pivot successfully?

4.   What does it mean to "work backward" from customer needs in your understanding?

5.   Do only startups "pivot or persevere"? Can you talk about examples from this chapter or from your own experience when a large company or a project had to pivot to address customers' problems?

User Research

In order to validate or invalidate a hypothesis, it is important to hear from customers. This is done via user research.

User research focuses on understanding user behaviors, needs, and observations through a number of techniques, from the observation of users in their natural surroundings to interviewing them about their experience with a working product and everything in between. It is an iterative and cyclical process.

User research is a significant and complex discipline and is the topic of a specialized course on User Experience and User Research. For the topic of Agile product management, we will cover the steps that are relevant to defining the product. In order to achieve validated learning from customers, four steps in regard to user research are most important:

1. Identify the right customer(s) representing the target persona(s) for your product.

2. Define the way of collecting this feedback (e.g., customer interview, observation of customer interaction with a prototype, surveys, or web analytics for online products).

3. Conduct the research.

4. Aggregate and interpret the data from the research to compare against the hypothesis in a nonambiguous way.

Tip   In this chapter, we cover the universal concepts of customer analysis and validated learning. These approaches apply to a product (a deliverable with its own life cycle, available to customers as long as there is a need for it), a project (an initiative of any size and scope with a specific outcome and specified constraints, such as budget, timelines, and scope), or a service (availability of a specific functionality to the customer via channels established within the customer's agreement with a provider). This is relevant for software, hardware, or any other undertaking. For the purpose of this chapter, there is no specific distinction between the types of the effort – customer analysis and validated learning are equally important, no matter what the goal is.

Let's review each of these steps:

1. **Identifying the customer(s).** In order to identify the right customer, it is important to refer to the target persona(s). The narrower this definition is, the more accurate the results are going to be.

   For example, for a financial services company offering banking services of 30,000–50,000 USD, it is not sufficient to talk about the mid-income revenue population. It is not sufficient to define their income as 50,000–150,000 USD per family in the United States. Depending on the type of financial services, target personas will be different. For a loan business, this would be people with medical bills or college loans to pay. They are most concerned about availability and convenience. For the insurance business, it would be families with children or one working family member who needs to protect their income. They are most concerned about insurance terms and conditions. For investment services, the customers are less concerned about convenience and more about the rate of return, as well as the security and liquidity of their investments. Depending on the nature of the product, project, or service, it is important to target the right customer.

"What people say is much less useful than what people do."

— David Travis, User Research and User Experience Strategist [11]

2. **Defining data to collect and the means of collecting feedback.** Once the customer audience is identified, it is important to define the question that needs to be answered, working backward from customer needs. Which problem needs to be validated? Are we defining whether customers lack transparency (in this case, there is a need to provide a comprehensive reporting tool) or have trouble managing dependencies (in this case, there is a need to provide a work visualization and alignment tool between multiple groups)?

Once the problem is identified, it is important to define how to measure it and how many respondents are required. If the user research method involves comprehensive interviews, then the number of customers participating in the research is significantly lower than a web analytics tool for an online tool or an app. Finally, it is helpful to identify success criteria: whether your hypothesis will be validated by a simple majority of respondents or you need a specific percentage of users to confirm your assumption.

The most important rule is to never ask questions starting with "Would you?" These responses do not validate customer behavior. Most customers would confirm that they are interested in using the tool because there is no obligation on their part. In addition, these types of questions cause respondents to guess about behavior rather than share facts about their actual behavior. You can show your customers a prototype of your product, followed by a set of questions, or simply observe their interaction with the prototype.

Alternatively, you can conduct interviews. A simple yet powerful interviewing approach is called a "three-point interview." It consists of three questions:

- Have you ever had <a problem>? (If they answer "No" at this point, the assumption is invalidated.)

- Tell me more about the last time you had <the problem>. What did you do?

- For you, what is the ideal solution in that situation?

3. **Conducting the research.** Customers have to be available and in agreement with the research. No matter whether they are internal or external, they need to be recruited. There are multiple ways of reaching out to customers and incentivizing them to participate in the research. In the case of external customers, you can offer them participation in a Beta product trial or a discount on your product for a specific period of time after launch. In the case of internal customers, you can incentivize them by supporting them in solving the actual problem they are facing.

Researchers need to have an interview script, allocate sufficient time for interviews, and make the participants comfortable and clear about the expectations. There are also legal aspects and other constraints. For example, you may want to ask external participants to sign a nondisclosure agreement (NDA) before showing them any prototypes of your product. All the results are accurately documented by interviewers in a predefined format.

Tips for conducting user interviews are as follows:

- The most effective interviews are with one person at a time because groupthink is misleading. Also, when there are multiple researchers, the respondents may feel uncomfortable.

- It is important to know the goals and questions ahead of time. A prioritized list of assumptions is used to generate the list of questions. It is advisable to clarify and adjust the questions based on the respondent, but there has to be a clear script to start with.

- Separate behavior interviews from feedback interviews. If the goal of the research is to understand customer needs, ask about the gaps between their needs and the available tools or functionality. If the goal is to get their feedback on features or on a specific prototype, ask about usability aspects.

- Stay open-minded and get excited about hearing hard truths. If you are invested in your product, project, or service, it is easy to overlook negative feedback and start "selling" your product to respondents or cause them to be unnecessarily polite. Encourage and embrace negative feedback – it will save you effort going forward.

- Active listening is the key. It is important to keep the questions short and unbiased. Open-ended questions are more effective than "yes/no" questions. If a customer pauses, do not try to fill in the gap. Give them time to think. The goal is to learn, not to market the product.

4. **Aggregating and interpreting the data.** This step is very important because the way the data is aggregated and presented influences the decision. This is one of the reasons why the metrics and success criteria are defined in advance. Based on the results, the decision is made whether to pivot (change the business model or one of the most fundamental assumptions) or persevere and proceed as originally intended. It is important to base decisions on data rather than speculations, even if these are coming from customers. As Henry Ford and Steve Jobs have shown, the features that customers ask for are never as interesting as to why they want them.

Topic for a Group Discussion   In groups, identify the key problem statement for the persona types you came up with in Chapter 2. How would you structure the experiment to validate this problem statement? What is the riskiest assumption? Who would you interview and what questions are you going to ask them? What would your success criteria look like?

Validation Canvas

In order to organize and structure validation experiments, companies use a simple template referred to as the "Lean Validation Canvas." This template allows them to make assumptions, validate hypotheses, and record pivot or persevere decisions (see Figure 4-4).

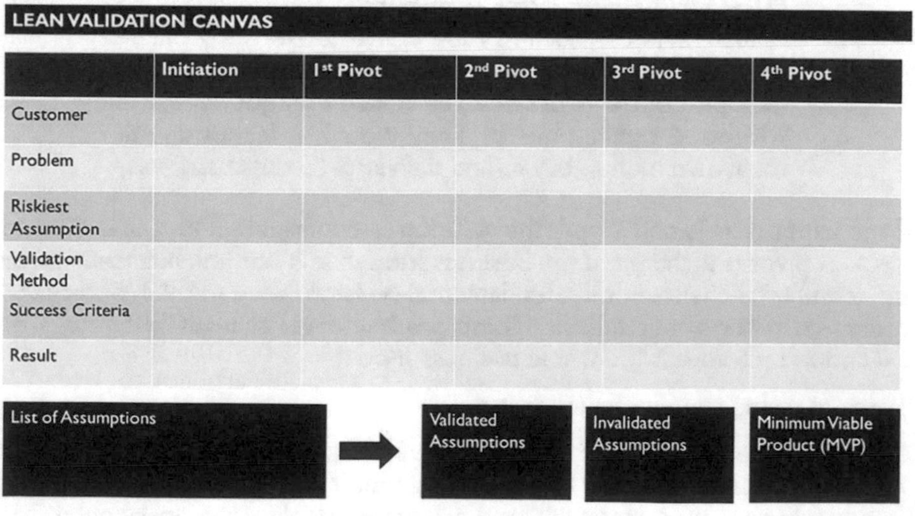

LEAN VALIDATION CANVAS

	Initiation	1st Pivot	2nd Pivot	3rd Pivot	4th Pivot
Customer					
Problem					
Riskiest Assumption					
Validation Method					
Success Criteria					
Result					

List of Assumptions	⇒	Validated Assumptions	Invalidated Assumptions	Minimum Viable Product (MVP)

Figure 4-4. Lean Validation Canvas

Step by step, the Lean Validation Canvas is used to record each customer's information, their problem to solve, the riskiest assumption, the experiment, and the results.

Major types of Lean startup experiments are the following:

1. Exploration: Exploration is an interaction with the customer that focuses on their problems, with the goal of understanding customer behavior. It is best done at the customer's location (in Lean, this is described by the term "Gemba" we mentioned before, which means "the actual/real place" in Japanese. In business, "Gemba" refers to the place where value is created). Besides observation, you can use interviews or a low-fidelity prototype, such as a paper drawing.

2. Pitch: Pitch is an interaction with the customer that attempts to sell the product to a customer in exchange for their time, work, or feedback. One of the possible approaches with this technique is to try to convince customers of the existing market leader that your proposed product is better.

3. Concierge: Concierge is the most elaborate type of Lean startup experiment. It includes delivering the product as a service to the customer to see if the delivery matches the customer's expectations. It is one of the most accurate as well. It frequently involves simulation or a minimum viable product built to validate only one out of multiple stakeholders. Concierge is a great way to validate services, such as food delivery. The early online food delivery companies, such as Seamless, conducted multiple concierge deliverables before they got contracts with food establishments. They would order food with their own money, buy it, and deliver it to the customer.

If the hypothesis is confirmed, the solution is confirmed. If not, it is time to pivot. A pivot is a change in the business model; it is not an enhancement or an incremental change – it is a fundamental revision. We can think of these as course-correction mechanisms. These are high-level changes in strategy or execution that impact the whole business model.

Types of pivots include the following:

Customers need pivot. If customer feedback shows that the problem that was assumed is not a major concern for them, it requires repositioning, or a completely new product, or finding a project that solves the actual need.

Zoom-in pivot. This pivot is used if the original feature becomes the whole product. It is done to deliver fast or because other features are not addressing customer needs. Earlier in this chapter, we reviewed the case of the Burbn app, which lost all its features except for those that were photo related and became Instagram.

Zoom-out pivot. This is a reverse pivot when a single feature does not cover major customer needs and thus is not sufficient to support a product. In this case, additional features are validated and introduced into the product.

Platform pivot. In this case, there is a change needed from an application to a platform or vice versa. However, most customers buy solutions, not platforms.

Channel pivot. "Channel," in sales terminology, is the mechanism by which a company delivers its product, project, or service to customers. Channel pivots usually require unique pricing, features, and competitive positioning.

Each of the experiments and its findings is recorded on the Lean Validation Canvas until the hypotheses get validated.

 Five key questions to review:

1. What is the goal of validated learning?

2. How does the Lean Validation Canvas help?

3. What are the three types of experiments?

4. What are the types of pivots described in this section?

5. There is another type of pivot, called the customer segment pivot. What do you think it means? Are you aware of any examples from your personal experience?

Design Sprints and Design Thinking

Design thinking is an iterative process focused on understanding the user and the user's problem. Design thinking helps identify strategies and solutions that might not be obvious based on observation and research. Design thinking is based on a deep interest in understanding customer needs. It is founded on questioning and validating the problem, its assumptions, and associated solutions. It is very useful when defining and validating a problem that is not well understood or is simply unknown by adopting a hands-on approach to testing and prototyping. It involves ongoing experimentation and brainstorming, including prototyping, sketching, testing, and validating ideas.

Design thinking is implemented in phases – from understanding customer needs to developing and testing solutions. Pioneers of design thinking include the company IDEO and Stanford's d.school (Hasso Plattner Institute of Design at Stanford,) who use their own definitions of this process. The process is not linear; it is repeated iteratively. d.school defines the following five phases of design thinking:

- Empathize – with your users
- Define – your users' needs, their problems, and your insights
- Ideate – by challenging assumptions and creating ideas for innovative solutions
- Prototype – to start creating solutions
- Test – solutions

Google Ventures created a methodology of design Sprints – five days of intense user research built on the five phases of design thinking. This methodology is described by Jake Knapp et al. in the book *Sprint: How to Solve Big Problems and Test New Ideas in Just Five Days* [12]. Design Sprint at Google Ventures is a unique five-day process for answering crucial questions through prototyping and testing ideas with customers. It's a combination of business strategy, innovation, behavioral science, and design packaged in a step-by-step process that anyone can use.

"Sprints can create those habits in your company. After your first Sprint, you might notice a shift in the way your team works. You'll look for ways to turn discussions into testable hypotheses. You'll look for ways to answer big questions, not someday, but this week. You'll build confidence in one another's expertise and in your collective ability to make progress towards ambitious goals."

— Jake Knapp et al. Sprint: How to Solve Big Problems and Test New Ideas in Just Five Days [12]

Design Sprints implement the Lean startup "build-measure-learn" feedback loop in a unique way that takes only five days. On Monday, participants map out the problem and pick an important place to focus. On Tuesday, they sketch competing solutions on paper. On Wednesday, they make decisions and turn their ideas into a hypothesis. On Thursday, they create a realistic prototype. On Friday, they conduct user research and test this prototype with potential customers (see Figure 4-5).

Figure 4-5. Google Design Sprint process

The five steps of the design Sprint are described in detail on the Google Ventures website. This method enables a thorough and structured way of conducting user research.

MVP (Minimum Viable Product)

Once the research is conducted, the time comes to define the minimum viable product, or MVP. MVP is an iterative, low-risk way of building a minimal valuable deliverable for the customer. It is a concept that stresses the impact of learning in product development. MVP is an early version of the product that has just enough features to satisfy early customers and initiate the feedback loop that will inform product development going forward. MVP minimizes risk because it helps test the assumptions about whether the product meets customer needs, and by doing this, MVP minimizes waste.

The most effective way to create an MVP is by prototyping the experience and simulating the use of the product or service in question. This includes low-fidelity prototypes, which are paper based, or high-fidelity prototypes simulating parts of the actual product or service. For software products, there are tools such as InVision, which allows you to create clickable prototypes in minutes. In their book *Lean UX* [13], Jeff Gothelf and Josh Seiden describe types of prototypes and discuss the choice of prototyping technique.

The authors describe two types of MVP: prototype MVP and nonprototype MVP. Prototype MVP is based on the customer response to a prototype. Nonprototype MVP is used to test the approach rather than specific features. Nonprototype MVPs include a landing page, Google AdWords, and the button to nowhere:

1. A landing page for click-through traffic from Google Ads is very helpful to validate the thinking.

2. Google AdWords allows you to assess interest by measuring click-throughs.

3. The button to nowhere is a fake control on a user screen that is used to measure the number of times it's clicked. Each click indicates the customer's interest in this feature.

Once MVP is defined, we can proceed with defining the product (see Chapter 5).

 Five key questions to review:

1.   What is design thinking?

2.   What are the five phases of design thinking according to d.school?

3.   What does it mean to ideate as part of the design thinking process?

4.   How does Google Ventures implement design thinking in their design Sprint model?

5.   Why is MVP so important in Agile product management?

Key Points

1.   Our understanding of what the customers need (or even who the customers are) is just an assumption, a hypothesis that needs to be validated.

2.   The Lean startup concept establishes the ability to validate a customer hypothesis before building new products or delivering complex business solutions. It is as applicable to Fortune 500 companies as it is to startups.

3.   This approach saves time and money, and helps shape and prioritize deliverables based on customer needs. It fits within Agile, flexible delivery and ensures that the organization is delivering the product that will be of value to customers.

4.   The biggest mistake that may happen while identifying the product or service, or defining the scope for an internal deliverable, is to focus on the solution. In fact, this is the way to create products and services that no one is interested in, except for their creators.

5.   The Lean startup approach relies on the concept of "validated learning." This principle describes learning generated by prototyping or by implementing an initial idea and then measuring it against customer feedback to validate its effect.

6. Based on user research and related hypothesis validation, product teams define MVP (minimum viable product) based on customer needs and identify all the necessary details to build a prioritized list of features to start execution. This is followed by relentless prioritization based on customer needs once MVP is delivered to the customer.

7. In order to validate or invalidate a customer hypothesis, it is not sufficient just to measure the outcomes. It is important to structure multiple "build-measure-learn" feedback loops to stage experiments, measure results, and "pivot" (switch to another product definition) or "persevere" (continue with the chosen product strategy).

8. In order to validate or invalidate a hypothesis, it is important to hear from customers. This is done via user research. User research focuses on understanding user behaviors, needs, and observations through a number of techniques, from the observation of users in their natural surroundings to interviewing them about their experience with a working product and everything in between. It is an iterative and cyclical process.

9. Design thinking is an iterative process focused on understanding the user and the user's problem in an attempt to identify strategies. It helps in questioning and validating the problem, its assumptions, and associated solutions.

10. Overall, incremental delivery proves to be the best way of minimizing risk over a period of time. By delivering a product incrementally, we learn from the customer and adjust the deliverables for the next iteration, depending on customer feedback.

Creating and Maintaining IT Requirements

This chapter compares Waterfall scope management and Agile product backlog practices. It addresses high-level software requirements elicitation, process modeling, UML principles and artifacts (use cases, data models, all relevant diagrams), UI wireframing, and UX design tools and covers multiple approaches to managing and defining requirements in IT. It will explain the logic behind Agile backlog development and prioritization practices: once product features have been identified, the next step is to create a prioritized list of features and split them into smaller requirements, referred to as "user stories." In addition, this chapter describes the product backlog taxonomy (epic, user story, subtask, bug, etc.), ongoing requirements maintenance, related roles, and stakeholder communication. Topics such as product backlog health, prioritization techniques, technical vs. functional requirements, and product backlog refinement are covered in detail.

© Mariya Breyter 2022
M. Breyter, *Agile Product and Project Management*,
https://doi.org/10.1007/978-1-4842-8200-7_5

Introduction

In Chapters 3 and 4, we discussed multiple techniques and frameworks of customer research. Using validated knowledge about the customers and their problem to solve, or Job-to-Be-Done, product features are sequenced and prioritized based on user needs. This information can be captured and documented in multiple ways.

Chapter 5 covers different frameworks and techniques for creating and maintaining requirements in IT – whether it is software or hardware development. It covers traditional requirements documents – how those are created, what information they cover, and how those are approved, updated, and maintained. As part of the requirements document, we categorize requirements into functional and nonfunctional and discuss software models as they apply to requirements definition. We will review use cases and user scenarios and cover UML (Unified Modeling Language) methodology and formal techniques for process modeling. In contrast to monolithic well-defined traditional requirements, we will review the details of the Agile approach to requirements gathering via collaboration, the role of IT professionals in the process, as well as continuous validation and adaptation that are happening in Agile delivery. We will review the concept of a product backlog, the taxonomy of its elements, and different techniques for creating backlogs, such as story mapping, as well as prioritization mechanisms that are used in product backlog management. We will talk about risk and dependency management as it applies to the requirements definition.

The following are the concepts we will cover in this chapter:

- Requirements in software development
- Software requirements specification
- Unified Modeling Language (UML)
- Agile requirements management
- Use cases and user stories
- Product backlog
- Product backlog taxonomy
- Requirements sequencing and prioritization in Agile
- Story mapping

Requirements in Software Development

Software requirements based on customer research and product definition are the basis of all software development work. Poorly defined or inadequate (inaccurate, incomplete, ambiguous) requirements are the major cause of poor-quality software. The goal of software requirements is to describe the capabilities, features, and constraints of the software products. Requirements contain information on how this product works, how users interact with the product, and, most importantly, what customer problem it solves.

The requirements are usually written in a language that everyone can understand. For many globally distributed teams, requirements are written in a natural language, frequently in English. However, some organizations use requirements templates and specialized techniques, such as UML (Unified Modeling Language) and RUP (Rational Unified Process), which will be discussed later in this chapter.

The goal of software requirements is to define what the system needs to do. It can be viewed as a checklist that designers, developers, and testers use to produce software products. Requirements are based on the vision, mission, organizational OKRs, market research, user research, and the validated problem that the product is solving for the customer.

The topics covered by requirements include

- Product features (capabilities provided to the user) that need to be developed, along with their priority
- Processes that need to be supported and key steps within each of those processes
- User groups and related access details
- What tasks the users will be able to perform
- Exceptions (what happens if users are not able to perform required tasks)
- Security and compliance requirements
- Hardware and infrastructure preferences or constraints
- Business logic (what type of processing happens behind the scene)
- Technology preferences or constraints
- Any third-party or existing systems that have to be integrated
- How fast the functionality has to be provided
- User load at any given point of time to be handled

and many other aspects of the system to be built.

A well-formed requirement is a statement that

- Can be verified
- Has to be met or possessed by a system to achieve a specific objective
- Is qualified by measurable conditions and bounded by constraints
- Defines the performance of the system when used by a specific user or the corresponding capabilities of the system [1]

"A requirement is a statement which translates or expresses a need and its associated constraints and conditions. This statement is written in a language which can take the form of a natural language. If expressed in the form of a natural language, the statement should comprise a subject, a verb and a complement. A requirement shall state the subject of the requirement (e.g., the system, the software, etc.) and what shall be done (e.g., operate at a power level, provide a field for)."

— ISO/IEC/IEEE 29148-2018 [1]

Requirements' format, elicitation techniques, documentation, and approval (sign-off) processes differ drastically among the organizations. In this chapter, we will review different methods in a historical sequence, starting with a traditional software requirements specification (SRS) document.

Requirements in Traditional Project Management

Requirements gathering in traditional project management is part of business analysis. It includes the following stages:

- Requirements gathering
- Requirements elicitation
- Requirements management plan
- Requirements analysis
- Requirements traceability
- Change control

The Project Management Institute (PMI) provides requirements management guidelines based on the Project Management Body of Knowledge (PMBOK). Requirements management is considered part of scope management and requires a detailed project management plan containing the following information:

- Requirements activities management (how requirements gathering, elicitation, analysis, and traceability will be performed)

- Configuration management activities (how the changes to the product will be initiated, approved, tracked, and reported)

- Requirements prioritization process (how requirements should be prioritized against each other)

- Product metrics (which metrics should be used to track requirements and related progress)

- Traceability structure (which requirement attributed will be captured on the traceability matrix with a complete audit trail of changes) [2]

Requirements traceability matrix is a list of requirements, their attributes (e.g., priority), references to test cases and validation mechanisms, status, and other relevant information. A sample traceability matrix template is provided in Figure 5-1.

Unique Req ID	Requirement Category	Requirement Description	Priority	Requested by:	Approved by:	Test Reference	Status
P001	Payments	Ability for customers to make a credit card payment onsite	Critical	Claims Department	Change Review Board (CRB)	Test Cases TP001, TP002, TP003	Done
P002	Payments	Ability for customers to make a cash payment onsite	Critical	Claims Department	Change Review Board	Test Cases TP004, TP005	In testing
P003	Payments	Ability for customers to defer the payment	High	Customer Forum	Change Review Board	Test Cases TP006, TP007, TP008, TP009	In development
N001	Notifications	Ability for customers to select payment notifications	Low	Customer Interview		Test Cases TN001, TN002, TN003	Scheduled for review by CRB
N002	Notifications	Ability for provider to setup periodic reminders for outstanding payments	Medium	Providers	Change Review Board	Test Cases TN004, TN005	Pending

Requirements Traceability Matrix: Medical Claims   *Date: January 15, 2021*

Figure 5-1. Requirements traceability matrix (RTM)

Topic for a Group Discussion   Review each field on the requirements traceability matrix format provided in the sample. Which data is informative and which can be replaced by other, more meaningful, data points? What information is missing? How would you optimize the template provided in this sample?

Software Requirements Specification (SRS)

In traditional project management (Waterfall), software requirements specification is a document that describes features and capabilities provided by the software along with its performance requirements. It also describes the functionality the product needs to fill the stakeholders' (business customers, end users, clients) need.

A software requirements specification (SRS) usually contains functional (customer-directed capabilities) and nonfunctional requirements (system-based features, such as availability, reliability, and security). Software requirements specification serves as a foundation for a handshake between the customers and the software provider on how the software product should function. The goal is to provide the relevant level of detail upfront to limit any redesign or changes to the list of required features. Usually, it is a comprehensive, well-defined document, which provides a clear and thorough understanding of the product to the development team.

In traditional project delivery, the communication between the development team and customer is limited throughout the development process, so SRS serves as an internal contract for the work that is being performed. Any changes to SRS are considered scope changes to the product and have to be reviewed and approved through the change management process based on the impact on product delivery that is estimated by the delivery team or the development lead.

Typically, SRS contains hundreds of pages of documentation, accompanied by appendices containing data models, descriptions of business logic, a set of assumptions, wireframes, and other relevant information. SRS is usually written and maintained by a product manager, business analyst, technical writer, or (in smaller companies) a systems architect or a software developer. SRS users include managers, software engineers, test engineers, maintenance engineers, customers, and managers.

Frequently, business analysts start their work on software requirements from the Business Requirements Document (BRD), which describes the high-level business needs. This document is extended by the Functional Requirements Document (FRD), which outlines the functionality required to fulfill the business need. Based on this information, they proceed to create SRS, which contains technical implementation details and serves as a primary input into the development. This nomenclature may differ depending on each company's internal processes and practices.

Software requirements specification structure is usually a variation of the following:

- Objectives (business objective, business processes and how the product will be used in this context, users for the software, and interaction with other systems)

- Functional requirements (statement of functionality, which can be viewed as a contract with customers)

- Nonfunctional requirements (performance, availability, usability, security, etc.)

- Appendices (used to capture any detailed information, such as UML diagrams, list of use cases, data models, lists, wireframes, repositories, and other relevant details)

There is an SRS standard developed by the Institute of Electrical and Electronic Engineers (IEEE), the world's largest technical professional organization dedicated to advancing technology for the benefit of humanity. The IEEE Recommended Practice for Software Requirements Specifications (IEEE Standard 29148-2018) [1] discusses a number of topics that should be considered during the creation of an SRS. The SRS is defined by IEEE as a specification for a particular software product, program, or set of programs that perform certain functions in a specific environment. IEEE advises that SRS writer(s) shall address the following:

a. Functionality: What is the software supposed to do?

b. External interfaces: How does the software interact with people, the system's hardware, other hardware, and other software?

c. Performance: What is the speed, availability, response time, recovery time of various software functions, etc.?

d. Attributes: What are the portability, correctness, maintainability, security, etc., considerations?

e. Design constraints imposed on an implementation: Are there any required standards in effect, implementation language, policies for database integrity, resource limits, operating environment(s), etc.?

IEEE provided the following samples of requirements:

Example 1. *When signal x is received [Condition], the system [Subject] shall set [Action] the signal x received by [Object] within 2 second [Constraint].*

Example 2. *At sea state 1 [Condition], the Radar System shall detect targets at ranges out to [Action or Constraint] 100 nautical miles [Value].*

Example 3. *The Invoice System shall display pending customer invoices [Action] in ascending order [Value] in which invoices are to be paid.*

Software Design Specifications

Software requirements document usually does not provide details of software design, that is, description of specific subcomponents of a system and their interfaces with other subcomponents. This includes descriptions of software architecture, its structural modules, data models, the flow of information or control between modules, and data structures.

However, in special cases, some requirements may severely restrict the design. For example, security or safety requirements may reflect directly into the design, such as the need to

- Keep certain functions in separate modules
- Limit communication between subsystems within the program
- Check data integrity for critical variables

Design constraints may be reflected in SRS as nonfunctional requirements.

 Five key questions to review:

1. What is a software requirement?

2. What is included in a software requirements specification document?

3. What is the difference between functional and nonfunctional requirements?

4. What is the relationship between a software requirements specification document and a software design specification document?

5. What are the topics that IEEE advises to cover in the software requirements specification based on Systems and Software Engineering – Requirements Engineering standard?

Use Cases

Requirements can be expressed in a natural language or in any agreed-upon format. Use case methodology is an effective approach for documenting requirements that originated in object-oriented programming. A use case is defined as a list of actions or steps defining the interactions between a role and a system to achieve a predefined objective. This could be a human or other external system.

The concept of use cases was introduced in 1987 by Ivar Jacobson, who described how this methodology was used at Ericsson to capture and specify requirements of a system using textual, structure, and visual modeling techniques to drive object-oriented analysis and design. In a nutshell, use cases are a methodology that allows for capturing, modeling, and specifying the requirements of a system. It is a combination of a software requirements specification and an implementation-based system requirements specification. According to the Software Engineering Body of Knowledge (SWEBOK) [3], these use cases belong to scenario-based requirements elicitation techniques, as well as model-based analysis techniques. In addition to that, use cases support narrative-based requirements gathering, incremental requirements definition, and modern testing techniques, such as acceptance-driven delivery.

A use case is a scenario that contains the following elements:

- Title
- Description
- Actors
- Trigger(s)
- Pre-conditions
- Postconditions
- Normal flow
- Alternative flows

Tip   Use cases are written in such a way that they are free of implementation details. The concept is to represent functionality rather than describing implementation. For example, the best practice is to specify that a user selects a specific option rather than stating that the user clicks a button.

In the following, we provide a sample use case for an online bookstore:

Title: *UC-1 Select a book to buy*

Description: *While browsing books in a bookstore, a user is able to select a book for purchase.*

Actors: *Customer, System*

Trigger(s): *A website provides a set of recommended books based on customer's preferences.*

Pre-condition: *A user has a profile set up with preferred book type and prior purchase history.*

Postcondition: *A user selects a book and places it in a shopping cart.*

Normal flow:

1. *The user views the proposed books.*

2. *The user chooses the book to view details.*

3. *The system presents book details and updates the set of recommended books based on the selection.*

4. *The user chooses to purchase the book reviewed.*

5. *The system presents a list of books that the users who purchased the originally selected book also have bought.*

6. *The user reviews the list and chooses a book to purchase without reviewing details.*

7. *The system allows for one-step addition of recommended items to the shopping cart.*

8. *The user selects an option to view the shopping cart.*

9. *Shopping cart content is presented to the user.*

Alternative flow:

2A.

1. *The user chooses to buy the book without viewing the details.*

2. *Proceed to step 7.*

4A.

1. *The user chooses not to purchase the book.*

2. *The user exits the system.*

4B.

The user chooses not to purchase the book.

The user is presented with a set of recommended books.

Proceed to step 1.

A set of use cases representing the complete functionality of a system is described in a use case diagram, as shown in Figure 5-2.

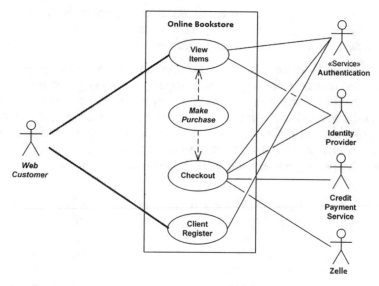

Figure 5-2. Online bookstore use case diagram, as modified from (1)

Topic for a Group Discussion   Review the use case diagram in Figure 5-2 and discuss who are the actors, how authentication is set up, and how payment is performed in this specific system. Review additional use case diagrams in the following UML tutorial and explain the functionality described there. Source: `www.uml-diagrams.org/examples/online-shopping-use-case-diagram-example.html?context=uc-examples`

Unified Modeling Language

Use case methodology laid the foundation of the Unified Modeling Language (UML). UML was invented in 1999 by Grady Booch, James Rumbaugh, and Ivar Jacobson (a.k.a. the Three Amigos), who did groundbreaking work in object-oriented analysis and design methods in the 1990s working at Rational Software.

Object-oriented analysis and design (OOAD) is an incremental approach to software delivery, which applies object-oriented programming principles to analyzing and designing software. It uses visual modeling (analysis modeling and design modeling) throughout the software development process to drive delivery. OOAD is based on the object-oriented programming (OOP) approach, which calls for organizing code into larger meaningful "objects" that model specific functionality. These objects combine all the necessary variables for describing each possible state of the model's components, as well as the methods (subroutines or functions) necessary to change each variable's data.

Alistair Cockburn, an American computer scientist, took this concept to the next level in 2000 by proposing a goal-oriented use case practice involving narrative descriptions of customer experience.

The goal of UML is to provide a visualization of business processes and software architecture. It's a graphical language providing a standard way to describe the functionality and create a system model covering conceptual ideas. It includes an integrated set of diagrams that describe and visualize the artifacts of software systems. It is also used for business modeling and other nonsoftware systems. The UML represents a collection of best engineering practices that have proven successful in the modeling of large and complex systems.

UML has been primarily used as a general-purpose modeling language in the field of software engineering; however, it has proven effective in documenting business processes, functional scenarios, and workflows. Since UML is agnostic of any specific programming language, there are tools that allow using UML diagrams to generate code in multiple programming languages or reverse engineer functional or system diagrams from the existing code. For example, Sparx Systems' UML Tool, Enterprise Architect, allows Java Binaries (JAR files) to be reverse engineered, creating code and UML diagrams. Developers can model UML classes, as well as dependencies to other classes.

UML is not confined to visualizing functionality only. UML diagrams include two types:

1. Behavioral UML diagrams:

   • Activity diagram (swimlane-based workflow used for business process modeling)

- Use case diagram (functional requirements scenario-based diagram discussed before)

- Interaction overview diagram (activity diagram providing details on relationships between actors)

- Timing diagram (activity diagram with timing between steps)

- State machine diagram (a.k.a. statechart diagrams, used to describe the different states of a component within a system)

- Communication diagram (a.k.a. collaborative diagram focused on communication between objects)

- Sequence diagram (business process design and implementation)

2. Structural UML diagrams:

- Class diagram (in software development, classes are considered abstract data types, whereas objects are instances of the abstract class)

- Object diagram (see the aforementioned text)

- Component diagram (it breaks down the system into smaller components. It is a useful way of representing multitier software architecture)

- Composite structure diagram (a rarely used UML diagram representing the internal structure of a class and relations between class components)

- Deployment diagram (used to visualize the relation between software and hardware)

- Package diagram (macro container for preceding deployment diagrams)

- Profile diagram (it provides additional notations, such as tags, constraints, and other extensive UML elements)

However, there is usually no need to use all these different types of UML diagrams to provide software specifications in each instance since some may not be applicable and some may contain an excessive level of detail. Use case diagrams, activity diagrams, class diagrams, and sequence diagrams are most frequently used in software specifications.

While UML was broadly used in the early 2000s, it is used significantly less nowadays. There are two primary reasons for that:

1. UML is based on object-oriented programming (OOP) practices. Object-oriented programming is still widely used. However, there is an increasing number of programmers who feel that this architecture is counterintuitive and error-prone. OOP was created when systems were single-threaded and objects were easily traceable. Nowadays, as the program executes, it is usually multithreaded.

   As a replacement for OOP, functional programming (FP) is continuously growing in importance and level of adoption, as well as procedurally oriented programming, data-oriented programming, compression-oriented programming, and data-driven design. The essential idea of functional programming is that a procedure should take input parameters and produce output with full predictability. This means it should not modify any variables that already exist. In this way, functional programming is similar to a mathematical function, which returns a consistent value that neither depends upon nor impacts anything outside the function scope. C++ provides an example of functional programming. However, UML is not suited for modeling functional programming languages [3a].

2. While it was recognized in UML that software engineering is typically conducted in an iterative and incremental way, there is no iterative process built into this methodology. The diagrams have to provide a sufficient level of details in a static way in order to be informative, so most of the requirements definition work was done upfront.

To address the problem of defining requirements without any feedback loop and to reflect the modern iterative way of developing software (and any IT product or service), a new customer-centric format has been adopted in Agile delivery, referred to as "user stories."

User Stories

User stories are short, simple descriptions of a feature told from the perspective of the actor who desires the new capability, usually a user or customer of the system. Each user story expresses one very specific need that a user has. It can be viewed as a minimum requirement focused on user needs.

User stories are used in the Agile development process to describe product features. They allow developers to focus on what the user need is. The best user stories are based on user research and market analysis, as described in Chapter 4 – they aren't "made up" and actually reflect user needs.

The difference between use cases and user stories is that user stories are written from the user perspective (hence the term "user stories") rather than that of a business analyst describing the system's functionality.

They are focused on outcomes rather than scenarios. And most importantly, they do not describe "how" to achieve the desired functionality; they focus on "what" this functionality should be. User story allows developers to design a functional solution to the user problem it presents.

User stories follow the standard format based on role–action-benefit (or "who–what–why").

It is important to keep in mind the following good practices:

1. A role ("who") represents a user type. It has to be as specific as possible. The system can be a role, but the development team or product manager cannot design the system for their own benefit.

2. The action ("what") describes the system behavior. It is usually unique for each user story. Actions are preferably written in active voice (buyer needs to purchase a book, rather than "a book needs to be purchased").

3. The reason or benefit ("why?) has to be specified (otherwise, the question arises why this feature is being developed at all). Multiple user stories may share the same benefit. The benefit may be for other users or customers, not only for the user in each particular story.

As a (role) I want (action/feature) so that (reason)

Some user story examples include the following:

As an online book shopper, I want to view the details of the book in an online store so that I can make an informed decision.

As a mortgage provider, I want to view the requestor's credit score so that I can approve or decline their mortgage based on the risk associated with it.

As a service provider, I want to authenticate my customers so that I can provide personalized service based on their subscription type.

There are several rules for a user story.

"3 C's" are an important characteristic of a user story that allows for keeping the purpose of the user story in perspective. This model was proposed by Ron Jeffries in 2001 [4]. These 3 C's include the following:

1. The first "C" is the user story in its raw form, the Card (i.e., index card). The concept is that the whole story has to be concise, that is, fit into a single index card. It also has to do with the way user stories are grouped together on a Kanban board (Kanban board is a way of visualizing work in progress based on user stories that are being delivered. The concept comes from Lean. In Japanese, "Kanban" literally means "visual card"). See an example in Figure 5-3.

TO DO	IN PROGRESS	DONE
Save the selection	Select book format	View books
As a book shopper, I want to save the sel	As a book shopper, I want to select the fc	As a book shopper, I want to view availab
□ ↓ - BOOK-5	□ ↑ - BOOK-3	□ ↑ - BOOK-1
View recent orders	View book recommendations	
As a book shopper, I want to view recent	As a book shopper, I want to view recom	
□ ↓ - BOOK-6	□ ↑ - BOOK-4	
Provide feedback	Pay for the books	
As a book shopper, I want to provide feec	As a book shopper, I want to pay for the I	
□ ↓ - BOOK-7	□ ↑ - BOOK-2	

Figure 5-3. Sample Kanban board

2. The second "C" is the Conversation. Conversations represent discussions between the project team, customers, relevant stakeholders, and business subject matter experts. In these conversations, stakeholders or team members exchange thoughts, opinions, and suggestions. While the conversation is largely verbal, it can be done in a digital firm (e.g., a distributed team may communicate via a persistent chat, such as Slack) and may be supported with documents or within requirements management tools, for example, via Slack Comments.

3. The third "C" is Confirmation. A user story is the start of a conversation. Once the need is articulated, the team raises a lot of questions, discusses them, and comes up with the best solution. The goal is to build a shared understanding.

   This agreement is being recorded as a set of so-called acceptance criteria, a set of success criteria to validate whether the user story has been successfully completed. These acceptance criteria are frequently used as an input into software test cases because they cover ideal paths and exceptions (alternative paths) for each user story.

   In software delivery, there is a programming practice that is based on acceptance criteria. It is referred to as "Acceptance Test-Driven Development" (ATDD). According to Scrum Alliance [5], these acceptance tests represent the user's point of view and act as a form of requirements to describe how the system will function as well as serve as a way of verifying that the system functions as intended. In some cases, the team automates the acceptance tests. Different flavors of ATDD are referred to as Story Test-Driven Development (SDD), Specification by Example, or Behavior-Driven Development (BDD).

There is an opinion that for ATDD, tests always have to be automated. This is not accurate. Despite us advocating for test automation and despite the tools, such as Fit/FitNess or Cucumber, ATDD is highly beneficial even if it is not automated (2).

ATDD is built on the concept of Test-Driven Development (TDD). ATDD process is built "backward." First, a developer writes a failing unit test that demonstrates that the existing code base does not fulfill the requirement. Once the unit test fails, they write the production code until the test passes the requirement. When the test is passing, they clean up the code and improve the design. Similarly, in ATDD, the team creates one or more acceptance-level tests for a feature before beginning work on it.

These tests are usually recorded when the team is working with the business stakeholders to understand this story. ATDD tests are heavily based on acceptance criteria for each story. Frequently, the team uses the Gherkin format for acceptance criteria that allows for directly translating acceptance criteria into an ATDD test. BDD (Behavior-Driven Development) is using the Given-When-Then test scenario format – this format is used in Gherkin, line-oriented language that is used in a tool called Cucumber. This format allows to describe scenarios by specifying pre-condition, action, and postcondition, as shown in Table 5-1.

Table 5-1. Acceptance criteria sample

Given	When	Then
User views online books	User selects a book to buy	It is visible in a shopping cart
User adds a book to the shopping cart	User views pricing	Cost is updated
User has a coupon	User adds a book to the shopping cart	Coupon is applied
User purchased a book	User is presented with a choice	Which book format do they prefer

Besides the title, description, and acceptance criteria described before, user stories may contain

- Component (database, UI, business logic tier)
- Category
- Priority
- Constraints (e.g., timelines based on market regulations or business conditions)
- Estimation of the complexity or time to completion
- Comments to establish a full audit trail
- Attachments (wireframes, data models, link to repositories and artifacts)

and many other relevant data points.

The acronym INVEST is a mnemonic introduced by Bill Wake, which helps to remember a list of criteria to assess the quality of a user story. The acronym represents the following qualities of a user story:

- Independent: User stories have to be as independent of each other and external prerequisites as possible. At the same time, when delivered independently, it should provide user value by itself.

- Valuable: The business value of any user story should be listed, and each story should be of value to a specific user type.

- Estimable: The effort required to complete this story can be estimated so that the team can plan their work successfully and establish the predictability of the delivery.

- Small: A user story should be small enough so that it can be completed within a short period of time (usually in days from start to finish).

- Testable: There has to be a clear way to verify whether the story has been completed, such as well-specified acceptance criteria.

If a user story is too large in terms of the effort required to complete it by the team, it has to be split into smaller independent stories, which is referred to as "user story decomposition." It is not always obvious how to split a user story; however, there is a set of possible parameters that allow successful decomposition. Some of these parameters include the following:

1. CRUD method (Create, Read, Update, and Delete). For example:

    As an online book store shopper, I want to manage my user profile so that I can view and update my account details and settings.

    This user story can be split into four:

    - I want to **create** a user profile.

    - I want to **view** my user profile.

    - I want to **update** my user profile.

    - I want to **delete** my user profile.

2. Business rules

As an online bookstore shopper, I want to search for books so that I can select an interesting book to read.

This user story can be split by business rules:

- I want to search for books **by the author**.
- I want to search for books **by title**.
- I want to search for books **by topic**.
- I want to search for a book **similar to the ones I've previously purchased**.

3. Workflow steps

As an online bookstore shopper, I want to buy a book so that I can start reading it. This user story can be split based on the sequence of the following activities:

- I want to **add the book to my shopping cart**.
- I want to **review the card**.
- I want to **confirm my selection**.
- I want to **pick payment type**.
- I want to **submit the payment**.

Other ways to decompose user stories are by user type (new vs. repeating user), by book type (paper vs. digital), by price, by geography, by language, and so forth.

 Topic for a Group Discussion Decompose the following user story and rewrite it as needed:

As a user, I want to log on to the online bookstore to check my order status.

The benefits of user stories include the following:

- **Customer-centricity** since stories keep the focus on the user. Apart from a list of tasks, user stories keep the team focused on user needs via delivering functionality.
- **Team empowerment and collaboration**, since stories define "what," not "how." Team members work together to decide how to implement specific functionality.

- **Creativity and innovation** since stories are focused on outcomes vs. outputs (tasks). Stories encourage the team to focus on solving customer problems.

- **Flexibility.** User stories can be tweaked on the fly unless they are already being executed – in this case, it will need a discussion and further analysis. They do not require any process-heavy change control. Once new information becomes available, the definition or acceptance criteria can be changed with a full audit trail.

- **Progressive elaboration.** User stories support an iterative and incremental approach to requirements gathering. They are prioritized top to bottom, from highest priority to lowest. The top-priority user stories are well defined, and acceptance criteria are provided. Lower-priority user stories do not need to be well defined since they may change or become obsolete by the time the team will start working on them. So why waste time – a definition might be sufficient until their priority changes. This reflects the "just-in-time approach" coming from Lean that eliminates any waste related to specifying details before it is required. This concept is similar to the "progressive elaboration" of requirements in traditional project management.

Five key questions to review:

1. What are user stories?

2. What is the difference between user stories and use cases?

3. What does the acronym INVEST stand for?

4. Why ATDD practice is driving quality improvement?

5. What are the benefits of using user stories vs. software requirements specifications? What are the drawbacks?

However, Agile requirements are not a collection of individual user stories. Given that for larger systems, there are usually hundreds of user stories developed, they need to be prioritized, sequenced, and organized in a meaningful way. This way of organizing, prioritizing, and maintaining user stories is called a product backlog.

Product Backlog

"A product backlog is a list of the new features, changes to existing features, bug fixes, infrastructure changes or other activities that a team may deliver in order to achieve a specific outcome.

The product backlog is the single authoritative source for things that a team works on. That means that nothing gets done that isn't on the product backlog."

— Agile Alliance: Glossary. Product Backlog [5]

The product backlog is a collection of prioritized discrete items of different types connected by parent-child relationships. Relationships between product backlog items are referred to as "product backlog taxonomy" shown in Figure 5-4.

Agile does not prescribe the types of elements in the product backlog; however, traditionally, functional requirements are represented in user story format. The team using the product backlog determines the format they choose to use and looks at the backlog items as reminders of the aspects of a solution the team may work on.

Besides user stories, other product backlog elements may include the following:

Epics. Epic captures a large body of work. It represents a feature that may be independently released to end users. It is usually written in the same format as a user story; however, this is not necessary. For example, "As a customer, I want to pick a flight ticket so that I can travel to a conference." This epic includes "selection" criteria, "view details" functionality, and "select functionality."

Technical Tasks. Tasks do not provide user functionality; however, they are necessary for software development. For example, deploying applications on the cloud, building test environments, implementing security features, upgrading software tools, and so forth.

Spikes. Spikes are research items. They are created to research the tool, define strategy, test performance, compare implementation methods, and so forth. They have an outcome, which is learning and potentially implementation or tooling decision, but they do not produce shippable products. If there are prerequisites to user stories, spikes usually address those prerequisites and precede user stories they are supporting.

Subtasks. User stories, epics, technical tasks, and sometimes even spikes may be broken down into subtasks (sometimes referred to as "tasks"). While each of these backlog item types either provides end-to-end functionality or provides an answer to a specific question, subtasks are used to divide responsibilities between team members in implementing any of these items, for example, coding, testing, designing, etc. Subtasks are helpful in planning and aligning as a team during execution.

Agile is a framework, not a methodology, so it does not prescribe specific taxonomies or formats for product backlogs. Each organization optimizes against its needs and processes. For example, there may be other item types in Agile organizations, such as bugs, risks, and so forth. It depends on organizational size, structure, reporting, and tracking. Since Agile assumes continuous improvement, many organizations experiment with the most efficient structure of the product backlog.

💡 **Tip**   Frequently, product backlog taxonomy is prescribed or configured within an organization by the software delivery life cycle tool that this organization is doing. To enable organizational-level transparency and reporting, it is important to standardize product backlog taxonomy across the organization. For example, if an organization is heavily regulated, it may implement Risk issue type or create a new one, for example, Compliance Approval. As long as there is consistency, training, and a glossary of product backlog elements, customization is encouraged. However, having more than five to seven item types is usually confusing and creates an unnecessary overhead.

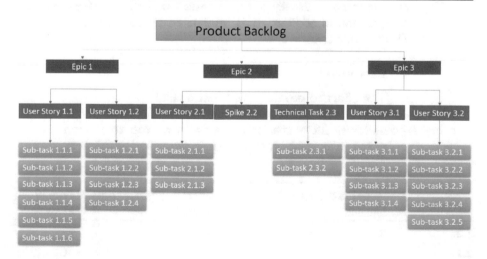

Figure 5-4. Product backlog taxonomy

It is important to prioritize elements in a product backlog top to bottom in a thoughtful and methodical way. Some common mistakes include the following:

1. **A product backlog item comes before its prerequisites.** For example, if there is a user story to select a book from a list, then a repository of books available for sale should be established first. As an exception, it is possible to test this user story with mock data. In this case, there should be a subtask to set up mock data in a relevant format for testing purposes.

2. **Product backlog items on the bottom of the backlog are defined in detail, while the items closer to the top lack acceptance criteria.** This violates the Lean "just-in-time" principle and creates waste since by the time the team gets to work on the lower-priority items, either the needs will change or there will be further details that will require rework.

3. **Prioritization is based on the "loudest voice in the room."** This happens when more senior stakeholders insist on prioritizing requirements that are considered most important, and the team does not argue because of their seniority. It is important to validate any assumptions with thoughtful user research, as described in Chapter 4.

4. **Prioritization is based on user value only.** Prioritization is usually a combination of two primary criteria, and in addition, it is influenced by constraints. The primary criteria are

   - User value

   - The effort to develop this functionality

The higher-value/lower-effort stories are prioritized top to bottom in the backlog. An effective prioritization technique is described as follows:

User Story ID	Value (from 1, lowest, to 10, highest)	Effort (1, highest, to 10, lowest)	Priority Index
3.2	8	9	72
2.1	6	8	48
1.2	10	3	27
1.1	7	3	21
3.1	8	2	16

However, this logic is impacted if there are constraints. For example, user story 1.2 describes a regulatory requirement that has to be implemented by a specific date. In this case, it does not matter that there is a significant effort to have it implemented, and this user story gets prioritized "just in time" based on the date when the regulation goes into effect and the estimation of the time that will require to deliver, test, and debug this user story.

While product backlogs represent a hierarchical structure with parent-child relationships, they are not usually created as such. An effective technique of creating a balanced, well-thought-through product backlog is referred to as "story mapping."

Story Mapping

Story mapping (a.k.a. user story mapping) is a valuable tool for software development. The concept of story mapping was introduced by Jeff Patton (3). In this process, the team explores the user story's life cycle, starting with opportunities and moving deeper into discovery and then sequencing these user stories into MVP and subsequent releases.

"User Story Mapping is a dead simple idea. Talk about the user's journey through your product by building a simple model that tells your user's story as you do. It turns out this simple idea makes working with user stories in Agile development a lot easier.

More importantly it'll keep your users and what they're doing with your product front and center in your products. That's better than getting lost in feature arguments – like what normally happens in software development. I'm not making any promises here, but if you use Story Mapping, I believe your products will ultimately be better."

— Source: Jeff Patton's blog [6]

💡 **Tip** Jeff Patton provides a quick reference to story mapping – a highly informative document, which serves as a foundation and a guide for the story map workshops. This reference can be downloaded from his website: `www.jpattonassociates.com/wp-content/uploads/2015/03/story_mapping.pdf`. Review the document and discuss practical takeaways from this approach.

In a nutshell, a story map tells a story about a type of person doing something to reach a goal. Story map represents features that comprise the major product features, which are later organized into subsequent product releases. A sample story map is provided in Figure 5-5.

It is a prerequisite to have a general understanding of the "big picture" in order to create an informed story map. The story mapping session usually starts with reviewing OKRs for the product, major functionality, persona types, and their needs and then moves top to bottom from requirements elaboration perspective: from "themes" (or functional categories) to product features, and sometimes even to user story level, so that the finished product may be used as a skeleton for creating a product backlog.

Flight Reservation System							
Traveler				Airline			
Search Flights	Select the Best Option	Pay for the Tickets	Access the Ticket	Confirm Purchase	Notify the Passenger	Access Cumulative Reports	
Search by date and destination	Provide all options	Pay by credit card or bank account	Provide a choice of mailing or e-mailing the ticket	E-mail confirmation			Release 1
Search by airline	Allow filtering by price and airline		Provide online access to the ticket from airline web site		Push notifications based on customer preferences		Release 2
Search by Flights previously purchased		Pay by Zelle or PayPal			Provide monthly report to airline HQ		Release 3

Figure 5-5. Sample story map for an airline reservation system

As it is shown in the preceding example, the user story map starts with the personas, defines epics (or sometimes collections of epics), and then decomposes those into features and user stories. Many story maps represent the product at the epic level and above, hence the term "story map" rather than "user story map."

 Five key questions to review:

1. What is a product backlog?

2. What is the structure of a product backlog?

3. Which elements are mandatory and which are recommended?

4. What is a story map? What are its elements?

5. Why is story map a more accurate term than "user story map"?

The benefits of story mapping include the following:

- Establishing team collaboration
- Ability to define MVP (minimum viable product) by sequencing and to prioritize features
- Exposing any dependencies, internal and external
- Developing a better, more user-centric product
- Focusing product development teams on features that provide customer value and improvement
- Enabling the prioritization process
- Enabling the delivery of incremental releases, early and often
- Setting realistic expectations with customers and stakeholders

Based on alignment and prioritization achieved with story mapping, the structure of the product backlog is shared between all stakeholders and can be used as a more flexible analog of a software requirements document.

Key Points

1. The goal of software requirements is to describe the capabilities, features, and constraints of the software products. Requirements contain information on how this product works, how users interact with the product, and, most importantly, what customer problem this software solves.

2. Requirements are based on the vision, mission, organizational OKRs, market research, user research, and the validated problem that the product is solving for the customer.

3. Requirements' format, elicitation techniques, documentation, and approval (sign-off) processes differ drastically among the organizations.

4. In traditional project management, the software requirements document is a comprehensive description of complete product functionality, requiring a lengthy elicitation process and a complex sign-off. The Project Management Institute (PMI) provides requirements

management guidelines based on the Project Management Body of Knowledge (PMBOK). Requirements management is considered as part of scope management and requires a detailed project management plan.

5. A software requirements document (SRS) usually contains functional (customer-directed capabilities) and nonfunctional requirements (system-based features, such as availability, reliability, and security). Software requirements specification defines the agreement between customers and the delivery team on how the functionality and performance of a software product.

6. Requirements in SRS can be expressed in a natural language or in an agreed-upon format. Use case methodology is an effective approach for documenting requirements that originated in object-oriented programming. A use case contains a list of actions or event steps that define the interactions between a role and a system with the purpose of achieving a specific goal.

7. Unified Modeling Language (UML) provides a visualization of business processes and software architecture. It's a graphical language providing a standard way to describe the functionality and create a system model covering conceptual ideas.

8. While it was recognized in UML that software engineering is typically conducted in an iterative and incremental way, there is no iterative process built into this methodology. The diagrams have to provide a sufficient level of details in a static way in order to be informative, so most of the requirements definition work has to be done up front. This does not address the incremental and iterative nature of software delivery.

9. In Agile, the construct that lies in the center of requirements definition is a user story. User stories are short, simple descriptions of a feature told from the perspective of the person who desires the new capability, usually a user or customer of the system. Each user story expresses one very specific need that a user has. It can be viewed as a minimum requirement focused on user needs.

10. Each user story specifies the value that this functionality provides to the customer. User story success criteria are defined in the form of statements referred to as acceptance criteria.

11. The acronym INVEST is a mnemonic, which is used to remember the criteria for a high-quality user story. If the story fails to meet one of these criteria, the team may want to rethink it. The acronym represents the following qualities of a user story: a user story should be independent, valuable, estimable, small, and testable.

12. Acceptance Test-Driven Development (ATDD) is a delivery technique that validates whether the system functions as intended. In some cases, the team automates the acceptance tests.

13. User stories support an iterative and incremental approach to requirements gathering. They are prioritized top to bottom, from highest priority to lowest. The top-priority user stories are well defined, and acceptance criteria are provided. Lower-priority user stories do not need to be well defined since they may change or become obsolete by the time the team will start working on them. This concept is similar to the "progressive elaboration" of requirements in traditional project management.

14. The product backlog is a collection of prioritized discrete items of different types connected by parent-child relationships. Relationships between product backlog items are referred to as "product backlog taxonomy." Agile does not prescribe the types of elements in the product backlog; however, traditionally, functional requirements are represented in user story format. The team using the product backlog determines the format they choose to use and looks to the backlog items as reminders of the aspects of a solution they may work on.

15. Besides user stories, product backlog may include epics (collections of user stories), spikes (research equivalent of user stories), technical tasks (which are technical requirements not providing immediate user value, such as upgrading a software tool or setting up a new environment), or subtasks (child item of user stories, spikes, or technical task, which enable team members to align on delivering each of their parent items).

16. Story mapping (a.k.a. user story mapping) is a valuable tool for software development. In this process, the team explores the user story's life cycle, starting with opportunities and moving deeper into discovery, sequencing these user stories into the minimum viable product (MVP) and subsequent releases. This technique allows the team to establish a "big picture" of product delivery and sequence it into releases, starting from MVP.

Building the Product RIGHT

In the first half of the book, we discussed how to build the right product. We used Lean startup techniques to validate whether our idea for a product or a product feature resonates with customers and whether the customers will be willing to use it and potentially buy or subscribe to it. We discussed how user discovery techniques, such as persona analysis and customer journeys, will help refine the ideas based on customer needs, and how to build a product backlog. Further, we discussed how to prioritize this backlog and create a set of discrete "user stories" that reflect user needs and address them feature by feature and how the development team takes an active role in defining acceptance criteria, which is also used in building test cases for the product. This happens iteratively throughout the life cycle of a product, which starts with innovators and early adopters until the majority of relevant users start using it before it sunsets when new, disruptive products get in their place. Part 2 of this textbook will focus on the IT delivery aspects of these products, starting with the description of delivery frameworks and the choices that need to be made in making decisions on product development and delivery to the customer.

Waterfall, Agile, and Hybrid Delivery Frameworks

This chapter covers major aspects of IT delivery, including Agile teams, roles, frameworks, and success criteria. Once the MVP is created, it is important to identify the delivery framework, whether it is Waterfall, Scrum, Kanban, Extreme Programming, or any other Agile framework. In this chapter, these frameworks will be described, compared, and discussed based on their fit to a company or a team, its culture, its products, and business objectives.

In Chapter 1, we provided a summary of the major delivery frameworks. To recap, traditional project management (informally referred to as "Waterfall") provides a list of consecutive steps in delivering the outcome. For example, if we want to build a house, we start with preparing the construction site and pouring the foundation; then doing framing, plumbing, electrical, and HVAC;

© Mariya Breyter 2022
M. Breyter, *Agile Product and Project Management*,
https://doi.org/10.1007/978-1-4842-8200-7_6

installing insulation; completing drywall and interior fixtures; doing exterior finishes and then interior trim; and so forth. We cannot start doing framing until the construction site is ready and the foundation is in place. In software delivery, traditional project management assumes that requirements are well defined before coding starts, testing starts after coding is completed, and the users do not see the finished product until it is ready.

There is a similar to the traditional approach to IT infrastructure management. The purpose of IT infrastructure management is to support technical operations. This usually involves hardware, software, and networks. In traditional project management, IT infrastructure projects are usually broken down by components, such as systems management, network management, and storage management. At the end of any relevant project, there are multiple integration and configuration requirements, such as deploying software on the new hardware or cloud storage, configuring the network, followed by access management, and so on. The whole project is not delivered until integration is complete. In traditional project management, there is even a specialization of an IT infrastructure project management, someone who has extensive experience with data center migrations, cloud implementations, software and hardware upgrades, integrations, and fixes.

For example, for a cloud migration project, the project starts by choosing the cloud solution provider and defining the hosting and architecture approach (level of cloud integration, single or multiple cloud providers, services, and KPIs, or Key Performance Indicators.) Then, companies negotiate and sign an agreement with the provider, establish performance baselines, define migration components, perform refactoring, create a migration plan, execute, integrate, and switch over to production, followed by monitoring and controlling.

In Agile delivery, the approach is different; it's incremental vs. the linear, sequential approach utilized in traditional project management. There is no need to wait until one phase is completed in order to start on the next one.

In both cases, the goal is value delivery. Business value is defined as the entire value of the business, the total sum of all tangible and intangible elements.

"A software product may be a proprietary product of the business and provide a major revenue stream for that business or business unit. In some cases, infrastructure and customer support software may be capitalized and deprecated over time. Software products are sometimes developed for use across multiple systems, thus increasing the business value of those products."

— Software Extension to PMBOK Guide, p. 13 [1]

PMBOK Sixth Edition [1] provides standards for project management practices from the Project Management Institute. It defines the project life cycle as a "collection of generally sequential project phases whose name and number are determined by the control needs of the organization or organizations involved in the project." It outlines traditional approaches to software development where the phases have typically followed the Waterfall methodology, interactive and incremental where product releases are delivered to users incrementally (phased approach), and Agile, which allows for making any functionality available to users as soon as it is developed and tested.

The Project Management Institute states that the process it describes can be applied to any project life cycle. In each Agile iteration, there are traditional Waterfall process groups:

- Initiation
- Planning
- Executing
- Monitoring and controlling
- Closing

However, the way of delivering value is significantly different between traditional project management and Agile. In traditional project management, the user is able to use the product at the end of each phase (usually months for software projects and even longer for network and infrastructure ones), while in Agile, the value is either delivered continuously or at the end of every short iteration (in Scrum, these iterations are called Sprints.) This can be compared in the following way (see Figure 6-1).

As shown in the picture, customers are able to use Agile software after MVP is developed, potentially from the first iteration. In every iteration, the team produces potentially shippable software. Once the minimum viable product is ready for delivery, Agile teams make it available to the customer upon testing and without waiting until the whole project scope has been delivered. Because of this approach, customer value is realized much earlier.

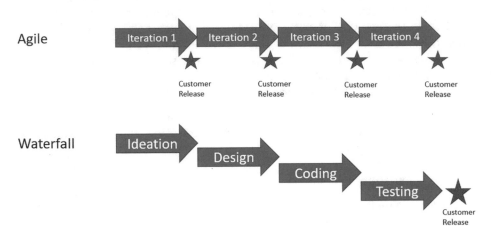

Figure 6-1. Comparison between Agile and Waterfall life cycle

There are other fundamental differences between Agile and Waterfall. Since the product in Agile is delivered incrementally, customers are able to provide their feedback on the product and its functionality from the very beginning. Then, the team is able to get on this feedback in the upcoming iteration(s) – no need to wait until the project is completed to hear customer feedback.

Another major difference is the collaboration between business and technology. In Waterfall, there are points of time throughout the project when the business is closely involved: in the initiation phase when business stakeholders are getting engaged in the project, during requirements gathering where the business stakeholders act as subject matter experts on the topic, and toward the end of the project, primarily during monitoring and controlling, when business stakeholders review the deliverable and sign off on the whole project. In Agile, business and technology are working together throughout the whole duration of the project via presentations of working software or the functionality that has been completed during the iteration.

One more difference is that in Agile, there are usually dedicated long-standing teams. This means that (1) the majority of the project team members are working full time on the project and (2) teams are not assembled for a specific project. They work together for a long period of time from the same backlog. In Waterfall, teams are created for the purpose of a specific project, and frequently, team members are multitasking, that is, working on several projects simultaneously. In Agile, the focus is on team-level delivery. Cross-functional teams are jointly delivering value to the customer. By cross-functional, we mean that the team members combined have all skills required for the end-to-end delivery (UX designers, user researchers, developers, testers.) Frequently, in an Agile environment, teams are allocated to a product; for example, in a health insurance company, one group will be working on claims, another on the patient portal, one more on the provider website, etc., for a long period of time, until this product is sunset. In Waterfall, projects are finite, so once the team completes a project, team members are allocated to other ones.

Some of the differences between Agile and Waterfall are described in Table 6-1.

Table 6-1. The difference between Agile and Waterfall

Parameter	Agile	Waterfall	Comments
Time from initiation to value delivery	One iteration. For example, in Scrum, it is one to four weeks	Large projects take months and sometimes even years	Agile minimizes risks and increases value delivery
The feedback loop from customers	After every iteration so that it can be immediately incorporated	At the end of the projects	Agile allows maximizing customer feedback throughout the delivery
Team type	Cross-functional teams working together on multiple projects	Team members come together for the duration of the project based on each person's competencies; they are frequently multitasking	
Dedicated vs. assembled teams	Long-standing dedicated teams capable of delivering end-to-end functionality	Teams are assembled for the project; team members are not used to be working together and move on once the project is completed	Agile provides a stable team environment so that the teams can go through Tuckman team stages [2] to become high performing
Product based vs. project based	Agile teams deliver products to customers providing the functionality that addresses customer needs. Multiple features can be delivered concurrently, and change in priorities does not cause major disruptions	Waterfall teams deliver projects; each of those addresses a specific need and has to be either completed and to end or closed without being completed. If priorities change, the project is closed, and a new one is initiated	Product-based delivery is customer oriented. A project-based approach addresses business needs rather than providing a holistic customer experience

(continued)

Table 6-1. (*continued*)

Parameter	Agile	Waterfall	Comments
Flexibility	Agile re-sets delivery plans every two weeks, so any change – in scope, priorities – can be seamlessly made every two weeks	Any change in scope or priorities has to be managed (this is referred to as "change management" with the review of the whole project)	Agile provides much more flexibility in planning and delivery than Waterfall
Team vs. collection of individuals	Teams are building an environment of collaboration and psychological safety	Teams are temporary and frequently go through a painful "storming" phase	In Agile, we deal with teams, and in Waterfall, there are collections of individuals rather than teams
Business and technology collaboration	Business and technology are on the same team and work jointly to deliver customer value	Technology is a service that delivers to the business, frequently resulting in tension and finger-pointing	Best products are a result of collaboration between business and technology

Topic for a Group Discussion   In groups, discuss other differences between Agile and Waterfall that are not mentioned in Table 6-1. Which one provides more flexibility and why?

How does Bruce Tuckman's concept for the stages of team development apply to Agile and Waterfall? Why is it important to understand development phases?

Many Waterfall concepts are not applicable to Agile. One of these concepts is scope. In Waterfall, the scope is an important constraint. Once the scope has been defined and signed off, all timelines and deliverables are defined based on the approved scope statement. Any change to project scope, for example, a new requirement or a delivery constraint (e.g., procurement and installation of a new plug-in, or a requirement to expose an internal network to a cloud solution, which has been missed at the beginning of the project), becomes a major obstacle to on-time delivery. In Agile, the scope is defined every iteration, so any change to scope can be seamlessly performed prior to any iteration. The concept of fixed scope in Waterfall is referred to as the iron triangle and is frequently represented as shown in Figure 6-2.

Figure 6-2. "Iron triangle" of the traditional project management

The challenge with this approach is that if any of these three major parameters changes (e.g., a team member gets sick or functionality has changed or the schedule is being changed by a vendor), there are two options:

(1) Having project team members work at an unsustainable pace to make up for additional requirements within the agreed-upon schedule.

(2) Initiate a change management process to assess the impact of the changed event; review project timelines, scope, or team composition; update the project plan; and get approval from senior stakeholders to change the baseline.

IT software management is a continuous learning process, and "known unknowns" (materialized risks, e.g., integration issues or data format inconsistencies) are followed by "unknown unknowns" that are almost impossible to foresee. Waterfall project managers invest a lot of time and effort in proper change management. The only continuous parameter in this construct is the quality because the teams are not expected to ever compromise on the quality of their delivery.

In Agile, the situation is different. There are obviously the same parameters – quality, cost, time (schedule), and scope – but they are fixed during the iteration only. For iterative Agile methodologies, such as Scrum, this is the duration of one Sprint (one to four weeks) – everything outside of the Sprint is going to be planned or adjusted before the new Sprint starts. It can be even more flexible since a new requirement can be taken into a Sprint while another one requiring the same effort is deprioritized. This can be shown with an inverted triangle where time and cost are fixed while the scope is highly variable. By making one of the parameters flexible, the stress is taken off the team, which now has full control in defining what can be delivered in a specific period of time. This paradigm shift is shown in Figure 6-3.

Figure 6-3. "Inverted triangle" of the Agile project management

Besides the three constraints mentioned before, it is important to understand who defines those parameters and when. In traditional project management, this process is orchestrated by a project manager who involves the stakeholders with relevant expertise: subject matter experts, development leads, software architects, and so forth. This estimation happens once at the beginning of the project and as needed during later phases of project delivery as part of the change management process. In Agile, planning is a continuous process that involves all team members who collaboratively make decisions on their deliverables based on team capacity and its historical delivery data.

Five key questions to review:

1. What is a project life cycle?

2. How is value delivered in Agile vs. Waterfall?

3. What are some differences between Agile and Waterfall?

4. What is an "iron triangle" and "inverted triangle," and what is the difference?

5. How is planning done in Agile vs. Waterfall?

Agile is much more than a project management framework; it is frequently defined as a mindset: a mindset of collaboration, self-organization, team collaboration, and customer-focused delivery based on the "build-measure-learn" loop. There is usually a question raised: when is Agile more appropriate, and when is Waterfall?

There are as many opinions on this topic as there are Agile practitioners and project managers. According to the PMI, Agile frameworks are more suitable for high uncertainty work, while traditional project management works well for well-defined projects, which are well understood with low levels of execution uncertainty and risk.

> "Project work ranges from definable work to high-uncertainty work. Definable work projects are characterized by clear procedures that proved successful on similar projects in the past... The production domain and processes involved are usually well understood and there are typically low levels of execution uncertainty and risk...
>
> High-uncertainty projects have high rates of change, complexity, and risk. These characteristics can present problems for traditional predictive approaches that aim to determine the bulk of the requirements upfront and control changes through a change requires process. Instead, Agile approaches were created to explore feasibility in short cycles and quickly adapt based on evaluation and feedback."
>
> — Agile Practice Guide, p. 7 (1)

Overall, according to the PMI, iterative, incremental, and Agile approaches work well for projects that involve new tools, techniques, materials, or applications, that is, for those projects that

- Require research and development
- Have high rates of change
- Have unclear or unknown requirements, uncertainty, or risk
- Have a final goal that is hard to describe (1)

Most agilists would argue with this statement. Agile is known to work well with any project at any time. Besides, most IT projects can hardly be referred to as "predictable": hardware has a limited life cycle, the software requires upgrades, network configurations need fine-tuning, and software needs refactoring. The level of uncertainty and flexibility is extremely high, even for repeatable processes.

Even in construction, where traditional project management originated, iterative delivery is highly successful. A foundation still has to be delivered before the walls are installed. However, this can be done in several iterations. Internal decoration can be done in iterations: if the first room is not successful, then decisions can be made by pivoting on style or on the team doing this work. This way, the customer would be able to review and advise on the next steps, thus establishing a short customer feedback loop. In its turn, the short feedback loop allows for fine-tuning the finished work to achieve customer satisfaction.

💡 **Tip**　We referred to Agile so far as a project management life cycle, a framework, a mindset, and a methodology. It is also sometimes referred to as a method, practice, or technique. What is it? It can be all of that depending on context. If we are planning an Agile iteration, we are using a process. If we align teams to work collaboratively throughout the organization, we are forming a mindset. If we use Agile estimation, it is a technique. In this book, we are specific on the aspect of Agile we are speaking about; however, following PMI guidelines (2), we are using the team "approach."

Agile Mindset

Most importantly, Agile is a mindset. It is drastically different from traditional project management because it is an adaptive (vs. predictive) people-first approach. While traditional project management assumes work assignments and follows up on deliverables, Agile empowers people who do the work and, most importantly, empowers them as a team to define their timelines, access capacity, and plan deliverables. It changes management thinking from top-down to bottom-up and changes managers' jobs from giving assignments to their staff to supporting them by removing impediments (delays, process inefficiencies, budget challenges, or external dependencies) and empowering their decision-making.

Besides the teamwork and collaborative bottom-up nature of the Agile mindset, it also assumes comfort with uncertainty. Some decisions and analyses are made iteratively, and Agile does not guarantee accuracy in longer-term estimations. Traditional project management attempts to achieve long-term accuracy (thus, it is referred to as a predictable model). However, studies show that this is only seeming predictability, and in fact, the accuracy of longer-term planning (over a quarter in advance) in traditional project management is still very low.

Besides people empowerment, Agile is a lightweight framework that allows for experimentation and gamification. Agile is built on inspiring and motivating people; this is why Agile teams are usually supportive and collaborative and enjoy working together. The challenges frequently come from middle managers who feel that they are losing power, so we recommend dedicated training to middle managers, starting with "why" (why their role is much more powerful than before when they were managing day-to-day work and includes leadership, people mentorship, talent development, and strategy definition.)

In his book *The Agile Mind-Set: Making Agile Processes Work* [3], Gil Broza speaks about beliefs that define the Agile mindset. Those can be summarized in the following way:

1. Motivation: Individuals are inspired and motivated to work.

2. Collaborative teams self-organize (define roles and processes, organize the work) toward value delivery.

3. Teams collaborate with their business stakeholders, and together they get direct feedback from their customers on whether they are solving their problems successfully.

4. Continuous feedback and reflection at intervals at multiple levels (internal to the team, team with its customers, managers, and team members) serve as a foundation of a successful team.

An important concept in Agile is servant leadership. The concept originates from Robert K. Greenleaf, who defined a servant leader as a "servant first," someone who has a natural feeling to serve [4]. In a nutshell, servant leadership is a philosophy where the main goal of the leader is to serve by supporting others rather than showcasing a person's own talents and capabilities. This concept is very important for Agile organizations. "Quiet leadership" is an important quality when the leaders give visibility and credit to others rather than emphasizing their own personality. They see their goal as supporting their team, helping them deliver products to customers, and staying in the background. Basically, servant leaders take a traditional power leadership model and turn it upside down. They are leaders and coaches first and executors second.

"If your actions inspire people to dream more, learn more, do more, and become more, you are a leader."

— John Quincy Adams (McCormick Center Library)

Agile Frameworks

There are multiple frameworks built on the Agile mindset with the values and principles of the Agile Manifesto in mind [5]. According to the latest State of Agile Report [6], the level of Agile adoption by enterprises is continuously growing. Ninety-five percent of respondents to the 2020 State of Agile Report indicated that their organizations practice Agile development methods. In most organizations, Agile practices are not limited to IT and include operations, marketing, human resources, sales, and others. The benefits realized by companies adopting Agile include [7]

- Ability to manage changing priorities
- Project visibility
- Business/IT alignment
- Delivery speed/time to market
- Team morale
- Increased team productivity
- Project risk reduction
- Project predictability
- Software quality
- Engineering discipline
- Managing distributed teams
- Software maintainability
- Project cost reduction

Topic for a Group Discussion   What is Agile as a mindset? What is servant leadership and how is it relevant to Agile?

Role-play within each team to discuss concerns of a middle manager, Steve. Steve is concerned about his job safety, if he has to become a servant leader instead of managing people and day-to-day work they do.

In terms of the Agile methodologies used, Scrum continues to be the most common Agile methodology used by organizations (58%), followed by Kanban (7%), Lean startup (1%), extreme programming (XP) (1%), and multiple iterative and hybrid methodologies. Let us review each of these methodologies.

Scrum

Scrum is by far the most popular Agile methodology. It was developed by Ken Schwaber and Jeff Sutherland, signatories of the Agile Manifesto, in the early 1990s to help organizations struggling with complex software development projects. The source of reference for this methodology is the Scrum Guide published online with regular revisions [8]. As of this time, the latest revision of the Scrum Guide was done in November 2020.

Scrum Guide defines Scrum as a "lightweight framework that helps people, teams, and organizations generate value through adaptive solutions for complex problems."

Scrum is

- Lightweight
- Simple to understand
- Difficult to master

According to the Scrum Guide, the "Scrum framework is purposefully incomplete, only defining the parts required to implement Scrum theory. Scrum is built upon the collective intelligence of the people using it. Rather than providing people with detailed instructions, the rules of Scrum guide their relationships and interactions."

Various processes, techniques, and methods can be employed within the framework. Scrum wraps around existing practices or renders them unnecessary. Scrum makes visible the relative efficacy of current management, environment, and work techniques so that improvements can be made."

While Scrum was initially used to deliver software, hardware, and networks, it has extended far beyond IT and is used for building autonomous vehicles, for managing schools, by the government, in marketing, for managing the operation of organizations, and almost everything we use in our daily lives, as individuals and societies.

"Scrum is founded on empiricism and Lean thinking. Empiricism asserts that knowledge comes from experience and making decisions based on what is observed. Lean thinking reduces waste and focuses on the essentials. Scrum employs an iterative, incremental approach to optimize predictability and to control risk. Scrum engages groups of people who collectively have all the skills and expertise to do the work and share or acquire such skills as needed."

There are three pillars in Scrum:

- Transparency: "The emergent process and work must be visible to those performing the work as well as those receiving the work. With Scrum, important decisions are based on the perceived state of its three formal artifacts. Artifacts that have low transparency can lead to decisions that diminish value and increase risk. Transparency enables inspection. Inspection without transparency is misleading and wasteful."

- Inspection: "The Scrum artifacts and the progress toward agreed goals must be inspected frequently and diligently to detect potentially undesirable variances or problems. To help with inspection, Scrum provides cadence in the form of its five events. Inspection enables adaptation. Inspection without adaptation is considered pointless. Scrum events are designed to provoke change."

- Adaptation: "If any aspects of a process deviate outside acceptable limits or if the resulting product is unacceptable, the process being applied or the materials being produced must be adjusted. The adjustment must be made as soon as possible to minimize further deviation. Adaptation becomes more difficult when the people involved are not empowered or self-managing. A Scrum team is expected to adapt the moment it learns anything new through inspection."

Scrum teams are usually small self-organizing cross-functional groups of individuals. These self-organizing teams make their own decisions on how to accomplish their work, rather than being told how to do so. Cross-functional teams have all competencies needed to accomplish the work without depending on other teams. Overall, the team model in Scrum is designed to optimize the software development flow, thus achieving higher quality and productivity. The most frequent team size is from three to nine people, but there is no strict constraint. Scrum values include commitment, courage, focus, openness, and respect, which are embodied and lived by the Scrum team.

Topic for a Group Discussion   What does it mean to be a self-organizing cross-functional team? Does it mean that there are no specific skillsets and everyone on the team can do each type of work? Does it mean that they decide what they are working on and not their business stakeholders? How do you understand those concepts and how are they different from the way you are familiar with in the organizations you've observed or worked at?

As described in the Scrum Guide, the Scrum team includes the Product Owner, the Scrum Master, and developers.

1. **Developers** are professionals who do the work of delivering a potentially releasable Increment of "Done" product at the end of each Sprint. Developers are empowered by the organization to organize and manage their own work. Developers are always accountable for

   - Creating a plan for the Sprint, the Sprint backlog

   - Instilling quality by adhering to a Definition of Done

   - Adapting their plan each day toward the Sprint goal

   - Holding each other accountable as professionals

2. The Product Owner is accountable for maximizing the value of the product resulting from the work of the Scrum team. How this is done may vary widely across organizations, Scrum teams, and individuals.

   "The Product Owner is also accountable for effective product backlog management, which includes

   - Developing and explicitly communicating the Product Goal

   - Creating and clearly communicating product backlog items

   - Ordering product backlog items

   - Ensuring that the product backlog is transparent, visible, and understood

   The Product Owner may do the preceding work or may delegate the responsibility to others. Regardless, the Product Owner remains accountable. For Product Owners to succeed, the entire organization must respect their decisions. These decisions are visible in the content and ordering of the product backlog, and through the inspectable Increment at the Sprint Review. The Product Owner is one person, not a committee. The Product Owner may represent the needs of many stakeholders in the product backlog."

3. The **Scrum Master** is a servant-leader for the Scrum team. While the Product Owner is responsible for "what" the team is building, the Scrum Master is responsible for "how." The Scrum Master's responsibility is in promoting and supporting Scrum as defined in the Scrum Guide. Scrum Masters do this by helping everyone understand Scrum theory, practices, rules, and values. The Scrum Master is accountable for the Scrum team's effectiveness. They do this by enabling the Scrum team to improve its practices, within the Scrum framework. Scrum Masters are true leaders who serve the Scrum team and the larger organization.

The most important feature of Scrum is its cyclical delivery within timeboxed iterations. There are Lean concepts – continuous improvement, ownership over defects, and customer-centricity – that serve as an inspiration for developing this timeboxed framework that allows for planning accuracy, high quality, and, most importantly, employee motivation.

"What Scrum does is bring teams together to create great things, and that requires everyone not only to see the end goal, but to deliver incrementally toward that goal."

— Jeff Sutherland, Scrum: The Art of Doing Twice the Work in Half the Time, p.20 (4)

A timeboxed iteration in Scrum is called a Sprint. Sprints are the heartbeat of Scrum, where ideas are turned into value. Sprints have consistent durations, usually two to four weeks. A new Sprint starts immediately after the previous one is completed. Sprint consists of Sprint planning, Daily Scrums, Sprint Review, and Sprint Retrospective. Scrum cadence is shown in Figure 6-4.

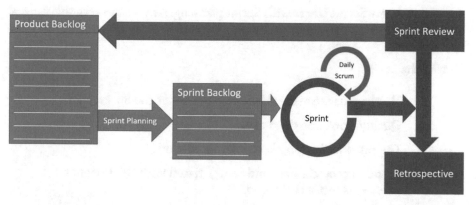

Figure 6-4. Scrum cadence

As a result of Sprint planning, the team sets a Sprint goal and takes on work into a Sprint. Once Sprint planning is completed, no changes are made that would endanger the Sprint goal. However, the scope may be adjusted between the Product Owner and developers as they learn more during the delivery process. Once the Sprint planning is complete and the team starts execution, they meet daily for up to 15 minutes to align on delivery and forecast upcoming work. These events are called Daily Scrum, and they focus on progress toward the Sprint goal. While there is no strict prescription, an effective format for Daily Scrums is having team members take turns to answer three questions:

- What did I do yesterday that helped the Scrum team meet the Sprint goal?

- What will I do today to help the Scrum team meet the Sprint goal?

- Do I see any impediment that prevents us from meeting the Sprint goal?

At the end of each Sprint, a team produces a shippable product that meets the "Definition of Done" and shows it to the stakeholders for their feedback. They also discuss any impediments and work that they were not able to complete. The result of the Sprint Review is a revised backlog and a shared understanding of the progress made by the team. Most importantly, the team gets feedback from their stakeholders.

Based on all the events and progress during the Sprint, the team conducts a Sprint Retrospective, which concludes the Sprint. A Retrospective is an internal team event, where the team members discuss how the completed Sprint went, what was accomplished well, and what needs improvement; decide on the action items to implement the most impactful of those improvements; and create a plan to implement those.

After this, a new Sprint starts with Sprint planning. As you can see, this cyclical structure allows for continuity, reflection, customer-centricity, and continuous improvement.

During the Sprint:

- No changes are made that would endanger the Sprint goal.

- Quality does not decrease.

- The product backlog is refined as needed.

- Scope may be clarified and renegotiated with the Product Owner as more is learned.

 Five key questions to review:

1. What is Scrum?

2. Why is Scrum by far the most highly adopted Agile methodology?

3. Why is Scrum both a framework and a methodology?

4. What is a Sprint?

5. How is a Sprint structured in Scrum?

Kanban

Kanban is the second Agile methodology after Scrum in terms of adoption. It originates from Lean manufacturing and is focused on optimizing the flow of value throughout the system, end to end. Kanban is based on "system thinking" when the value delivery process ("the flow") is optimized throughout delivery, from the initial input to customer delivery.

In his book *The Principles of Product Development Flow*, Donald Reinertsen explained the challenge of many companies who manage timelines instead of managing product development queues. Project managers focus on managing timelines instead of optimizing the delivery process. According to Donald Reinertsen, the secret to high performance is to optimize queues rather than driving toward timelines. Timelines are a lagging indicator. Once the timeline is in jeopardy, the process is already close to delivery. In contracts, the queues are leading indicators of future cycle-time problems. By controlling the batch size and limiting work in process, we get better control of the deliverables (5).

Kanban allows to define the flow, control the batch size, and ensure the optimal pace of delivery. The goal of Kanban is to visualize the body of work and define the optimal way of producing a desirable outcome. Every process has its flow – a step or consecutive steps to deliver a product or a service. Companies such as Microsoft, Sprint, and Motorola use Kanban for their software development process. As opposed to Scrum, which requires significant organizational changes upfront, Kanban is an evolutionary method that is built on optimizing delivery, reducing waste, and maximizing value. Kanban can be used by itself or combined with another methodology, such as Scrum. The combination of Scrum and Kanban is referred to as Scrumban. It includes optimized flow combined with timeboxed iterations.

There are several principles in Kanban:

1. Flow optimization by reducing waste and maximizing value. There are multiple ways to achieve this goal. Let us review the following example:

    A company called FlowChart Associates was involved in processing legal documents online. When a document was created, it had to undergo multiple compliance reviews. Reviews were done by specially designated people having different skills and subject matter expertise. One of them was responsible for the national copyright law, the second was responsible for international IP Property rights, and the third was responsible for confirming that the document does not violate any general regulations related to its content or the place of resolution that was stated in the document. There was also a rule that prior to each of the reviews, any document is reviewed by an editor and a proofreader.

    It took about three weeks on average to process all documents, and FlowChart was losing business because their clients complained that they were not willing to wait three weeks for a document review. The company CEO invited Alicia, a Kanban consultant, to help out with the problem. The first thing Alicia did was invite everyone into a room and draw a workflow diagram of this process, end to end. On this diagram, she mapped the time when work was performed as well as the gap time between the steps, which was used for handovers. Most of the gap time, though, was caused by the fact that the next person in the chain was busy doing other work, so the whole process stopped, given how busy everyone was. When they calculated the time spent doing work (reviewing and analyzing documents or editing and proofreading them), it took six to eight hours between all the participants. The gap time between every step was measured in days, not hours. On top of it, the third reviewer was a constant bottleneck in the process since they had to review documents coming from both the first and the second reviewer. This visualization of work Alicia called a **value stream map**.

When participants looked at this value stream map, they clearly saw three big loops when after being edited, the document went to the first reviewer, then went back to be proofread and went to the second reviewer, and then went to the third reviewer before undertaking final editing and proofreading. The third reviewer was backed up with a pile of 10–15 documents at any moment of time, so customers started raising quality-related complaints. As it turned out, the third reviewer was so stressed that they missed issues trying to catch up with the work, which generated quality concerns. This was the first time that metrics were collected related to this process.

Alicia suggested optimizing several things:

1. Instead of three loops, cross-train reviewers in their adjacent areas of competency. This would immediately remove the bottleneck.

2. Have one person review the document for all three sets of issues: local copyright, global IP, and execution – this eliminated the gap time between multiple loops.

3. Establish a work in process (WIP) limit so that the work is "pulled" once the person has the capacity, rather than pushed each time new work is required.

4. Implement process automation so that basic checks are done algorithmically.

5. Visualize all work via a comprehensive Kanban board.

6. Start relentlessly collecting metrics, such as cycle time and lead time, and focus process improvements on improving outcomes.

The training and knowledge sharing took about two weeks, and the new process started. In the second week, the average cycle time was reduced by 50%. This was done by removing a bottleneck, consolidating three loops, and implementing WIP limits for each of the processes. At the end of the process, proofreading and editing were done only once. Within several more weeks, the same group of people was processing an average contract within one workday.

2. In order to implement process changes, it is important to visualize the work being done. This is done with a visual board. Many people think that this board equals Kanban; however, it is one of multiple techniques and artifacts used in Kanban. A similar board (but not identical) is used in Scrum and many other frameworks.

    Kanban literally means visual board (see example in Figure 6-5). The goal of a daily Kanban meeting is to remove bottlenecks every step of the way, walking Kanban board right to left and visualizing any bottleneck in the flow. Kanban uses work in process (WIP) limits to establish maximum load on each of the process steps within the flow.

    A fable based on the concept of "flow" was presented by Eliyahu Goldratt in 1984, who has shown that the only way to optimize flow is to remove the bottleneck, which is followed by finding out which is the next most limiting constraint [6]. This highly effective approach to flow optimization is referred to as the theory of constraints. Eliyahu Goldratt challenged a well-established perception that a system has to be full to capacity. If a road is full to capacity, it creates a traffic jam. If a person is filled with work to capacity, they will become a bottleneck, while if challenged, they will come up with innovative out-of-the-box solutions.

    While Goldratt's book, *The Goal*, was based on manufacturing examples, his theory of constraints is universally applicable to software development. Adding resources to any step of the process except for the bottleneck, does not address a constraint; it just increases pressure on the bottleneck and makes it slower.

Figure 6-5. Sample Kanban board

Five key questions to review:

1.   What is Kanban?

2.   What is the difference between Scrum and Kanban? Can they be used together?

3.   What is the flow and how is it visualized?

4.   How is a Kanban board created?

5.   Why is the theory of constraints so important in process optimization?

Case Study: Project Phoenix.   In their 2013 bestseller IT fiction, Project Phoenix (6), Gene Kim, Kevin Behr, and George Spafford tell a story of DevOps having a major impact on application workflow management. The main character, Bill Palmer, has recently been named VP of IT Operations, and he is facing an urgent need to change ineffective software delivery and release processes for his company, Parts Unlimited. Bill has 90 days to fix an overbudget, low-quality failing project with a code name The Phoenix Project.

Bill's role is to change end-to-end processes to become effective, manage the quality of delivery, upgrade failing systems, and enable efficient on-time delivery.

The most important part of the vision that Bill brings in is that IT operations are no longer seen as a support function to the business. The work is performed in collaboration between business and IT. All the IT employees are part of delivery against the business objective. There is no longer a customer/vendor relationship; there is collaboration between a cross-functional team of individuals.

The key to Bill's success in turning the company around is not in technology and even IT operations per se. He introduced DevOps as the application of Lean manufacturing methods to the world of software development and operations. First, he focused on system thinking. He did not try to optimize every step of the delivery process but rather identified the bottleneck, which was one critical area of expertise that was represented by an overworked engineer who was unable to provide high-quality work by working at an unsustainable pace. Once he forced this employee to go on vacation, others had no choice but to build their own areas of expertise in this area.

By focusing on the flow of value delivery from start to finish, Bill was able to establish trusting relationships with business partners, so the relationship was built on collaboration rather than business providing requirements to IT and not participating until the software was ready.

Bill implemented a pull-based Kanban process, created transparency, enabled groups to align, and motivated people by delegating solutions to those who were doing the work. He promoted a sense of ownership and accountability through the concept of flow: focusing on speed of delivery to create value for the business.

Extreme Programming

Extreme programming, also known as XP, is a discipline in software development that focuses the whole team on feasible reachable goals. In his book, the creator of extreme programming, Kent Beck, defined XP as an attempt to bring accountability and transparency into software development [9]. Many practitioners think that XP is primarily focused on technical practices, such as pair programming and test-driven development. This is correct, but first of all, XP is about social change. As Kent Beck states, "it is about letting go of habits and patterns that were adaptive in the past, but now get in the way of us doing our best work" [10, p. 1].

XP is a "style of software development, focusing on the excellent application of programming techniques, clear communication, and teamwork, which allows us to accomplish things that we previously could not even imagine" [10, p. 2]. Similar to Scrum, it is based on short iterations of software development.

Organizational Structure and Team Topology

The organizational model and team structure have been an important topic for Agile companies. Given that teams stay together for a long time, it is logical to have a team as a nuclear structure within an organization. However, the question then arises: How is this team going to fit within the organization as a whole – not just by role and function, but also in terms of skills that its members bring to this group?

In traditional project management, there are eight organizational types, according to PMBOK:

- Organic or simple organization
- Functional or centralized organization
- Multidivisional organization
- Matrix organization
- Project-oriented (composite or hybrid) organization
- Virtual organization
- Hybrid organization
- PMO

Out of these eight, there are three major categories:

1. Functional or centralized organization: This is the most frequent organizational structure. Those companies include departments where people have the same skillset, for example, developers, testers, business analysts, system administrators, and project managers. This structure is represented in Figure 6-6, example 1.

2. Multidivisional organization: This type is based on divisions building products with adjacent functionality serving the same market, for example, consumer banking vs. investment banking vs. investment management. This structure is represented in Figure 6-6, example 2.

3. Matrix organization: Matrix organizational structure is when each employee reports to multiple managers; one is usually a competency manager (e.g., Head of a Project Management Office for project managers, Tech Lead for developers, and so on), and the other is the functional manager, depending on a division (e.g., in a bank, it would be commercial banking, consumer banking, investment management, or private wealth management). Matrix organizational structure was developed in the aerospace industry in the 1950s and is still widely adopted in multiple industries. This structure is represented in Figure 6-6, example 3.

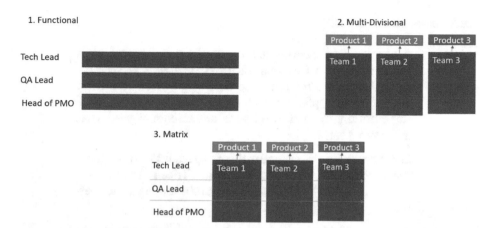

Figure 6-6. Organizational structure

This organizational typology is only the first step to creating a healthy organization. In 1968, Melvin Conway, a computer researcher, published an article entitled "How Do Committees Invent?" In this article, he stated that organizations that design systems are constrained to produce designs that are copies of the communication structure of these organizations [11]. Fred Brooks quoted this paper in his book *The Mythical Man-Month* by referring to this statement as the Conway Law. This statement emphasizes the human factor in organizational design that further reflects on system design.

The Conway Law is a significant consideration in organizational design. For example, if an organization is built based on competencies (separate group of project managers, developers, testers, and analysts,) the major challenges will be "system thinking" and end-to-end delivery. If an organization is built on "component" teams responsible for different systems – data, business logic, messaging and notification, transaction processing, user identity management, and so forth – the major challenge will be integration. The most efficient way to build an IT project is to have an organization that is structured in sync with product functionality – the teams within such an organization are referred to as "feature" teams.

The team structure is discussed in detail in the book by Matthew Skelton and Manuel Pais, *Team Topologies*, published in 2019 [12]. In this book, the authors analyze organizing business and technology teams for fast flow. They come up with four fundamental typologies for IT teams:

- Stream-aligned team (a.k.a. feature team)
- Enabling team
- Complicated-subsystem team
- Platform team

Let's review these types:

- A stream is a continuous flow of work aligned to a business domain or organizational capability. A stream-aligned team is a team aligned to a single value stream of work, for example, product or service. In a modern IT organization, most of the teams are stream aligned, that is, feature teams.

- Enabling team is composed of specialists in a given technology or product domain. These teams are responsible for the strategy – research, tooling, practices, frameworks, and training.

- The complicated-subsystem team is responsible for building and maintaining a part of the system that depends heavily on specialist knowledge to make any changes. This could include a mathematical model and transaction reporting system for financial services or a face recognition system.

- The platform team enables the stream-aligned team to deliver work with substantial autonomy. They own building, running, and fixing their application in production.

An interesting matrix-like organizational structure was introduced at Spotify in 2012 (8). The Spotify model was developed by Henrik Kniberg and Anders Ivarsson. Instead of groups and divisions, Spotify implemented a people-driven approach based on the number of people, and the nature of the product, for example, a popular audio streaming subscription service (9).

Case Study: Spotify. Spotify is a company that provides music subscriptions on demand. To sustain its rapid growth and give autonomy to its teams, Spotify created a multidimensional model of a Scrum organization. There are four types of groups: Tribes, Squads, Chapters, and Guilds.

1. The major unit is a **Squad**. A Squad is similar to a Scrum team: it's a cross-functional dedicated team. Spotify compared it with a mini-startup.

2. Collection of Squads is called a **Tribe**; it usually includes up to 100 people. An example of a Tribe is a music player. The tribe is seen as an incubator for mini-startups.

3.   Chapters and Guilds are the glue that holds the company together. A **Chapter** is a group of people having similar skills and working within the same general competency area, within the same Tribe. They regularly meet to discuss their area of expertise and build sustainable practices and processes. Members of a Chapter report to their line manager who has traditional responsibilities, such as developing people and deciding on compensation and promotions, as well as hands-on responsibilities of a team member.

4.   **Guilds** are more organic communities of interest, where people want to learn and share knowledge, tools, and practice. Chapters are always local to a Tribe, while Guilds cut across the whole organization. Examples include the tester guild, Agile coach guild, and database guild. They meet for conferences and other events to share their experience.

This structure supported Spotify's rapid growth (in two years, they have grown from 30 to 350 people in tech) and allowed for autonomy, mastery, and purpose of the team members.

Source: Henrik Kniberg, Anders Ivarsson. Scaling Agile @ Spotify with Tribes, Squads, Chapters, and Guilds. October 2012. `https://blog.crisp.se/wp-content/uploads/2012/11/SpotifyScaling.pdf` as retrieved on September 5, 2020

 Five key questions to review:

1.   What types of organizational structure are you familiar with?

2.   How does software design reflect the culture of an organization?

3.   What is a matrix organization?

4.   What organizational structure did Spotify come up with?

5.   How many managers does each employee have on Spotify?

 Topic for a Group Discussion   Do you find Spotify organizational culture effective, and why?

Roles in Agile

Roles in Agile are focused around three major areas.

Agile teams are self-organizing for value delivery. It is important that team members complement each other and they are able to produce value end to end. For example, if a team is involved in software delivery, they have development, testing, and analytical skills on the team. These skills would be represented by a small number of people (five to nine), but there are no constraints that Agile would impose specific to skill distribution. Team members actively participate in backlog refinement and have direct access to customers.

Besides the Agile team composition, there are two areas:

1. Building the **RIGHT** product. The role is responsible for "what?" This is where the Product Owner's expertise, prioritization, and ability to communicate clearly with the stakeholders are key.

2. Building the product **RIGHT**. This role is responsible for repeatable lightweight processes with continuous improvement.

Scrum Guide defined Agile roles on a Scrum team in the following way.

The Scrum team [8] consists of a Product Owner, the developers/testers/designers, and a Scrum Master:

1. The Product Owner is responsible for maximizing the value of the product resulting from the work of the Scrum team.

2. The Scrum team includes professionals who do the work of delivering a potentially releasable Increment of "Done" product at the end of each Sprint. A "Done" Increment is required at the Sprint Review.

3. The Scrum Master is a servant-leader for the Scrum team. The Scrum Master helps everyone change these interactions to maximize the value created by the Scrum team.

The Scrum Master serves the Scrum team in several ways, including

- Coaching the team members in self-management and cross-functionality

- Helping the Scrum team focus on creating high-value Increments that meet the Definition of Done

- Causing the removal of impediments to the Scrum team's progress
- Ensuring that all Scrum events take place and are positive, productive, and kept within the timebox

The Scrum Master serves the Product Owner in several ways, including

- Helping find techniques for effective Product Goal definition and product backlog management
- Helping the Scrum team understand the need for clear and concise product backlog items
- Helping establish empirical product planning for a complex environment
- Facilitating stakeholder collaboration as requested or needed

The Scrum Master serves the organization in several ways, including

- Leading, training, and coaching the organization in its Scrum adoption
- Planning and advising Scrum implementations within the organization
- Helping employees and stakeholders understand and enact an empirical approach for complex work
- Removing barriers between stakeholders and Scrum teams

However, Agile roles are not limited to three primary roles defined in Scrum. In many frameworks, there are other roles – Product Manager, Business Analyst, Tech Lead, and so forth. Let us review the roles, their differences, and the ways they support each other, starting with the Product Owner.

According to the Scrum Guide, the Product Owner is the sole person responsible for managing the product backlog. Product backlog management includes

- Clearly expressing product backlog items
- Ordering the items in the product backlog to best achieve goals and missions
- Optimizing the value of the work the Scrum team performs

- Ensuring that the product backlog is visible, transparent, and clear to all and shows what the Scrum team will work on next
- Ensuring the Scrum team understands items in the product backlog to the level needed

The Product Owner may do the preceding work or have the Scrum team do it. However, the Product Owner remains accountable.

This does not mean that the Product Owner is the only person who provides input into the product backlog. Representing the customer and being the voice of the customer, the Product Owner conducts analysis to define customer personas, understand their needs, and combine this knowledge with a deep understanding of the subject matter areas and the business. At the same time, the Product Owner is a person, not a group or committee. Based on all inputs, the Product Owner makes prioritization and scope decisions related to the product.

An important concept is an empowered Product Owner. If a person in this role is not empowered to make decisions, they will not be successful. The organization must respect the decisions of the Product Owner, and the changes in priorities or features delivered should be presented to the Product Owner for their decision.

In large organizations, there may be Product Owners on Agile teams and Product Managers who are responsible for the product's business success: P&L, or profit and loss – the business success of the product summarizing revenues, costs, and expenses related to creating, marketing, and distributing the product along with its sales; for the sales, marketing, and all related activities; for the relationships with the customers and envisioning new products and businesses. The role of the Product Manager is outside of the boundaries of any delivery framework, including Agile.

An example of a product manager was Steve Jobs, who synthesized a deep understanding of customers and their needs with his revolutionary vision. He was focused on the "what" and the "why" rather than the "how." His vision was a world where everyone had access to the best computers. He also built stories around that vision that got others excited. People who got excited about his vision bought his products and built upon his vision as their own. This is the function of the Product Manager – to envision, get others excited, and help them make this product their own.

One of the most respected authorities on the topic of product management, the founder of the Silicon Valley Product Group, Marty Cagan, wrote an iconic book, *Inspired: How to Create Tech Products Customers Love* [13]. In this book, Marty shared that behind every great product, there is someone – usually, someone behind the scenes, working tirelessly – who led the product team to combine technology and design to address customer needs that meet the need of the business. This person is the Product Manager.

The second role on the Scrum team is the team itself. The Scrum Guide refers to it as a "Scrum team." Scrum teams are self-organizing. They are structured and empowered by the organization to organize and manage their own work in delivering the product. According to the Scrum Guide, "Scrum teams have the following characteristics:

- They are self-organizing. No one (not even the Scrum Master) tells the Development Team how to turn product backlog into Increments of potentially releasable functionality.

- Development Teams are cross-functional, with all the skills as a team necessary to create a product Increment.

- Scrum recognizes no titles for Development Team members, regardless of the work being performed by the person.

- Scrum recognizes no subteams in the Development Team, regardless of domains that need to be addressed like testing, architecture, operations, or business analysis.

- Individual Development Team members may have specialized skills and areas of focus, but accountability belongs to the Development Team as a whole."

The size of the Scrum team is usually 5-7 +/- 2 people; however, different organizations have specific rules related to structuring and organizing their teams [14].

The Scrum Master role is frequently referred to as "Agile project manager." However, there is a fundamental difference between a Scrum Master and a project manager. The project manager is responsible for delivering a project. In this sense, it is a management role where the project manager has to use a "command-and-control" approach to set tasks, define timelines, and follow up on completion. The Scrum Master role is the opposite. Scrum Master helps everyone understand Scrum theory, practices, rules, and values. It is a servant-leader role where Scrum Master helps the team to be self-organizing and create high-value products. Scrum Master does so by removing impediments to the progress of the Development Team; promoting Scrum values of commitment, courage, focus, openness, and respect; and coaching the Development Team in organizational environments in which Scrum is not yet fully adopted and understood. Scrum Master ensures that the product scope, goals, and domain are understood by the Development Team, helps the

Development Team understand and collaborate with the Product Owner on the product backlog, and helps the organization in understanding and practicing agility.

This is one of the least understood Agile roles and one of the most critical ones. As good sports coaches, there are Scrum Masters who make any team successful, no matter where they go and what they do. Similarly, there are Scrum Masters who continuously fail in creating a productive Agile environment and blame it on their team members or organizational level of agility. In reality, there are no bad or perfect teams or organizations. The role of the Scrum Master is to patiently and passionately support their team's and organization's journey to agility.

This role is frequently misinterpreted as a facilitator and almost like a team secretary: someone who books meeting rooms, maintains schedules for team meetings, schedules events, facilitates them, maintains repositories, and is responsible for vacation calendars. This cannot be farther from the intent of this role. Scrum Master is a coach who educates the teams, challenges them when they become complacent, supports team members when they are discouraged or demotivated, and leads them to success when things are hard. It is a leadership and coaching role as much as it is a servant role to the team and the Product Owner [15].

While Scrum Master is the most controversial and least defined role in Scrum, it is crucial for the success of the Agile enterprise adoption. It is a recent trend that Scrum teams do not need a dedicated Scrum Master, and this role can be played by delivery leads. The practice shows time and again that the organizations that do not value a role of a dedicated Scrum Master are significantly less successful than the ones that have this role filled with people who are passionate about the "how": how to build a self-organizing team, how to position it for success, how to support it when there are major impediments in place, how to optimize delivery and target it better to customer needs, and many other questions that the Development Team has to continuously solve in a changing delivery environment.

In his article, "The Tao of Scrum" (10), Michael Spayd uses inspiration from Tao Te Ching to discuss Scrum concepts from Tao's perspective.

The roles are defined in the Scrum Guide and interpreted by Michael Spayd in connection to Scrum (10):

1. The Product Owner decides the "what" of the Way.

2. The Team decides the "how" and "how much" of the Way.

3. The Scrum Master serves the Way and tells others when the Way has been lost.

Now that we've established tools and roles, we are going to move on to the most complex element of Agile: estimation and planning (see Chapter 7).

Key Points

1. The Project Management Institute states that the process it describes can be applied to any project life cycle. In each Agile iteration, according to PMBOK, there are traditional Waterfall process groups: Initiation, Planning, Executing, Monitoring, Controlling, and Closing.

2. Many Waterfall concepts are not directly applicable to Agile. One of these concepts is scope. In Waterfall, the scope is an important constraint. Once the scope has been defined and signed off, all timelines and deliverables are defined based on the approved scope statement.

3. According to the latest State of Agile Report, the level of Agile adoption by enterprises is continuously growing. Ninety-five percent of respondents to the 2020 State of Agile Report indicated that their organizations practice Agile development methods. In most organizations, Agile practices are not limited to IT and include operations, marketing, human resources, sales, and others.

4. Project managers in Waterfall invest a lot of time and effort in proper change management. The only continuous parameter in this construct is the quality because the teams are not expected to ever compromise on the quality of their delivery.

5. Agile is a mindset. It is drastically different from traditional project management because it is an adaptive (vs. predictive) people-first approach. While traditional project management assumes work assignments and follows up on deliverables, Agile empowers people who do the work and, most importantly, empowers them as a team to define their timelines, access capacity, and plan deliverables.

6. While Scrum was initially used to deliver software, hardware, embedded software, and networks of interacting functions, it has extended far beyond IT. It is used for building autonomous vehicles, for managing

schools, by the government, in marketing, for managing the operation of organizations, and almost everything we use in our daily lives.

7. There are three pillars in Scrum:

    - Transparency: This includes repeatable shared processes, common language referring to these processes, and the shared Definition of Done, which defines the completed product ready for sign-off by the business or the customer.

    - Inspection: Scrum is built on continuous improvement. This includes relentless progress toward the stated delivery goals.

    - Adaptation: Quality is important in Scrum, so there is a continuous adaptation based on the variability and related failures.

8. Kanban is the second Agile methodology after Scrum in terms of adoption. It originates from Lean manufacturing and is focused on optimizing the flow of value throughout the system, end to end. Kanban is based on "system thinking" when the value delivery process ("the flow") is optimized throughout delivery, from the initial input to customer delivery.

9. Kanban allows to define the flow, control the batch size, and ensure the optimal pace of delivery. The goal of Kanban is to visualize the body of work and define the optimal way of producing a desirable outcome. Every process has its flow – a step of consecutive steps to deliver a product or a service.

10. Roles in Agile are focused around three major areas: Development Team (The Team), Product Owner, and Scrum Master.

11. Agile teams are self-organizing for value delivery. It is important that team members complement each other and they are able to produce value end to end. For example, if the team is involved in software delivery, they have development, testing, and analytical skills on the team. These skills would be represented by a small number of people (five to nine), but there are no constraints that Agile would impose specific to team distribution. Team members actively participate in backlog refinement and have direct access to customers.

Agile Estimation and Planning

This chapter discusses the topic of estimation and planning in Agile. It explains how the Sprint structure is used to estimate effort and plan delivery. It talks about short-term and long-term planning, story point estimation, Definition of Ready, and Definition of Done. The five levels of Scrum planning ("Agile onion") are discussed based on a case study.

In Chapter 6, we covered the difference between multiple delivery frameworks. We also learned that Scrum is by far the most popular Agile framework, and one of the reasons for this is that Scrum allows for the most accurate planning, short term and long term, thus establishing predictability that far surpasses traditional project management. This statement may not seem immediately intuitive. In traditional (Waterfall) project management, a lot of time and effort goes into planning. Opinions of senior leaders in each area are collected, the experience of prior relevant projects is studied and analyzed in depth, and a lot of time is spent creating work breakdown structures, which list all tasks that need to be done to complete the project. All those efforts create a sense of thoughtful, reliable planning.

However, in real life, this level of predictability is a myth. The most thorough, well-thought-through project plans collapse when they meet reality. According to a 2018 PMI's Pulse of the Profession report [1], 12% of IT projects fail. However, this number only represents total failures. Of the projects that

© Mariya Breyter 2022
M. Breyter, *Agile Product and Project Management*,
https://doi.org/10.1007/978-1-4842-8200-7_7

didn't fail completely, 22% did not meet their goals, 33% exceeded their budgets, and 36% were late. So with all the thorough planning that went into them, why are more than a third of all projects late?

💡 **Tip**　It is important to understand why predictability is important in IT overall and especially in software delivery. Imagine a stakeholder is asking a brand-new team about their estimation to deliver a specific product. The team does their estimations and promises to deliver within six months. The sponsor allocates a six-month budget, informs the management, does external marketing, and in six months finds out that the product is not even close to being ready. The sponsor is not willing to invest more, and the product never gets delivered. Or the sponsor requests additional budget, the team completes the product and launches it in 12 months, but no customers are willing to buy it because the company lost their credibility with them, or because another company has already launched their product to the market. Next time, the same team decides to play it safe ("underpromise and overdeliver") and inflates their original estimation for a similar project telling the stakeholders that it is going to take 18 months. Do you think the stakeholders will be happy when the product is actually delivered within 12 months? Unfortunately, not, because they decided not to proceed with such a lengthy and expensive endeavor. Our responsibility is to provide accurate and thoughtful estimations, and Agile provides a way to do so.

So why are the estimations so difficult to make accurately? The answer is straightforward: project delivery is nontrivial. A good way to visualize this is a traditional project management matrix depicting "knowns" vs. "unknowns" in project delivery. This tool is frequently referred to as the Rumsfeld matrix, named after US Secretary of Defense Donald Rumsfeld, who used it in his Department of Defense news briefing in 2022. He mentioned that there are known knowns: the things we know that we know. There are known unknowns: things we do not know. There are also unknown unknowns – the ones we don't know, we don't know, and these are the most difficult ones. However, the idea of "unknown unknowns" was invented in 1955 by two American psychologists, Joseph Luft and Harrington Ingham, in their development of a well-known analysis technique referred to as the Johari window [2], named as a combination of their first names. Johari window is a technique that helps people better understand their relationship with themselves and others by using a two-by-two grid to map how we see ourselves vs. how others see us. A template for the Johari window is presented in Figure 7-1.

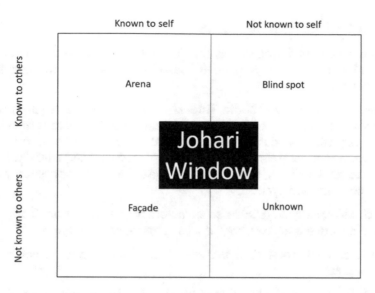

Figure 7-1. Johari window

In project management, this framework is used for risk management. Each project has its known knowns that are reflected in a project plan, known unknowns (the risks to watch for), unknown knowns (the information that exists elsewhere but is not known to the project team, e.g., government regulations that may not be public at the time of the project planning), and unknown unknowns that are impossible to predict or plan for. This is reflected in the project management variation of the Johari windows (Figure 7-2).

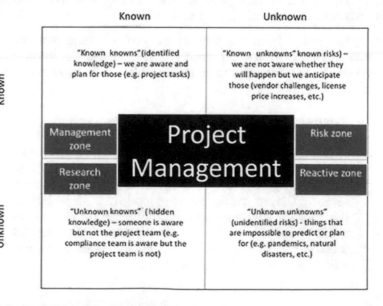

Figure 7-2. Project management risk classification

Planning Fundamentals

It is important to understand that the duration of the project is not equal to the duration of its constituents. In Lean manufacturing, there are three distinct terms.

In terms of an assembly line, the **Takt time** describes the required product assembly duration end to end. Takt time is defined as the average time interval between sequential production of two similar units, for example, two engines on an automotive assembly line, if those are produced sequentially. It is also referred to as a delivery heartbeat that we'd like to synchronize with the product consumption cycle.

Cycle time is the time it takes to complete a cycle of action, from start to finish. An example is an assembly of a car engine, start to finish.

Lead time is the total time between the initiation and completion of a project or a task.

Usually, lead time includes all sorts of overhead, referred to as "waste" in Lean manufacturing. This includes waiting between the dependencies (e.g., testers are available but there is no code available to test yet or code is available but there is no test environment to deploy it to); resources, especially those with rare skills (the sole UX designer on a team got sick or took a vacation); requirements not available; design decision that has not been approved; and so forth. According to different sources, the actual time when team members work on the project tasks is up to 60–85% of the lead time for a medium-size project, while up to 40% is the waste due to mismanaged dependencies, resource constraints, blocked process flow due to quality issues, unbalanced supply, delayed decision-making, and so forth.

All of these factors influence the accuracy of planning, whether it is in traditional or iterative project management. However, iterative project management is significantly more predictable. This happens for several reasons:

1. Iterative planning allows to take "known knowns" and "known unknowns" into account and adjust timelines and targets based on the new data. This can be compared to the difference between a static roadmap and Waze app (see Figure 7-3). In a dynamic roadmap, besides selecting the preferable route and mode of transportation, the route is continuously revisited based on changes in traffic situations within the constraints of the selected preferences, thus resulting in a better predictable and much faster trip to the destination.

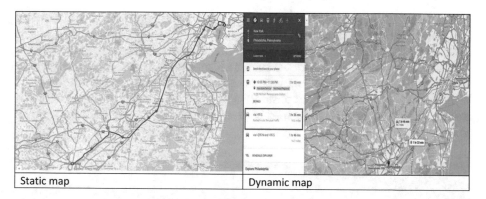

| Static map | Dynamic map |

Figure 7-3. Benefits of incremental planning vs. static plan

2. There is no need for change management to account for any changes in the project plan, as it is being revisited at regular short increments, so the planning time and related efforts are reduced by default. This flexibility reduces planning overhead and makes changes in planning seamless and easy to manage.

Incremental Planning

What does this all mean from the project planning perspective? Most importantly, it means that it is dangerous to predict project duration based on the duration of its tasks. In traditional project management, this is sometimes done by adding a specific extra time and budget to the project plan, up to 50% of project duration for the most complex projects with multiple dependencies. This differs by industry. For construction projects, for example, project managers usually add 5–10% of the total budget and duration to determine contingency. However, this number is arbitrary and is never accurate since it is not clear when this contingency should be added to the project: in the beginning, in the middle, or prior to completion. At the same time, it is known that there will be "known unknowns," "unknown knowns," and possibly even "unknown unknowns" that will influence the project through its life cycle. How is this issue addressed in Agile?

First, the answer is incremental planning. The plans are refined given the "cone of uncertainty." The closer to the project completion, the more predictable the timelines are. Given that the cone of uncertainty in Agile is initiated with every iteration, there is full predictability related to each iteration being achieved at the end of this iteration. This allows for increment-managed predictability and increment-based planning.

Second, the answer is replanning, which happens in every iteration. Based on the outcome of each subsequent iteration, the plan is revisited, and the empirical data observed in prior iterations is used for future planning. For continuous delivery frameworks, such as Kanban, this planning adjustment is happening in a continuous manner so that all the unknown unknowns can immediately be taken into consideration. The sense of urgency in these implementations can be compared to the war strategy that allows an army to win the war.

"There are known knowns. There are things we know we know. We also know there are known unknowns. That is to say, we know there are some things we do not know. But there are also unknown unknowns, the ones we don't know we don't know."

— Donald Rumsfeld, U.S. Secretary of Defense [3]

Topic for a Group Discussion   In groups, compare static planning done in traditional project management and iterative planning done in an Agile environment. What are the benefits and drawbacks of each approach? Why do agilists say that traditional project management promises stakeholders peace of mind but fails miserably most of the time?

Multilevel Planning

From this perspective, Agile planning includes multiple levels, moving from long-term planning (company's mission and vision) to short-term time planning (daily meeting with Scrum where participants discuss what they were doing yesterday and their plans and impediments for today). These levels are also referred to as an "Agile planning onion" because they can be represented as a set of layers from long term to short term, resembling the process of peeling a metaphorical onion (see Figure 7-4).

Figure 7-4. The "planning onion" in Agile

How to interpret the planning onion? In Agile, planning happens continuously at multiple levels. It starts with the **company's strategy**, aligned with its mission and vision. Many companies use OKRs (see Chapter 1) to establish long-term business goals focused on customer success, such as customer satisfaction increase or business targets. These goals are established for longer-term intervals, usually for one or several years, and reflected in product roadmaps. They focus on "why" rather than "how." If a company launches a new product and this product does not perform as expected, it can pivot by launching another one or enhancing its existing product portfolio within the same set of OKRs.

The next level is the **product portfolio**. For a bank, the product portfolio would include all the products and services it provides – checking and savings accounts and related services, loans (home, auto, and any others) investment products and services, and so on. It is an important decision on which products to provide as part of the portfolio, which to sustain, which to sunset, and which new ones to launch to disrupt the current product line. This level of planning is aligned with the strategy and is also usually done long term. It affects product roadmaps and defines execution.

For each of the products within a portfolio of products and services, there is a **product roadmap**. The product roadmap reflects the product life cycle. Each product experiences multiple phases within its existence, which need to be managed, from its inception, through design, development, adoption, maintenance, and sunset. This cycle varies for each of the products and depends on its adoption rates, business success, customer feedback, overall market status, company policy, and a lot of other factors, which directly or indirectly affect it.

While the concept of a project is not directly relevant in an Agile environment, it is frequently used in large enterprises to define major feature **releases**. Frequently, a concept of the release is confused with software deployment. It is important to distinguish between the two: software deployment results in making a software system or any relevant functionality available for use. The general deployment process includes multiple activities that result in the ability of the customer to use the software. Those can be frequent, especially when those are automated and deploy minor changes on a continuous basis. For example, Netflix engineers deploy code thousands of times per day. Google deploys sofware many times per day, and so do many other companies that implement the DevOps strategy of continuous deployment. However, a deployment that makes specific functionality possible does not constitute a major feature release.

A major software release means a new version of the software that includes significant architecture changes or new features on top of the original functionality. For example, if an online bank provided checking accounts only, providing savings accounts would be a major feature. Even in an Agile environment, those are usually referred to as projects because there is a stated business goal and defined (though flexible) scope, and frequently, there is a timeline, whether it is based on vendor agreement, business expectations, or a new regulation. These releases are usually announced to customers and stakeholders in advance with a specific commitment. This can be compared with major releases of new iPhone models and related iOS, starting from the release of the original Apple iPhone in 2007. These are usually listed as a milestone on the product roadmap.

In order to deliver the functionality of the product within the forecasted milestones, many Agile frameworks use incremental delivery where planning is done in short time frames, referred to as **increments** (or Sprints in Scrum). As we discussed, Sprint duration in Scrum is usually two to four weeks. During this time, delivery teams make a commitment based on their prior capacity and their delivery history. Using this empirical data, they are able to accurately predict the work they will be able to accomplish during the Sprint. Based on the results of the Sprint, they adjusted their estimation for the upcoming one. Because of the consistency of team composition and the availability of empirical data for analysis, the accuracy of Sprint planning on mature Agile teams usually exceeds 80%. We will discuss this process in more detail further in this chapter.

However, as much as the team is able to predict its delivery within an iteration, known unknowns and even unknown unknowns may happen. These include new market entrants that disrupt existing competition, government regulations, changes in vendors, staff attrition, and many other unexpected circumstances. For this reason, team members meet on a daily basis for a brief daily meeting (referred to as "Daily Scrum" in Scrum) to align on all the tasks they are working on and support each other in resolving impediments. This represents the daily level of planning, which allows for day-to-day alignment between the team members. In larger organizations, Scrum Masters for every team meet for Scrum of Scrums to resolve intrateam dependencies and remove shared blockers.

Topic for a Group Discussion   It is a known belief that there is no planning in Agile. In every iteration, a new plan is created, which can change at any time. This makes planning look fluid and unreliable. The timelines seem to shift all the time based on the current state, while in a traditional project management plan, every single task is accounted for, durations are defined, sequencing is provided, and the overall timelines are clearly stated, along with the people who are responsible for working on them. Discuss this statement in your group: Do you agree with this point of view or disagree with it, and why?

Tip   Planning does not happen in a vacuum. It is important to establish a credible intake process – how the ideas are captured, assessed, prioritized, and sequenced. Planning will not be successful if the intake process is not well thought through, communicated, established, and followed through. It usually depends on the organizational culture, size, industry, nature of the business, and other parameters. We covered different intake and prioritization techniques in the first part of this book on how to build the RIGHT product. In any organization, thoughtful and relevant intake is a prerequisite for any planning to be successful. Ensure that the intake and prioritization process is well defined before engaging in planning activities.

To summarize, there are multiple simultaneous levels of planning in Agile, also referred to as "planning horizons":

I. **Long-term planning, which allows one to plan against business objectives and create reliable roadmaps.** At this level, we do not usually speak about commitment since we understand the level of complexity and the number of unexpected factors that may influence the plan. Instead, we are talking about the forecast – the best level of predictability based on empirical data and existing knowledge. This includes planning against strategic objectives – from a product and business perspective.

2. **Medium-term planning, which usually includes a quarter ahead in software delivery.** While it is still a significant time frame for a commitment, the level of certainty is significantly higher at this level since the scope is better defined, and the risks are more predictable and easier to control. This is especially important if there are multiple delivery teams working on the same feature since they have to coordinate delivery between them, known as dependency management. When there are multiple teams working on the same product, it is referred to as "scaled Agile." This topic will be covered in detail in Chapter 10. In the Scaled Agile Framework (SAFe), one of the most widely adopted Agile scaling frameworks, this level of planning is defined as the program increment (PI) planning (1).

3. **Short-term planning, or Sprint planning in Scrum.** This is the most predictable level of planning where each delivery team is planning its work for the upcoming iteration, usually two to four weeks. They discuss the requirements and internal and external dependencies, brainstorm on solutions, agree on the division of work between team members, and assign ownership. They use this opportunity to raise risks and discuss issue resolution and sequence delivery within the Sprint. In his book *Agile Estimating and Planning* (3), Mike Cohn discussed the philosophy of Agile estimation and planning and showed in real-world examples and case studies why this methodology works.

Five key questions to review:

1. Why conventional prescriptive planning fails and why Agile planning works?

2. What is the meaning of the "planning onion" in Agile?

3. What are the three planning horizons in Agile?

4. Why do we talk about commitment for a short-term plan and forecast for longer-term plans?

5. Is it possible to deliver on time, on budget, and within the original scope?

Estimation in Agile

In order to achieve predictable planning outcomes, Agile teams estimate their work based on their capacity. In Agile, team capacity is referred to as "velocity." The definition of velocity is the number of units of work completed in a given time. The units of work are usually measured in abstract measurement units, referred to as "story points." A story point in Agile is a metric used to estimate the effort required for implementing a given user story. This includes the work required to complete the story and any approvals and decisions that have to be completed as part of the implementation, any external dependencies, and other relevant factors, such as the lack of team members' experience with this specific type of work, or limited subject matter expertise in the area.

Story points do not equate to hours directly since the effort does not include the time required to produce the output. It accounts for all the elements discussed before, including dependencies that need to be satisfied, the learning and experimentation that has to happen, solutions involved, and so on. Given that story points provide a holistic estimation of the effort, they are much more accurate than time estimates that take only "known knowns" into account by adding the time required to complete each of the tasks that have been identified.

Agile estimation is done by the whole development team (developers, designers, testers, etc.) so that each team member brings their own perspective of the product and the work required to deliver each user story. For example, if a Product Owner would like to make a simple screen change to one of the user profile fields, it may require performing full regression testing for the whole product, given that this parameter is being used throughout the whole application, and the testers would be able to indicate that.

While traditionally, software estimation is done in a time format (months, days, hours), story points are usually using a Fibonacci-like scale: 1, 2, 3, 5, 8, 13…. This level of abstraction is important because it pushes the team to make difficult decisions around the effort required to complete the work. There are multiple reasons to use story points:

1. As stated before, story points account for dependencies and other nonproject work that takes time from the team.

2. Story points help drive cross-functional collaboration.

3. It takes less time and effort to do story-points estimation than other methods.

4. Relative estimations provide direct and straightforward comparisons (e.g., Is user story A more complex to implement than user story B? rather than How long will it take user story A to be completed?).

5. Each team is estimating their velocity at a different scale, so comparisons between teams or pressure to get specific features delivered before the delivery team finds it feasible is meaningless.

A helpful technique in facilitating story point estimation in Fibonacci numbers (1, 2, 3, 5, 8, 13...) is referred to as the planning poker. All team members select a playing card with the story point estimation they suggest for each user story. If all team members vote for the same value, it is assigned to the user story. If not, then team members with the highest and the lowest score provide their reasoning, and the whole group votes again until they reach a consensus. If they do not reach a consensus, different teams have their own agreements on how to resolve minor discrepancies. For example, some teams always agree to honor the higher estimate if there is only one degree of difference after several conversations and voting cycles (e.g., 2 and 3 or 3 and 5). During the conversation about user point discrepancies, a lot of helpful facts get discovered that some team members are aware of and some are not. It is a helpful collaboration technique and not just an estimation technique.

Since the length of each iteration (Sprint) is fixed, each team develops its average velocity over the course of several Sprints (usually, 2–4 latest Sprint average is most meaningful). For example, if team A had a velocity of 18, 20, and 22 story points over the last three Sprints, respectively, without changes to the team composition, they would commit to a maximum of 20 points for their next Sprint. However, if one of the days of their two-week (ten working days) Sprints is a holiday, they would commit to 18 story points only for that Sprint. The same type of logic applies to vacations, sick days, and other changes in team capacity or composition.

☀ **Tip**   A good illustration of relative estimation is a fruit salad exercise. In this exercise, team members are presented with identical set of fruit (apple, pear, grape, strawberry, etc.) and a "Definition of Done" for a fruit salad; for example, all fruits are washed, peeled, deseeded, and cut into salad. They are informed that their Sprint velocity equals 20 story points and asked to estimate the fruit they will be able to make a salad from. Usually, they start with a grape or a strawberry estimating those at 1, then apple or pear at 5, and, finally, pineapple at 13. This leaves them with a combination of one grape, one strawberry, one apple, and a pineapple, or another variation that is estimated up to 20 story points.

The most important rule is to learn from past estimates and adjust the current estimates based on this learning.

As an example, team A's historical estimates are as follows (we refer to the following table as a "calibration banner" because it serves as an estimation reference for team A):

Story Points	1	2	3	5	8
User story examples	As a website customer, I want to view my user profile so that I can confirm that all information is relevant	As a website customer, I want to update my profile as needed so that I can keep my data up to date	As a web shopper, I want to search for the items by keywords so that I can select the best matching product to buy	As a web shopper, I want to log onto the shopping website so that I can use my profile data to make purchases	As a web shopper who made a purchase, I was to modify my order within 24 hours after the purchase so that I did not need to cancel it after it arrives

In this case, when a new user story needs to be worked on, it is estimated by comparing it with the ones on this banner. For example, if there is a need to search by brand, the effort may be seen as similar to keyword search (hence estimated as three story points). If there is a need to delete the profile, it may be seen as similar in size to updating it (hence estimated as two story points) and so forth. The nature of the work performed may be completely different, but the effort related to getting it done is seen as a similar one.

The next question: What happens if the set of the stories pulled into a Sprint one by one does not fit within the velocity estimated for the upcoming Sprint? Let's review a sample product backlog structure with estimates below:

User story 1	5
User story 2	2
User story 3	2
User story 4	3
User story 5	3
User story 6	5
User story 7	1
User story 8	2

If the team's velocity for the upcoming Sprint is 18, the team pulls stories from the top of their backlog into the Sprint until they reach 18. In this case, user stories 1–5 get pulled and reach the total estimate of 15 (5+2+2+3+3). The next user story is #6, which is estimated at 5 story points. In this case, team

B will skip user story 6 and pull user stories 7 and 8 into the Sprint. If the Product Owner thinks that user story 6 is the absolute priority over 7 and 8, they can "decompose" user story 6 into several smaller size stories. For example, if user story 6 is to search for a product, they would decompose it into search parameters (by name, by category, by manufacturer, etc.). For user forms, they can decompose by "create, read, update, and delete" (CRUD) functionality and so forth. In either case, the story has to satisfy INVEST criteria.

 Exercise   Split in teams and try an equivalent of the fruit salad exercise with dogs: Chihuahua, Poodle, Beagle, Bulldog, Collie, Labrador, Golden Retriever, Great Dane, Mastiff, and Greyhound. The Definition of Done in this case is adopting the dog, so the comparison will be between sizes, temperaments, cleanliness, and other relevant features.

🔆 **Tip**   There are five steps in Sprint planning:

1. Refine the backlog in advance to be prepared with data and estimated story points.

2. Confirm estimated story points for the top items in the backlog (ideally, at least one Sprint ahead).

3. Determine the team's capacity for the upcoming Sprint (velocity).

4. Based on the team velocity, move items from the top of the backlog into the upcoming Sprint, thus creating a Sprint Plan.

5. Review the resulting Sprint scope and confirm team's commitment.

Medium-scale estimation. Frequently, Agile teams are asked to provide estimations when specific features or releases will be completed. There are two possible approaches to answer this question:

- Estimate the feature based on comparing it with similar features previously delivered.

- Break the feature into user stories and estimate them individually. The following calculation is straightforward: if a given team delivers 20 user points on average per Sprint and a specific feature is split into user stories that are estimated at 400 story points total, it would take this team 20 Sprints (or 40 months in case of two-week Sprints) to deliver this feature.

The approach to estimate feature size in story points and convert them to time duration at the time of estimation has proven to be inaccurate because it requires time-based estimations, which are usually inaccurate because they do not account for all the effort required for delivery. At this level, aggregated story points are the best measure of predictability.

During release planning, an Agile team schedules delivery into iterations, or Sprints. They use the prioritized user story backlog to move user stories (and sometimes epics, especially for the further timelines) into a specific iteration, based on the effort required and team velocity. This is described in Figure 7-5.

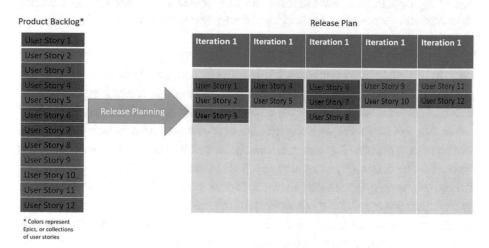

Figure 7-5. Release planning in Agile

A good example of medium-scale planning in Agile is the PI (program increment) planning in the Scaled Agile Framework (SAFe) (4). It is a cadence-based planning event that aligns all Agile teams to a shared mission and vision. It implements the Agile Manifesto principle that "the most efficient and effective method of conveying information to and within a development team is a face-to-face conversation." PI is a large-scale planning event based on the premise that people who do the work plan the work. PI planning has a standard agenda defined in SAFe. It includes a presentation of business context and vision, followed by team planning breakouts. In these breakouts, the teams create their iteration plans and objectives for the upcoming program increment (many companies plan in quarterly program increments).

PI planning is an asynchronous, usually two-day, event with the participation of all members of delivery teams within the program, though it is often extended to accommodate remote planning across multiple time zones. It allows establishing face-to-face communication (frequently virtual) across all team members and stakeholders. In addition, it aligns development to business goals with the visual context, vision, and program objectives; identifies dependencies across multiple teams; provides an opportunity to discuss high-level solutions and make decisions on architecture, UX, and other guidelines and solutions that match demand to capacity to minimize work in process (WIP); and allows for fast decision-making.

Its outputs include committed PI objectives (a set of SMART – Specific, Measurable, Achievable, Realistic, and Timely – objectives) that are created by each team with the business value assigned by the business and the program board highlighting the new features and forecasting delivery dates, featuring dependencies among teams, and identifying relevant milestones.

💡 **Tip**   To ensure planning accuracy, it is important for each team to establish their Definition of Ready and Definition of Done. The Definition of Ready provides a set of criteria that are sufficient for a user story or a task to be taken into a Sprint by a Scrum team. For example, if acceptance criteria for a user story are vague, it may result in a lot of confusion during the Sprint, and the team won't be able to complete it as expected. Similarly, the Definition of Done provides a set of clear expectations for a user story about what does it mean that it is considered done. Frequently it includes both process-related items (all acceptance criteria are satisfied, the user story is accepted by the Product Owner, and similar expectations) and technical items (the user story is deployed into the production environment and the functionality is integrated with downstream systems or nonfunctional requirement related to performance and resiliency).

Large-scale planning. There is a belief that Agile is failing in large organizations because strategic planning conflicts with short planning horizons in Agile. As stated in the Forbes article "Is Agile Failing Long-Term Planning" [4], Pradeep Ittycheria, a Forbes Technology Council member, argues that "there's no doubt about it: Agile works. There are many stories of companies that have benefitted from going Agile. However, Agile is failing to meet expectations in larger organizations; in many cases, it is failing because established strategic planning conflicts with the notion of a Lean enterprise and Agile planning (with very short time horizons).

In my experience, capital allocation decisions are typically made six to twelve months in advance. Investors and management teams want to carry out strategic planning for an entire year. Financial targets are yearly targets. Planning for a year in the future is not a time horizon that fits the scheme of Agile."

This opinion is a well-known Agile myth. As we saw from the "Agile onion," there are multiple concurrent levels of planning in Agile, which are executed in parallel. Specifically, for the long-term estimation and planning, a product roadmap is usually created based on prior data and subject matter expertise, which is broadly shared with the stakeholder for their input and feedback. No matter how Agile a project is, there is always a need to manage scope, resources, and time when planning a strategic vision. There are four steps to achieve an accurate long-term estimation in Agile:

Step 1: Start with the big picture. Based on OKRs, define actions and milestones. Setting your high-priority themes will help you focus your time and energy on the high-priority work that matters. For large-scope estimation in Agile, T-shirt sizes (Small, Medium, Large, XL) are used more frequently than Fibonacci numbers. These sizes usually translate directly into the timelines.

Step 2: Identify high-priority work items. Identify the most important items to be completed and achieve consensus with the stakeholders on this prioritization.

Step 3: Decompose these items. In this step, we need to break the work for the larger initiative into more consumable work items, such as epics. This will provide a granular view into all the work that needs to be completed and makes estimation tangible.

Step 4: Create a roadmap. Establish a roadmap based on the decomposed items by comparing them with previously delivered work units. Because estimating requires knowledge of similar efforts in the past, it is helpful to compare this project to the ones previously completed. The product roadmap outlines the progress of a product over time. Iterations are translated into timelines, and timelines indicate feature delivery to the customer. A product roadmap template is presented in Figure 7-6.

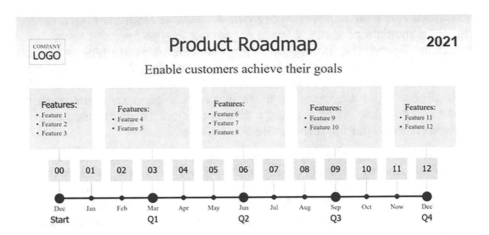

Figure 7-6. Example of a product roadmap

Once the roadmap is agreed upon, it is shared with the entire product team so that everyone understands the vision, deliverables, and dependencies. It becomes the delivery guideline, which is being updated on a regular basis to reflect progress with delivery and changing business priorities. Product Owners usually own the roadmap, whether it is a static representation of feature delivery, as shown before, or a dynamic roadmap created with one of the specialized tools, such as Jira, ProductPlan, Aha!, Productboard, Trello, and Roadmunk.

In sum, Agile enables companies to execute planning not at the project level, as in the traditional project management – it allows to plan at multiple levels in parallel, continuously narrowing the "cone of uncertainty" to achieve predictability and allow for live updates. In addition, the planning is not happening project by project using arbitrary start and end dates defined by project managers; rather, it enables planning at the value stream level. A value stream is a term coming from Lean that shows how customer value is being created – from the start of the value chain until the delivery to the customer. It allows to establish a customer-centric delivery process and plan for the delivery of products and services rather than planning for a specific set of deliverables that may or may not achieve customer and business value.

"A key tenet of Agile estimating and planning is that we estimate size but derive duration."

— Mike Cohn. Agile Estimating and Planning (3)

Five key questions to review:

1. What is a product roadmap?

2. Why multiple planning horizons are possible in Agile?

3. Who is responsible for creating and maintaining the roadmap?

4. What is the difference between Sprint planning and PI planning?

5. How Scrum teams plan their dependencies on each other and external providers?

Case Study: Sprint Planning in a Health Insurance Company. SolidHealth, a small health insurance company, decided to purchase and customize its medical claim system. The system that they selected was robust and contained most of the features they needed; however, it was geared toward large insurance providers working with thousands of clients and hundreds of employers. There were numerous forms to fill out for each retail provider, complex claim entry screens, and overcomplicated patient forms for each claim. This level of complexity was excessive for SolidHealth that was geared toward small businesses. It provided two insurance plans (SolidHealth HMO and SolidHealth PPO) and covered vision benefits only for the geography in question.

The vendor for the system agreed to provide multiple customization opportunities to SolidHealth, some of them by exposing their APIs for the SolidHealth development team to write their own code, some of them through their user-friendly administrative module, which allowed to turn on and off specific functionality and configure the software. SolidHealth had a small IT department of 24 individuals: developers, testers, UX designers, automation engineers, and system administrators who also performed release management functions. The vendor gave SolidHealth six months of IT support to complete all customizations and launch their software.

In this situation, time was of the essence. SolidHealth IT team decided that they wanted to use Scrum to deliver the new system to the organization. They had to move fast because they needed to process data, create or simplify several user screens, customize the user experience with their company colors and logos, and provide a user experience that was familiar to their customers. They had to make multiple engineering decisions while defining and minimizing functionality to exclude any features they did not need, given the small size and limited business features their company required. They also had to ensure proper security of their systems, given that there was protected personal information involved. The timelines looked aggressive given the uncertainty and the pressure.

To assess the feasibility of this deployment, they did a long-term assessment. SolidHealth has recently implemented a pharmaceutical claim system in a different geography, similar in scope to the vision one. They even considered reusing it for this initiative, but it was completely geared toward the pharmaceutical industry and provided in a specific region different from the one in question. However, the scope and the level of customization were quite similar, and the same team worked on the implementation. As a result, they felt that the six-month timeline was feasible. Then, they did user story mapping to define the scope of customization that was required. They clearly marked which features needed development and which would be configured.

To execute this initiative, SolidHealth decided to use Scrum. They chose two-week Sprints. Their logic was that one week created planning overhead, and anything longer than two weeks would not give them the flexibility to build, assess, and make decisions on how to proceed, given the uncertainty of their own needs and their lack of familiarity with the new product. They made a decision to release software into a production-like environment every Sprint and then launch a basic but already usable version of the system after three months, which they referred to as MVP (minimum viable product), so that they keep refining it and adding features over the subsequent three months. They also decided to launch it at least one month (two Sprints) before their support from the vendor expires so that they can learn from its real-life use what the problems are and correct those before the vendor leaves.

Based on these assumptions, they created a draft product roadmap whether they called their first Sprint "Sprint zero" because they were not planning to produce any software and wanted to answer basic decisions: which hosting model to select, that is, virtual private cloud (VPC) or Software as a Service (SaaS) implementation, and which technical stack to choose, including their continuous deployment pipeline, so that they do not need to manage their releases manually and can automate testing to validate that the change to the code base is correct and stable and ensure immediate autonomous deployment to their production environment. They chose to use Jenkins, an open-source automation server, which enabled them to automate software development as it relates to building, testing, deploying, facilitating continuous integration, and continuous delivery. This approach is frequently referred to as CI/CD, or continuous integration and continuous deployment. They also made a decision to use Test-Driven Delivery (TDD) so that they run automated tests before and after the developers write code to showcase the functionality being built. There were multiple other solutions for them to figure out, so these two weeks provided a good jumpstart for them.

During these two weeks, SolidHealth formed three teams, which remained dedicated to this and the future initiatives throughout the company. Each team was cross-functional; that is, it included three developers, one tester, one test automation engineer, one UX designer, and one DevOps engineer who ensured a proper software delivery pipeline. DevOps engineers also monitored their infrastructure and supported configuring the system via its Admin module. In addition, Sprint zero provided an opportunity for the group to run their first Sprint planning session. Prior to the session, Orla, their assigned Product Owner, created and prioritized the backlog as well as provided acceptance criteria for each user story or task she created. She also categorized product backlog items into three categories: user, claim, and payment.

The decision was made that the first team will be responsible for everything related to users (authentication, user profile, individual insurance type, and user eligibility); team 2 will be responsible for claims processing to run each claim against user insurance, define eligibility, and send related communications; and team 3 will work on payment processing. They contemplated whether they needed a program increment planning given that all three teams would be working on the same code base. Finally, they decided that given that there was an existing product already and that the three separate categories allowed avoiding multiple interteam dependencies, they could do Sprint planning independently and resolve any upcoming questions via their daily Scrum of Scrums.

Prior to each of the Sprint planning sessions, each of the teams spent several hours with Orla refining the backlog, discussing and solidifying acceptance criteria, and making high-level implementation decisions. On the first day of Sprint 1, each team met for two hours for Sprint planning. They were excited about this Scrum event because it gave them an opportunity to come together virtually and get a shared understanding of what they will work on during the upcoming two weeks. Sprint planning started with Orla communicating the Sprint goal for each of the teams. The user management team got a goal of automating user data feed from their core database to the new system. The claims team got a goal of creating claims validation logic based on the dataset already available in the vendor system, and the payment team had a goal of integrating credit card payments into their existing payment portal.

Team members provided active input into the acceptance criteria, discussed solutions, estimated user stories, and aligned them with the team capacity. They also identified some dependencies on other teams and got immediate answers related to their questions. Based on the answers, the payment team decided to move one of the user stories to the subsequent Sprint so that the user management team could deliver the required data in Sprint 2 for proper end-to-end testing. Based on team capacity, team 3 committed to delivering four user stories from the top of the backlog; they had to move one of the user stories that Orla was hoping to get done into Sprint 2, based on their capacity. Orla asked why they had to do so and, after the explanation, acknowledged that she did not understand all the complexity given that payments had to be integrated into the credit card vendor payment system, which would take at least four weeks of development. Based on this information, Orla was able to split this user story into four, separately for each credit card they were accepted for payments.

Team members felt excited and empowered by this planning session. They were able to align themselves between each other and the other teams. In addition, they discussed implementation details and assigned ownership over user stories, so they felt responsible for delivery. They also felt motivated because the outcome was clearly defined, and there was a plan for them to follow. They were excited and challenged to achieve their Sprint commitment. When the Sprint was over, teams 1 and 2 achieved their commitment, and team 3 was able to complete only three user stories. However, there was no blame. In their Retrospective on the last day of the Sprint, they discussed the reason and agreed that they just ran out of time, so the decision was made to take only 17 story points of work into the second Sprint vs. 20 that they took on for their first Sprint and were able to complete only 17.

In addition, all three teams provided a demo of the new functionality to their key stakeholders, and Orla found out that the primary form of payment was a bank transfer, given that most vision services were provided to retail customers. As a result, she prioritized bank transfers over credit cards payment for team 2 in the upcoming Sprint. Overall, the stakeholders provided positive feedback, which created even more excitement among the team members. They were looking forward to their Sprint 2 planning!

-ᕦ- **Tip**   Longer-term planning requires that there are business priorities defined for a noticeable period of time (at least one quarter) and there is enough consensus on the features to be delivered and the priority of their features. Sometimes, especially in the case of startups or the companies launching new product lines, this level of certainty is not possible. This does not mean that these companies should not strive to provide longer-term visibility. A good practice in this case is to establish "rolling wave" planning, which means that features and feature sets are planned as they arise, with all the prerequisites and dependencies being properly planned and any risks being assessed and mitigated.

Key Points

1. In traditional (Waterfall) project management, a lot of time and effort goes into planning. Opinions of senior leaders in each area are collected, the experience of prior relevant projects is studied and analyzed in depth, and a lot of time is spent creating work breakdown structures, which list all tasks that need to be done to complete the project. All those efforts create a sense of thoughtful, reliable planning, which can be relied upon. However, in real life, this level of predictability is a myth since projects face "known unknowns" and even "unknown unknowns," which are impossible to predict.

2. Iterative planning allows to take "known knowns" and "known unknowns" into account and adjust timelines and targets based on the new data. This can be compared to a static roadmap and a dynamic one, such as Waze. In a dynamic roadmap, besides selecting the preferable route and mode of transportation, the route is continuously revisited based on changes in traffic situations within the constraints of selected preferences, thus resulting in a better predictable and much faster trip to the destination.

3. In Agile, replanning happens in every iteration. Based on the outcome of each subsequent iteration, the plan is revisited, and the empirical data observed in prior iterations is used for future planning.

4. Agile planning includes multiple levels, moving from long-term planning (company's mission and vision) to short-term time planning (daily meeting with Scrum where participants discuss what they were doing yesterday and their plans and impediments for today). These levels are also referred to as "Agile planning onion" because they can be represented as a set of layers from long term to short term, resembling the process of peeling a metaphorical onion.

5. Agile planning starts with the company's strategy, aligned with its mission and vision. Many companies use OKRs to establish long-term business goals focused on customer success, such as customer satisfaction increase or business targets. These goals are established for longer-term intervals, usually for one or several years, and reflected in product roadmaps.

6. The next level is the product portfolio. It requires a decision on which products to include in the product portfolio, which to sustain, which to sunset, and which new ones to launch to disrupt the current product line. This level of planning is aligned with the strategy; it affects product roadmaps and defines execution.

7. For each of the products within a portfolio of products and services, there is a product roadmap. The product roadmap reflects the product life cycle. Each product experiences multiple phases within its existence, which need to be managed, from its inception, through design, development, adoption, maintenance, and sunset.

8. The next level is release planning (not to be confused with each deployment). A major release means a new version of the software that includes significant software architecture changes or new features and functionality on top of the original functionality of the preceding software if any.

9. In order to deliver the functionality of the product within the forecasted milestones, many Agile frameworks use incremental delivery where planning is done in short time frames, referred to as increments (or Sprints in Scrum).

10. Scrum team members meet on a daily basis for a brief daily meeting (referred to as "Daily Scrum" in Scrum) to align on all the tasks they are working on and support each other in resolving impediments. This represents the daily level of planning, which allows for day-to-day alignment between the team members.

11. There are multiple simultaneous levels of planning in Agile, also referred to as "planning horizons": long-term planning, medium-term planning, and short-term planning.

12. To enable planning and increase accuracy, the effort is estimated in Agile using abstract relative units of measurement, referred to as story points. The team makes their delivery commitments based on their velocity per Sprint, that is, the cumulative number of story points they are able to deliver historically.

13. To ensure planning accuracy, Agile teams establish their Definition of Ready and Definition of Done. The Definition of Ready provides a set of criteria that are sufficient for a user story or a task to be taken into a Sprint by the team. The Definition of Done provides a set of clear expectations for a user story, defining what it means that it is considered completed.

14. There are four steps to achieve an accurate long-term estimation in Agile: start with the big picture, identify high-priority work items, decompose these items into granular requirements, and create a roadmap based on the estimation of effort to deliver those items.

15. Agile enables companies to execute planning not at the project level, as in the traditional project management – it allows to plan at multiple levels in parallel, continuously narrowing the "cone of uncertainty" to achieve predictability and allow for live updates.

Incremental Delivery and Continuous Improvement

This chapter covers delivery, reporting, and continuous improvement. It provides examples of Agile metrics for Scrum and Kanban teams and reviews software delivery and product satisfaction metrics. It discusses team empowerment, feedback loops, and Retrospective techniques. In addition, it discusses the concept of a product life cycle and how it affects incremental delivery.

In Chapter 7, we covered the topic of estimation and planning in Agile. We discussed three planning horizons (short-term, medium-term, and long-term planning) and reviewed the approach that is used to estimate effort and plan delivery. We covered story point estimation and discussed why this type of estimation is more accurate than a calendar-based one and how to convert story point estimations into predictable roadmaps. We also covered multiple concurrent levels of Agile planning (referred to as "Agile onion") and explained how to establish predictability of delivery in the Agile environment.

In this chapter, we are going to move into execution and discuss how incremental delivery reduces risks and enables fast feedback loops from the customers. We will also cover how the feedback – internal and external – can be used to refine and enhance execution and shape delivery models. In order to encourage open feedback, we will review multiple techniques for conducting Retrospective sessions. We will cover Lean concepts of quality and quality-related outcomes. Finally, we will review incremental delivery from the product life cycle perspective. Throughout this chapter, we will reemphasize Agile culture, that is, team empowerment, accountability, and customer-centricity.

Incremental Delivery

First, we need to define incremental delivery. It is important to distinguish between incremental delivery and continuous delivery. **Continuous delivery** is the process when features deployed into production are released incrementally or immediately to customers based on business needs (market demand, seasonal release dates, business timelines, or other reasons). Continuous delivery should not be confused with continuous deployment, which means that any change is automatically deployed to production by delivering it to a production-like environment. Continuous delivery allows for business decisions related to making specific functionality available to the customer.

Incremental and **iterative delivery** supports feature-based delivery vs. a "big bang" phase-based "Waterfall" approach. Prioritized features are made available to end users once they are developed. There is a difference between incremental and iterative delivery. Jeff Patton described it very well by showing the Mona Lisa picture [1]. He explained incremental development as incrementally building software, similar to adding bricks to a wall. For a Mona Lisa painting, it would be painting the head, then the upper body, the hands, etc. Paint-by-numbers artists work this way.

Iterative delivery means gradually building up functionality, so if development takes longer than we expect, we can release what we've incrementally built so far. For a Mona Lisa painting, it would mean a pencil draft, then a few basic shades, then the colors, then finishing – each of those steps requires work on all the painting, just at a different level of detail. For example, if we are building a website and need to provide logon functionality, we may start with a simple database encrypted login and further progress to a single sign-on solution.

"We iterate to find the right solution. Then given some good candidate solution, we might then iterate to improve a candidate solution. We use incrementing to gradually build up functionality so that we can release what we've incrementally built so far. We release incrementally so that we actually **get that business value we're chasing**. Because, we don't really get return on investment till people begin to use the software we've built.

In Agile development we actually conjoin these two tactics. Where things really fall apart in Agile development is when no one plans to iterate."

— Jeff Patton, Don't Know What I Want, But I Know How to Get It [1]

It is important to understand that Agile is both iterative and incremental: teams deliver slices of functionality in priority order while prioritizing key functionality and deprioritizing extra features. Then we deliver this software to customers at regular intervals, called Sprints in Scrum, or continuously, which is referred to as Kanban.

Topic for a Group Discussion   What are the benefits of incremental and iterative delivery compared to a phased Waterfall delivery? How are those conceptually different? When are the scope and product features defined? Which one allows to learn from customer feedback and adjust the scope of subsequent delivery? Which companies are known for that? Share any examples that you are aware of or do the research to find up to three relevant examples.

Product Roadmap and Release Plan

In order for iterative, incremental delivery to be meaningful for the customer, the delivery team needs to be clear on what they are delivering and when they will make this functionality available to their customers. They need to provide visibility into the upcoming functionality to their current and potential customers. For product companies such as Apple, launch announcements are big events awaited by millions of their loyal customers. Prior to these events, there are always rumors and excitement from official media and their social media fans. As an example, rumors about upcoming 2021 iPhones started in 2020 and received a lot of publicity [2]. Apple frequently holds "One More Thing" events, in addition to their major product unveiling events, well familiar to all of us by Steve Jobs' announcement of the iPhone at the Apple's Macworld conference.

At this conference on January 9, 2007, Apple CEO Steve Jobs introduced the new iPhone, which will combine a mobile phone, a widescreen iPod with touch controls, and an Internet communications device with the ability to use email, web browsing maps, and searching. He informed that iPhone would start shipping in the United States in June 2007. As we can see from this example, products are usually introduced significantly prior to being released. This requires delivery teams – software and hardware – to be able to predict when specific features, devices, or network configurations will be completed and become available to the end user. This information governs marketing, sales, customer support, and multiple other customer-facing events and activities, and predefines the market strategy for the product or the whole product line.

This means that IT teams and organizations need to be highly predictable about what and when is being delivered. Imagine what would happen if, in the preceding example where Steve Jobs made a promise to deliver iPhones in June 2007, the phones would not pass testing and delivery would be delayed until 2008. Apple's reputation and the trust that the company has with its customers could be damaged with a long and painful path to recovery. Apple's track record of predictability of delivery is stellar. It does not mean that they deliver on expected timelines at a 100% rate or that each of their products is commercially successful.

Release planning is a longer-term (usually one quarter and longer) planning that enables delivery teams to answer the questions when specific features or new products are going to be delivered, or released, to the customer. The questions customers are asking may vary from "When will this be ready?" to "Which features or products will we get by the end of the quarter? End of the year?" Business stakeholders will ask: "How much will it cost? How will it impact other products? Who will work on this?" In a nutshell, release planning involves product delivery, capacity planning, budget allocation, dependency management between multiple teams and frequently parts of the large organization (e.g., software and hardware for smartphones), prioritization, alignment, and many other processes that allow for smooth and synchronized delivery.

In different project management methodologies, release planning is done in different ways. The frequency of releases varies as well. In many Scrum organizations, new product features are released to customers every Sprint (two to four weeks). In some large engineering or pharmaceutical organizations, there are longer, monthly, and even quarterly releases. Even for Scrum organizations, many teams group the results of multiple Sprints into one release or do the opposite: release continuously as soon as a feature is completed, which is known as continuous delivery. For large organizations that practice scaled Agile frameworks, discussed further in Chapter 10, there are structured activities such as PI (program increment) planning or a Big Room Planning. Both terms refer to a cadence-based (usually quarterly) event that aligns all teams within a large program to a shared release plan.

Some of these release planning approaches are described in Figure 8-1.

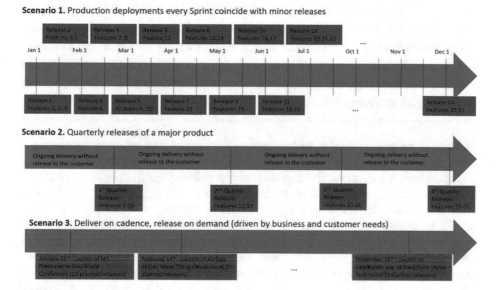

Scenario 1. Production deployments every Sprint coincide with minor releases

Scenario 2. Quarterly releases of a major product

Scenario 3. Deliver on cadence, release on demand (driven by business and customer needs)

Figure 8-1. Most common release planning scenarios

🖳 **Topic for a Group Discussion**   Compare scenarios 1, 2, and 3 described in Figure 8-1. What type of companies and products would benefit from each of the scenarios? Complete scenario 3, which is a hypothetical example for customer-based and market-based releases, with the examples that you are aware of (or research on the Internet). Describe each of the scenarios in your own terms.

Scenario 1 shows a release plan where each deployment at the end of the Sprint delivers value to customers. This happens with startups or smaller products without major dependencies. The second scenario shows a cadence-based (in this case, quarterly) release plan, which is suitable for major endeavors, such as commercial engineering products of a significant scale. The third scenario utilized by most consumer-driven technology product companies is based on customer demand and market triggers. However, even in this case, there are specific patterns. For example, Apple maintains a cadence of announcing new iPhones around the second or third week of September and releasing them one or two weeks later.

🔆 **Tip** It is important to understand the difference between production deployments of software and release of software to the customer. Similarly, the product deployment or manufacturing dates (for hardware) are not the same as release dates. Multiple deployments usually lead to a release of an IT product or a software-powered device. Ten or fifteen years ago, many organizations did not distinguish between production deployments and releases of their software to customers; however, these days are long gone. There are multiple software release models that gradually transfer user traffic from a previous version of a website, an app, a database, or a microservice to a near-identical new release – both of which are running in production. By swapping alternating production environments or toggling specific features, delivery teams fully decouple production deployments from customer releases.

Release plans are created based on a combination of two primary parameters: capacity and scope. While the terminology is different in Agile and Waterfall, the approach is the same: the capacity of the delivery team (assuming that this is a long-standing dedicated team or a group of teams) needs to be aligned with the scope of delivery. Agile provides a mechanism for alignment and flexibility of planning, which makes release planning much more accurate. Predictability can be based on a structured planning effort where all features are being discussed, and dependencies and risks identified and aligned quarterly, such as in Scaled Agile Framework (more on this in Chapter 10), or a lightweight quarterly planning effort where high-level features are estimated using T-shirt sizes and pulled into releases based on prior velocity. For example, for each Sprint, the team delivers one large, three medium-size, and six small features on average, or three large features, or two large, one medium, and five small, and so on. Whichever way of release planning an organization chooses, it is important to apply it consistently: days, story points, and T-shirt sizes are effective only if those are based on empirical data when there is a historical record and an established baseline. In Waterfall, estimations are usually provided by tech leads in days and sequenced on the calendar.

A lot of factors influence how each organization does release planning – some organizations focus on feature delivery, and some more traditional organizations focus on value predictability. The mandate from the leadership frequently defines the thoroughness and the overall effort invested in planning. Program increment planning in SAFe allows for higher predictability for larger organizations with less flexible products, but as soon as anything changes, the plan requires major rework. A more flexible T-shirt-based estimation approach does not take as much time but does not prevent surprises where seemingly simple features become gigantic and super complex, some features get overlooked, or sequencing is off because a major dependency has been missed. In most cases, organizations try several ways of planning for their releases until they come up with one that works best.

Once the release plan is created, product managers publish the roadmap for each of their products. The roadmap shows which features are going to be delivered and when. It is usually targeted toward internal stakeholders. However, many companies proudly display their roadmaps to the customers to be absolutely transparent and to receive immediate feedback.

We define a **product roadmap** as a shared source of reference for a product that outlines the vision, direction, priorities, and deliverables (functional or nonfunctional) of a product over time. Many organizations use product roadmaps as a means of alignment across the company in terms of short- and long-term goals for the product. In Agile software development, a roadmap provides the context for the team's or program's everyday work while pivoting based on the market and customer needs. Multiple Agile teams may share a single product roadmap if they work on the same product. A sample roadmap is provided in Figure 8-2.

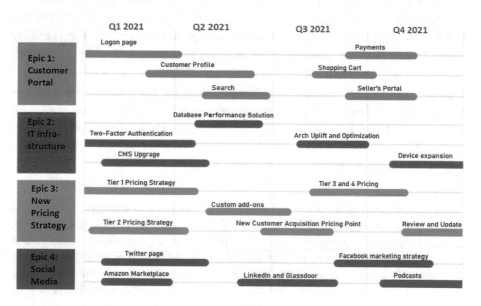

Figure 8-2. Example of a product roadmapc based on quarterly planning

The product roadmap is not set in stone, and it is changing based on new information, customer feedback, competing priorities, and multiple other factors. While the usual time frame for a product roadmap is one year, it may differ based on products and companies. While the roadmap seems straightforward, it is a complex strategic tool that involves thoughtful planning, analysis, research, prioritization, dependency management, alignment, risk analysis, and numerous discussions. If done well – in a collaborative and thoughtful way – the roadmap impacts alignment, buy-in, strategic prioritization, and product success overall.

The product roadmap is aligned with the release schedule; however, it serves a different purpose of explaining to the business and to the customer why a specific direction has been chosen and how the product is going to evolve over time. The product roadmap is owned by a product manager (Product Owner in Scrum); however, it is a result of alignment with the business and the broad group of stakeholders, and its goal is to work backward from customer needs to innovate on behalf of the customers.

There are multiple software tools – Aha!, Asana, Productboard, monday.com, Roadmunk, Jira Plan, and many others that provide advanced road mapping functionality [3].

Topic for a Group Discussion   We established that while the product roadmap is a simple artifact, it's a result of comprehensive research, analysis, and discussions. High level of complexity leads to the failure of product roadmaps. To be effective, a roadmap needs to accomplish a number of strategically important tasks, such as communicating product strategy and vision, prioritizing delivery, creating expectations on timeline and validating those to ensure feasibility, empowering the teams to define how they will accomplish these strategic goals, creating a single point of reference for business and delivery teams, and many others. The goal of this group discussion is to address multiple factors that may go wrong. We will start by listing a few: roadmap was created but it was not communicated, roadmap is based on unrealistic expectations and forces people to work around the clock to meet the deadlines, and so forth. For each of the reasons for failure you come up, discuss the impact and the way it could be avoided.

Once the roadmap is established, there are specific expectations set with the business and the customers related to feature and product delivery. With multiple planning horizons, we are looking at commitment near term (upcoming Sprint in Scrum or one to three months for multiteam programs) and forecast longer term, since a lot of changes and discoveries are made outside of the quarterly time frame. Self-managing teams organize and plan their delivery, and this level of empowerment comes with a similar level of accountability for delivery.

The question that comes up next is the following: How do we know that we are executing the right features at the right pace, and how are we progressing toward executing the roadmap overall? To accomplish this purpose, companies use a set of metrics.

Agile Metrics

In traditional project management, there are usually not that many metrics involved since delivery progress is driven by status updates. Every activity is shown in a specific color (the default is RAG – red, amber, green, or "traffic light colors") based on its status. Green if on track, amber if there is a risk or delay, and red if it cannot be delivered as planned. Once the impediment is resolved and the timeline is adjusted, the activity goes back into green or amber status. This status metric is very straightforward, so you may be confused as to why it is not sufficient or what is wrong with it. The best way to answer this question is to state that **all we can do with the status is to worry**.

Amber or Red statuses provide an important signal; however, this signal is not actionable. Instead of preventing the issue by adjusting expectations or changing the release plan, status provides visibility into the current state but does not answer many fundamental questions. RAG status updates are known for the surprises they frequently bring when the status is green for many months in a row and then it suddenly changes to red. It is referred to as a "watermelon status." It is all green on the surface, but once you cut deeper, it is all red inside.

In Agile, there is a lot of data being collected: number of user stories delivered during a Sprint, number of story points being completed by a team (team velocity), number of defects during a Sprint, and many other numbers. However, this is all being referred to as "vanity metrics," which do not provide any meaningful or actionable information and can, in fact, be quite damaging.

Instead, the most useful approach is to **collect the metrics that are important to the company**. For example, if there is an issue with meeting predefined timelines, then it is a good approach to measure predictability of delivery. In Scrum, a frequent metric for that is the "commitment rate," which is a percentage of work delivered over work committed, in story points. For example, if a team committed to delivering 100 story points worth of work in one Sprint and delivered only 80, the commitment rate equals 80%. Anything within the range of 80–120% is considered healthy (software delivery may be quite unpredictable; however, velocity keeps adjusting every Sprint to make delivery as predictable as possible). Anything outside of this range requires a thorough analysis of the reason for the deviation and potential action items to prevent this from happening in the future. Some teams continuously overcommit and underdeliver – sometimes the reason is their fear to say "no" to increased demands. Some teams continuously overdeliver – this is also not optimal because it is hard to predict delivery in this case. In both cases, it makes sense to discuss the lack of accuracy in a Retrospective, identify potential root causes, and agree on the action plan to increase predictability.

"Predictability builds and holds trust, a core Agile value, better than does delivering more with less reliability."

— David J. Anderson, Kanban: Successful Evolutionary Change for Your Technology Business [7]

According to the Agile Manifesto, **the primary measure of progress in Agile is working software**. As a result, the number of user stories delivered per Sprint or epics delivered over a longer period of time is a valid metric. However, the complexity of stories differs significantly, so either this metric is used over a large number of teams or a long period of time or there is a T-shirt sizing of stories, which helps establish higher accuracy with "translation" rules between small, medium, and large stories or features.

Since the software is delivered to customers, the most important subjective metric is customer satisfaction. Comprehensive web analytics is the key to understanding **customer behaviors in using the software**. Companies such as Google are driven by web metrics. The following are some examples of web metrics in Google Analytics:

- Sessions: Measures the volume of visits to the website

- Users: Measures unique visitors to the website

- Page views: Measures the total number of pages viewed on the website

- Average time on page: Measures the amount of time (on average) users spend on the website

- Bounce rate: Measures the percentage of sessions that leave the website without taking any additional action

- Entrances: Measures the entrance points (i.e., your homepage, pricing page, etc.) users visit the website through

- Exit rate: Measures the rate at which visitors leave the website from specific pages [5]

Subjective customer data are also extremely important. Through customer observation, pop-up satisfaction screens, customer satisfaction surveys, and NPS (Net Promoter Score), companies collect data to align their software with customer needs.

In addition, since it is important to maintain and develop the business, product success and, specifically, P&L (profit and loss) data are very important. These data indicate **commercial success** (or failure) of a product.

There are also so-called **"vanity metrics,"** introduced in Chapter 4, which are frequently collected but are not directly actionable. For example, team velocity (cumulative number of story points delivered within a Sprint) is a helpful metric for a team that allows them to plan the next Sprint but is not informative or actionable outside of the team. Moreover, velocity is a relative metric, so comparing velocity between teams is meaningless. At the same time, velocity at the team level indicates team productivity, so capturing velocity trends within one team is informative. For example, if a team delivered 100 points in Sprint 1, 110 points (given the same composition and time off between its members) in Sprint 2, and 121 points in Sprint 3, the team is consistently increasing its velocity by 10%. On the contrary, if a team is losing velocity, there is a reason to perform root cause analysis and find out what is wrong and how to support them.

Another common parameter that companies care about is **quality**. There is little value in measuring defects within a Sprint since any defects are immediately corrected as part of the collaboration between developers and testers (or in the case of CI/CD and test automation, developers become aware of defects upon integrating their code and fix the defects right away). However, production defects that leak to the customer are extremely important, and the company's reputation depends on that. As a result, measuring the number of production defects (or so-called "escaped defects") is very important, especially if it is presented as a trend over time.

Topic for a Group Discussion   Consider a company that struggles to deliver software on time and is having multiple customer issues related to software quality with each release. Which three to five parameters would you suggest them to track on a consistent basis?

Tip   For each company, it is important to identify data being collected, implement software to eliminate manual data collection, and make these reports transparent to the organization. While publishing this data (usually as a dashboard representing live data), it is important to never use this data to threaten or shame the teams who need support; rather, it is important to provide them with help and coaching to get back on track.

In terms of software being used, Jira provides easy Dashboarding and Reporting functionality, especially in combination with scaling Agile software, Jira Align, which helps to analyze software delivery data at scale as related to organizational roadmaps, OKRs, and financials as well as manage dependencies at scale. Figure 8-3 shows an example of a Velocity Chart, prebuilt for Scrum teams in Jira. As you can see, in the first Sprint, the team significantly undercommitted, so they took more work into the second Sprint and delivered exactly as much as in the second.

Figure 8-3. Sample Velocity Chart generated by Jira (Atlassian tool)

Topic for a Group Discussion   What happened to the team whose Velocity Chart is shown previously in the third Sprint and what could be the root causes?

A more comprehensive dashboard can be created in Jira, visualizing almost any data to help a team stay on track throughout the Sprint. Figure 8-4 shows a fragment of such a dashboard.

Figure 8-4. Fragment of a sample Jira dashboard

While velocity and commitment rate are relevant in regard to Scrum, what do the Kanban teams measure? Metrics in Kanban are focused on measuring "time to value" or "time to market" as leading indicators for market value.

Lead time and **cycle time** mentioned in previous chapters are the two most important Kanban metrics. They show how long work items stay in the workflow until they are completed. As discussed in Chapter 7, lead time is the total amount of time a task spends from order to delivery in the system. Cycle time is the amount of time that is spent actively working on it. It is important to understand the difference between the lead time and cycle time. The lead time starts when a new task is requested and ends when it is complete. The cycle time begins when someone actually starts working on the task, which is also known as a commitment point. We use the lead time to analyze if work items wait for too long before they are taken on. On the other hand, cycle time helps us understand the amount of time needed for the actual completion of a given task, as shown in Figure 8-5.

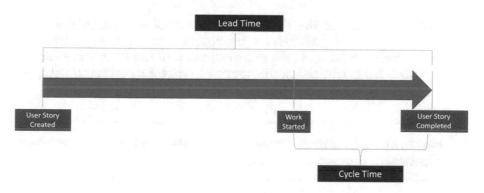

Figure 8-5. Lead time vs. cycle time in Kanban

Some other types of standard Kanban metrics include queue length, number of queues, and wait times. This allows to measure the effectiveness of the flow and calculate the cost of delay based on wait times and system throughput.

Standard diagrams to measure progress include the **Cumulative Flow Diagram** (or the **CFD**), **cycle time control chart** or **average time diagram**, and **lead time distribution chart** [6].

It is important to establish a different level of metrics collection. For example, during a Sprint, each team measures its progress toward successful delivery at the end of the Sprint. To do so, they use the burndown chart, which shows how the work progresses throughout the Sprint by subtracting the number of story points (or user stories) completed during the Sprint. The ideal burndown line is going down in a straight line from top left to bottom right (flat on weekends). This indicates a healthy project and a well-functioning Scrum team. Value is being delivered constantly in a linear way. If the burndown chart is a flat line, the team is not completing any work. Figure 8-6 shows a sample burndown chart.

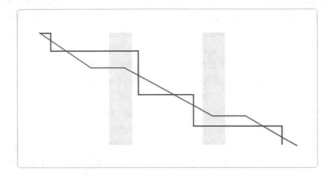

Figure 8-6. Sample burndown chart

This data is relevant to the team level and not of interest to the whole organization. For an organization, it is important to focus on metrics that matter: customer satisfaction, the quality of the software being delivered, the speed of delivery, predictability, the speed of refactoring technical debt, and other organization-level reporting.

 Topic for a Group Discussion   Discuss which metrics are relevant for the company level or team level and which metrics are relevant for both.

There are comprehensive tools that measure the level of organizational agility, such as AgilityHealth [8]. AgilityHealth is a measurement and continuous improvement platform providing insights into Agile maturity.

Five key questions to review:

1.   What metrics are relevant in Scrum? Kanban?

2.   What makes Agile metrics meaningful?

3.   What is the difference between lead time and cycle time? Why are those parameters important?

4.   What is the burndown chart and when is it used?

5.   What are the levels of scaling metrics in an Agile enterprise?

Continuous Improvement and Retrospectives

Once areas of improvement are identified, the goal is to implement relevant improvements. The teams are empowered in deciding how to prioritize these improvements and which techniques to use. Every Sprint, they conduct a Retrospective, where they prioritize areas of improvement, analyze root causes, and agree on a small number (usually three to five) of action items that they want to commit to as a team during the upcoming Sprint.

After implementing these improvements for a Sprint, the team starts the next Sprint Retrospective by discussing whether the action items they've implemented brought them the desired results; if yes, they persevere and make these decisions a part of their process, and if not, they discuss how to pivot and try other measures. This short feedback loop allows the teams to be productive and nimble in addressing productivity, quality, and other concerns. It also allows for an honest conversation between the team members since Retrospectives are internal to the team.

There are multiple techniques that are being implemented to enable inclusive and open discussion during a Retrospective. A standard technique for Retrospective has three steps:

1. Silent brainstorming: Participants write their comments on two topics – "What went well last Sprint?" and "What are the improvement opportunities?" – on post-its (physical or virtual) and post them on the Retrospective board. Once items are posted on the board, team members group them into categories.

2. Prioritization: Each team member gets an equal number of votes and places their votes (dots) on the groups of items they would like to prioritize.

3. Action items: The whole team discusses the highest voted groups and agrees on three to five action items they'd like to implement in the upcoming Sprint to address these. Usually, each item is owned by one of the team members who continuously updates the team on their progress.

Topic for a Group Discussion   Do a Retrospective on the latest class assignment you've done as a team. What went well? What are the improvement opportunities? What would you like to do as a team before next class to address these opportunities?

Tip   Having the same format for Retrospectives every Sprint may become boring and unproductive. Frequently, teams use a gamified approach to Retrospectives. A popular format is "Sailboat," where a Scrum Master or a team member paints a picture of a boat and asks questions to the group: What is a tailwind that accelerates our movement and what is the anchor that holds us back? They also analyze rocks, which are impediments preventing them from success. From this discussion and the subsequent voting, they move to the same action items conversation as in the standard format described in this chapter. There are many other formats described here: www. tastycupcakes.org/

There are many other creative formats used for Retrospectives.

These formats include "Glad, Sad, Mad," where team members start by silently brainstorming on three topics based on their observations from the prior Sprint, describe them to each other, group, and vote, similar to the original format as shown in Figure 8-7.

Figure 8-7.   A sample Retrospective format

Another popular format is "Start. Stop. Continue," where the team reflects on three topics:

- What should we start doing?
- What should we stop doing?
- What should the team continue doing?

Team members add their post-its to each category, followed by a discussion.

The foundations of Retrospectives are described by Esther Derby and Diana Larsen in their book, *Agile Retrospectives: Making Good Teams Great* [10].

In a remote environment, Retrospectives can be as much productive, collaborative, and fun as in physical. Virtual Retrospective boards are available in Mural, Miro, InVision Freehand, and in many other formats. There is helpful advice on making remote Retrospectives efficient and inclusive provided by multiple practitioners [9].

In summary, irrespective of the standard, the goal of a Retrospective is to align as a team in improving their process and delivery outcomes and commit to actionable items to achieve those improvements.

Product Life Cycle

From the product perspective, it is important to consider the product life cycle as part of the continuous improvement process. The life cycle of a product is associated with development, marketing, and investment decisions within the business. All the products go through five primary stages: development, introduction, growth, maturity, and decline. These phases are repeatable in an Agile environment within the course of the use of the product. However, from a macro perspective, each product goes from its beginning stages all the way through its decline and eventual retirement.

This means that we should not be investing in a product that is nearing its retirement in terms of new features and drastic improvements in its functionality. We should, though, ensure that it provides a continuous, high-quality experience to the customers.

Product life cycle management (PLM) process manages the entire life cycle of a product from inception, through inception and high-level design and manufacture, to service and sunsetting of the manufactured products. PLM is a key process within the information technology structure, so while the processes continuously improve, product development and research reflect the phase the product is in.

In sum, continuous improvement is a must for modern businesses. Improvement is related to continuous process improvement in Scrum via Retrospectives. In addition, improvement is being made to products and services in a different manner, with consideration of the product life cycle practices.

To summarize, incremental and iterative delivery is a must for a modern business. It allows to align delivery with business needs, focus on solving customer issues, and align deliverables within a large organization. However, it is not a "one-and-done" effort; the goal of an Agile enterprise is to continuously improve and pivot if the customer or business expectations are not met. From a product and team perspective, Agile delivery is a continuous learning and thoughtful improvement every step of the way.

Key Points

1. Incremental and iterative delivery allows feature-based delivery vs. a "big bang" phase-based Waterfall approach. Prioritized features are made available to end users once they are developed.

2. In order for iterative, incremental delivery to be meaningful for the customer, the delivery team needs to be clear on what they are delivering and when they will make this functionality available to their customers. They need to provide visibility into the upcoming functionality to their current and potential customers.

3. **Release planning** is a long-term (usually one quarter and longer) planning that enables delivery teams to answer the questions when specific features or new products are going to be delivered, or released, to the customer. Release plans are created based on a combination of two primary parameters: capacity and scope.

4. A **product roadmap** outlines the vision, direction, priorities, and feature delivery of a product over time. The roadmap defines the plan of action that aligns the organization around short- and long-term goals for the product. In addition, it contains high-level information on how these goals would be achieved. In an Agile environment, a roadmap provides primary context for everyday work while pivoting based on the market and customer needs. If multiple Agile teams work on the same product, they share a roadmap.

5. To ensure that teams are executing the right features at the right pace and assess how they are progressing toward executing the roadmap overall, companies use a set of Agile metrics.

6. The most useful approach to Agile metrics is to **collect the metrics that are important to the company**. For example, if there is an issue with meeting predefined timelines, then it is a good approach to measure the predictability of delivery.

7. **The primary measure of progress in Agile is working software.** As a result, the number of user stories delivered per Sprint or epics delivered over a longer period of time is a valid metric. Other parameters include quality and customer satisfaction. Another important metric in Scrum is the "commitment rate," which is a percentage of work delivered over work committed in story points.

8. Lead time and cycle time are the two most important Kanban metrics. They show how long work items stay in the workflow until they are completed. Lead time is the total amount of time a task spends from order to delivery in the system. Cycle time is the amount of time that is spent actively working on it.

9. The teams are empowered in deciding how to prioritize these improvements and which techniques to use. Every Sprint, they conduct a Retrospective, where they prioritize areas of improvement, analyze root causes, and agree on a small number (usually three to five) of action items that they want to commit to as a team during the upcoming Sprint.

10. From a product perspective, it is important to consider the product life cycle as part of the continuous improvement process. The life cycle of a product is associated with development, marketing, and investment decisions within the business. All the products go through five primary stages: development, introduction, growth, maturity, and decline. These phases are repeatable in an Agile environment within the course of the use of the product.

Agile Implementation Beyond IT: Budget Management, Risk Management, and Procurement Management in Agile

This chapter covers the topic of delivery beyond software or hardware products. It demonstrates that project management covers all areas of work, including marketing and finance, human capital management, the services industry, and beyond. It covers cultural aspects of project management and organizational change management, leadership, and influence without authority. It also addresses traditional management areas, such as budget management ("beyond budgeting" principle), risk management via impediment resolution, and procurement management.

© Mariya Breyter 2022
M. Breyter, *Agile Product and Project Management*,
https://doi.org/10.1007/978-1-4842-8200-7_9

In Chapter 8, we covered the topic of Agile execution and discussed how incremental delivery reduces risks and enables fast feedback loops from the customers. We also covered how the feedback – internal and external – can be used to refine and enhance execution and shape delivery models. In order to encourage open feedback, we reviewed multiple techniques for conducting Retrospective sessions. We covered Lean concepts of quality and quality-related outcomes. Finally, we reviewed incremental delivery from the product life cycle perspective. Throughout this chapter, we reemphasized Agile culture, that is, team empowerment, accountability, and customer-centricity.

In this chapter, we will review how Agile is used outside of IT – in sales, marketing, HR, finance, and, overall, across the organization. Then, we will talk about an Agile organization overall: organizational change management, leadership, continuous improvement at the organizational level, and the impact of Agile adoption on people, their roles, expectations, communication mechanisms, alignment principles, and leadership paradigm. Finally, we will review how traditional project management areas of knowledge, such as budget management, risk management, and capacity management, apply in Agile.

Agile Beyond IT

The Agile concept of incremental and iterative delivery of value to the customer, internal or external, applies to almost any industry, company, or professional. As a result, Agile and Lean concepts are used in many areas: from executives running their companies to sales, marketing, or human capital organizations, and even in personal life.

The concept of **extending Agile implementation** beyond IT and engaging the whole organization to be able to quickly and flexibly respond to customer and market needs is known as business agility. **Business agility** is the ability of organizations to quickly adapt to market changes in a productive, customer-centric, and cost-effective way without compromising the quality delivered to the customer.

There are two well-known and frequently quoted interesting facts:

- Fifty percent of companies that were in the Fortune 500 in 1995 had dropped off the list by 2015.

- The average life cycle of a company in the 1960s was 67 years – today, it's 15 years, and it's falling [4].

The modern business world has changed. Whether a company considers itself a technology company or not, technology has fundamentally disrupted the business landscape. In order to compete, companies need to innovate and continuously change the way they work.

The reasons why business agility is so powerful are the same as in software delivery:

1. Focus on delivering value by solving customer problems.

2. Team-based work where the unit of delivery is not an individual; it is an empowered team.

3. A short feedback loop that allows for pivoting to better address customer needs.

4. Low risk related to validation of outcomes at regular short intervals.

5. Higher employee engagement because of their ownership of the work performed and related outcomes.

In 2016, the Business Agility Institute (BAI) was formed to address the lack of conferences, resources, and overall awareness of business agility. BAI supports business agility research around the world. In their 2020 Business Agility Report, BAI emphasized the positive impact of business agility during the global pandemic. While some businesses were devastated, some were able to sustain and grow. According to BAI, one characteristic that was common among the latter group was that they benefited from the fact that they were, for the most part, practicing principles of business agility – an obsession with delivering value for customers, drawing on the talents of their staff, and working as networks of competence [1].

Based on the information from 433 respondents from 359 organizations, the 2020 Business Agility Report mentioned before identified three key predictors of business agility:

1. Relentless improvement: By encouraging a culture of learning and experimentation to thrive, organizations will continuously improve both what they do and, more importantly, how they do it, reducing costs, improving efficiency, and delivering greater value to customers.

2. Funding models: By funding business outcomes, rather than specific work outputs or projects, organizations can quickly and easily invest in new products or services as soon as market opportunities arise and, with the right governance, just as quickly stop or change work that is not delivering the expected business value.

3. Value streams: By designing flexible work processes that are both efficient and customer-centric, organizations can structure teams at all levels in a way that maximizes value creation for the customer.

In 2021, the Business Agility Institute further investigated how organizations adapted to the disruptions of the COVID pandemic and what effect this had on their business agility. They found out that business agility transformations had an overwhelmingly supportive impact on responding to and coping with COVID. Over 87% of organizations reported increases in business agility throughout the COVID disruption. In addition to reporting increases in business agility since March 2020, 82% of participants believed that they would sustain the level of agility developed during the pandemic. For many organizations, their business agility practices were directly credited as the reason why they were still in business. Some respondents indicated that they continually realigned or refocused around their most valuable customer streams. Beyond survival, there was a marked shift to accelerate digital and online activities, including the move to remote working and a substantial change in how products and services are delivered to customers [2].

In addition, they analyzed the impact of COVID on over 6,000 Agile team members. They identified that since the start of the pandemic, team performance has improved across several key measures: Workspace, Happiness, Predictable Delivery, Quality, Value Delivered, Response to Change, and Time to Market, as shown in Figure 9-1.

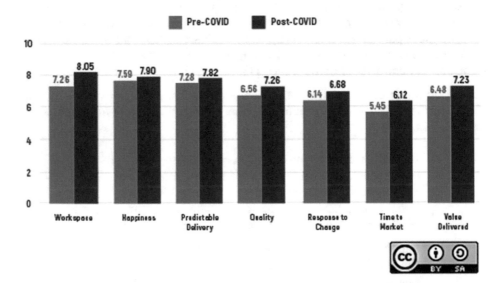

Figure 9-1. Resiliency of Agile teams during COVID. Source: Business Agility Institute [2]

"Business agility is the ability of a business to **realize and sustain its full potential both in terms of its profits and its people, regardless of internal or external environment changes**. It enables organizations to innovate and deliver more effectively, thus turning market disruption into competitive advantage, while thriving in complex environments."

— SolutionsIQ blog, April 2019 [3]

Let's review some of the case studies of Agility within different groups and organizations.

Case Study 1: Company-Level Agility. Adoption of business Agility at Moonpig [4]. Moonpig is an Internet-based business whose head offices are situated in London and Guernsey. The company's business model is mainly selling personalized greeting cards, flowers, and gifts. Having achieved a measure of success adopting Agile practices within their product engineering team, Moonpig's leadership was keen to see if the rest of the organization could also benefit from Agile adoption.

Business agility at Moonpig started with WHY. It did not start with Scrum practices or Kanban boards. It started with the mindset so that people across the company understood why they were making the changes and what the benefits would be. The goal was to understand that these changes were not introduced by executives; they were driven across the industry and within the company and were underpinned by solid principles and reasoning.

Moonpig started its Agile journey focusing mainly on software development by adopting cross-functional teams, leveraging Agile and DevOps practices to improve delivery capability, and introducing a Lean approach to product development – using data to form hypotheses and test assumptions. This way of working allowed to improve efficiency, deliver better outcomes, and grow the business. In addition, teams leveraging Lean-Agile practices also showed significantly higher levels of engagement.

Software delivery teams were able to realize the benefits of Agile while their business counterparts could not. In marketing and commercial functions, the situation was different. They did a Retrospective, and the feedback was as follows:

- "Everyone works in silos."

- "There is no communication within teams."

- "We have too many objectives."

- "Lack of trust to let people do their jobs."

- "There's no collaboration across teams."

- "We have conflicting objectives."

It manifested in the company having two separate cultures – one in software delivery (collaborative, transparent, customer focused) and one on the business side (siloed, misaligned, and lacking trust).

Topic for a Group Discussion   In groups, discuss the best way to proceed in this situation, given that the company is still commercially successful. Should they maintain status quo and focus Agile implementation on software delivery? Would it be safe to disrupt the positive software delivery culture to align business and technology in Agile approach? What are the advantages and risks of each of these two major options? If moving forward with business agility, what would be the major barriers? What metrics should be used to measure success?

The decision was made to implement business agility. To do so, the following mission statement was created: "I want to design a tailored system of work that optimizes the entire organization, allowing Moonpig to innovate and move fast at scale, whilst still ensuring it is a place that people love to work."

At the next steps, success criteria were defined. It was decided to look for specific outcomes rather than Agile maturity levels. They wanted to become better, faster, cheaper, and happier and summarized it into three outcomes:

- Better: Better outcomes leading to increased Return on Investment (RoI)

- Faster: Reduced cycle time across all value streams

- Happier: Higher employee engagement

They selected the following measurements for these outcomes:

Getting better by

- Embedding a customer-focused, data-driven, experimental approach to minimize wasted investment. Understanding where we create value and reduce time wasted on low-value output

- Increasing innovation through the collaboration of people with different skills and expertise

Getting faster by

- Aligning relevant people around key outcomes and removing conflicting priorities and dependencies

- Leveraging Lean working practices – visualizing work, reducing work in progress, and focusing on finishing

- Championing a culture of collaboration and cross-functional working where team success comes before individual glory

- Embedding a continuous improvement mindset, seeking to constantly optimize our working processes. Empowering and supporting teams to self-organize, removing dependencies and bottlenecks around senior management

Getting happier by

- Developing a safe-to-fail environment where people can take risks

- Ensuring our teams have clear goals and are supported to achieve them

- Creating a culture of autonomy where teams are empowered to use their collective skills to deliver outcomes

- Encouraging a growth mindset and making learning a central part of our working life

As the next step, they developed the roadmap, which consisted of four steps:

1. Alignment (reorganizing around clear goals into cross-functional teams by value stream)

2. Working processes (reducing cycle time by embedding the culture of continuous improvement)

3. Experimentation (creating "fail fast" culture by implementing customer-focused, data-driven experimentation)

4. Culture of learning (implementing growth mindset and collaborative learning)

Each of these steps was nontrivial. For example, one of the key challenges in step 1 was resource bottlenecks. Copywriting was one area in particular where they lacked resources. At that point, they had three immediate solutions: accept that delivery will be delayed, hire additional resources, or do fewer things. Another, longer-term, solution was to invest in people and train some of their marketers and UX designers to write the copy themselves. This wouldn't remove the need for dedicated copywriting experience but would provide flexibility because simpler copy tasks could be handled by other team members. The decision was made to resource the outcomes in the order of their priority, similar to a product backlog in software development. Once capacity is achieved, the rest of the work remains in a backlog. This allowed marketing and commercial teams to generate the most impact fast. The understanding that was formed is that the faster you deliver prioritized outcomes, the faster you get to the next items of the backlog.

Each of the cross-functional teams contained a product function, marketing function, creative function, and engineering function. All together, they worked on new products, marketing campaigns, financing, sales, and so forth. These teams implemented daily standups for collaboration and alignment and biweekly Retrospectives for continuous improvement. They used the Kanban board to align their activities and dashboard to continuously capture metrics in each category. For happiness, they measured "mastery, autonomy, and purpose," according to Daniel Pink's findings [5]. A clear purpose lets people know what is expected of them. Autonomy empowers people to achieve the purpose and serves as the antidote to micromanagement. Mastery gives them the necessary skills to achieve that purpose.

In addition to these key principles, leveraging Lean and Agile working practices, which were introduced to increase speed, was also intended to promote a sustainable pace of work and better work-life balance. In addition to improved quality of work experience, it was also hoped that a sustainable pace would provide people with more time to learn. Another opportunity was in developing a clear career progression. To address this, the leaders developed a competency matrix against which they could align roles and provide clear guidance for individuals to develop and progress.

In the first six to eight months, the company was able to achieve success in getting better, faster, and happier across the whole organization. Realigning the teams and bringing agility to the business improved cycle times dramatically in some areas, particularly in the delivery of their marketing content, where they saw cycle times reduced from months to days. People were happier and more engaged, and retention increased. At the same time, the leaders came up with several opportunities for improvement, such as coaching leadership, defining the outcomes early to collaborate with the business, having Agile coaching in place, and relentlessly focusing on prioritized work.

"My exploration of business agility began two years ago. Back then, I wasn't even conscious of the term "business agility"—I was simply exploring the possibility of adopting Agile practices and processes in different contexts... and now I cannot see past business agility! My experiences in the last few years have taught me that it has enormous potential, and anything less now feels sub-optimal. As long as Agile remains a "tech thing", we consign ourselves to optimizing a single corner of an organization. Lean and Agile comprise a set of principles which are ultimately agnostic of technology—every part of the organization can benefit. There is no one-size-fits-all. The basic principles may apply to all, but designing a better system of work for your organization means experimenting to create a tailor-made system that works for you."

— Amanda Colpyos, Case Study: Adopting Business Agility at Moonpig [4]

Example: Agile HR. The Human Resources (HR) function in multiple organizations around the globe is moving toward agility. This includes multiple areas:

1. Performance management
2. Learning and talent development
3. Compensation
4. Recruiting

Agile for HR looks at how HR can apply an Agile mindset and various working methods within their own teams and products, as well as across the whole organization. Agile for HR has the potential to reinvent human capital organizations' operational model and modernize HR as a profession. Any organization can realize the benefits by applying some basic concepts in their everyday work.

This includes focus on outcomes vs. processes, focus on the team vs. individuals, and continuous improvement to achieve efficiency and alignment. Agile includes an Agile mindset, Agile ways of working, organizational design of Agile (cross-functional teams), and the establishment of psychologically safe organizations via collaboration and team empowerment.

In order to develop a model for developing and sustaining the Lean and Agile culture in the organization, HR professionals need to answer the following questions [7]:

> **What does it mean to be an Agile/Lean professional?** Rather than looking for people with the words "agile" and "lean" in their titles, the recruiting function needs to look for people with a Lean-Agile mindset. This includes people who are customer oriented and team driven, the ones who

have had a chance to work in a similar environment. Too often, the hiring process at any level becomes heavily based on referrals and behavioral interviews to reveal the servant/leader nature of the individual, in addition to job-specific competencies. Within Agile and Lean frameworks, a good topic for a behavioral interview is job dynamics and team-level collaboration. For example: talk about a situation where you disagreed with your team's decision and whether you ended up following the team or confronting the decision.

What does it mean to be an Agile/Lean HR function? Nowadays, the performance review process morphed into a continuous feedback process. For example, Scrum builds feedback into its cadence. At regular intervals of time, the team meets, and team members provide direct process improvement feedback, resulting in two to three action items they agree to implement within the next iteration. This process is ongoing. Meanwhile, team performance is intentional: driven by Objectives and Key Results, teams self-assess their performance against predefined objectives (quality, productivity, predictability, customer satisfaction, employee happiness); also cascading goals are used, and the results are transparent across the organization. Continuous feedback is the center of the performance review process, with the feedback coming from leaders, peers, and clients.

How does an Agile/Lean organization handle compensation, recognition, and awards? There are two major changes in the Lean-Agile approach to employee recognition: First, recognition comes from peers and customers rather than managers. Second, awards are no longer individual and depend on the team's success. In his book *Managing for Happiness*, Jurgen Appelo describes multiple ways of recognition in an Agile environment. An interesting example that he provides is a peer-to-peer bonus system which he calls "merit money," where team members reward each other with credits (later translated into bonus money) for their collaboration and support. He provides the following example: "Last month on my team, Jennifer gave 15 credits to Lisette 'for being the backbone of the organization.' Lisette gave 25 points to Sergey 'for all the feedback and support.' Sergey gave ten credits to Chad for his 'terrific illustrations.' And Chad gave 20 credits to Hannu for his 'friendliness and clarity of communication.' And on and on it went..." [6]. At the same time, in the learning culture, there is no shame for failure – mistakes are seen as a learning opportunity; hence "fail fast, succeed faster" approach to failure is taken. Some companies even establish "failure walls" where employees share their failures to allow others to learn from their mistakes.

How does an Agile/Lean organization implement titles and promotions? Lean-Agile culture requires different thinking about organizational hierarchy and the role of management. Managers are no longer assigning work or evaluating performance; rather, their role is to support employee development and growth and provide tools for issue resolution and team-based delivery. In most instances, midlevel managers are "playing coaches" on their teams. This philosophy goes all the way to C-level management. This principle is sometimes referred to as an "inverted pyramid," where the role of an executive is to support and enable from the bottom of the inverted pyramid where employees are the ones on top of the pyramid. While the managers no longer assign work to individual team members, this does not mean that there is chaos or anarchy with everyone doing what they like. With a clear definition of the company's objectives and team's goals, there is a clear understanding of outcomes, alignment of deliverables, and transparency about the progress.

How to create an HR Ecosystem in an Agile and Lean enterprise? We need to think of HR as the backbone of the Lean and Agile ecosystem – empowering employees and teams and providing all the underlying functions, from employee hiring development to team enablement and recognition, is the key to a Lean enterprise. This is one of the reasons why the success of Lean-Agile transformation for a modern enterprise is measured by two sets of parameters: The first set is in relation to business objectives and product delivery metrics, such as time to market, quality, and customer satisfaction; the second set is employee driven and is represented as "employee happiness," collaboration within the teams, and employee retention rate. This is also why work-life balance and sustainable pace for teams and individuals have become so important. Especially with the global pandemic affecting all the people and organizations in an unprecedented way, we do not talk about "work-life balance" where there is a 9 AM–5 PM "workday" but rather a "work-life fusion" that allows a person to dedicate time to the family. This can be done with the aid of modern technology and communication, which allows for building high-performance globally distributed teams. See Alberto Silveira's book, *Building and Managing High-Performance Distributed Teams*, on excellent tips and guidelines for creating a successful work ecosystem and empowering employees to seek the North Star (5).

Another key item is employee "self-selection" into teams. There are multiple examples of how thoughtful and well-executed self-selection mechanisms take teams to the next level in terms of their productivity and work happiness. In her example of how HBC Universal ran their self-selection campaign, Dana Pylayeva outlines a thoughtful, step-by-step orchestrated process that provided a platform for team self-selection at an organizational level [8].

How to create a culture of continuous learning?
Learning and continuous growth when managers become coaches in this process vs. task givers and evaluators are some of the keys to the Agile HR approach to personnel development. AI is being used to customize training to individuals, with gamification based on simulations and experiential learning being at the center. Many companies, such as IBM, make a shift by redesigning all aspects of their people management systems to build a culture of continuous learning, innovation, and agility. They change the nature of HR organizations by incorporating ML/AI and process automation across all offerings, resulting in hundreds of millions of dollars of net benefits. At IBM, Diane Gherson, Head of HR, was the one who championed the company's global adoption of design thinking and Agile methods at scale [9].

Topic for a Group Discussion   In groups, discuss the difference between traditional HR functions and Agile HR. What are the benefits of Agile HR? What shift is required to implement Agile HR? Where do you expect resilience? How would you address it?

Organizational Management and Agile Leadership

Business agility demands new ways of organizing businesses – from startups to multithousand-employee corporations. It is imperative for businesses nowadays to be flexible and respond quickly to shifts and changes in the market environment. Agile organizations are able to rapidly change their business processes to satisfy customer needs.

This approach is significantly different from Taylorist organizations as described by an American mechanical engineer, Frederick Taylor, who came up with the concept of scientific management that optimized labor productivity using a scientific approach to effectiveness and efficiency. Taylor believed that it was the role and responsibility of manufacturing plant managers to determine the best way for the worker to do a job and to provide the proper tools and training. This approach supports organizational hierarchy, command-and-control management style, and top-down work allocation [10].

Agile organizational structure, management, and leadership approach are fundamentally different. In the 2018 McKinsey & Company article, "The Five Trademarks of Agile Organizations," the authors summarize the trends that are brought by the "digital revolution" that is transforming industries, economies, and societies:

- *"Quickly evolving environment.* All stakeholders' demand patterns are evolving rapidly: customers, partners, and regulators have pressing needs; investors are demanding growth, which results in acquisitions and restructuring; and competitors and collaborators demand action to accommodate fast-changing priorities.

- *The constant introduction of disruptive technology.* Established businesses and industries are being commoditized or replaced through digitization, bioscience advancements, the innovative use of new models, and automation. Examples include developments such as machine learning, the Internet of things, and robotics.

- *Accelerating digitization and democratization of information.* The increased volume, transparency, and distribution of information require organizations to rapidly engage in multidirectional communication and complex collaboration with customers, partners, and colleagues.

- *The new war for talent.* As creative knowledge- and learning-based tasks become more important, organizations need a distinctive value proposition to acquire – and retain – the best talent, which is often more diverse. These 'learning workers' often have more diverse origins, thoughts, composition, and experience and may have different desires (e.g., millennials)" [11].

These trends require new paradigms where organizations are viewed as living organisms. They respond quickly and are nimble and ready to act. In short, they respond like living organisms.

This shift reflects the transition from bureaucracy to focusing on action, from top-down hierarchy to leadership. It shows direction and enables managers to act as coaches and leaders, to move from silos to collaboration, from detailed instruction to building teams around end-to-end predictability. An interesting fact is that when pressure is applied to an Agile organization, it responds even faster and in a nimbler way. This focus on outcomes vs. hierarchies allows the companies to achieve greater customer-centricity, faster time to market, higher revenue growth, lower cost, and a more engaged workforce. There are fewer silos, more collaboration. Less command-and-control managers, more empowered engineers. Less hierarchy and more accountability.

The ultimate way of structuring and running an organization that replaces the conventional management hierarchy is holacracy [12]. Instead of operating top-down, power is distributed throughout the organization – giving individuals and teams freedom while staying aligned to the organization's purpose. These organizations are fully purpose driven. They focus on purpose at every level of scale: organizational purpose, team purpose, and individual purpose are all explicit and aligned. Every team member directs their energy in alignment with the broader mission, unlocking their organization's full potential. They see their role in being responsive, that is, turning their challenges and opportunities into improvements for the organizations. Holacracy is Agile: small, incremental decisions replace large-scale organizational transformations so that the company can respond quickly to a shifting environment and maintain agility as they grow.

"In Holacracy, you see groups making proposals to revise the design of their group and of the broader organization. They're making decisions that a typical organization—a hierarchical organization—only makes at the management and senior management level."

— Dr. Michael Y. Lee, Assistant Professor of Organizational Behavior at INSEAD [13]

Using Agile in Sales

Agile is broadly used in sales and marketing. Marina Alex is an Agile coach who introduced SWAY (Sales with Agile), her proprietary sales system founded on self-organization, cross-functionality, and value. According to her website [14], the effectiveness of SWAY has been proven in practice. It has been successfully utilized in more than 20 countries around the world. Sales volumes increased primarily due to the effectiveness of the system, creating value for the client, and day-to-day interaction between sales and marketing. SWAY users have observed sales growth from 43% to 127% within a 12-month period.

SWAY is the composite of Scrum, Agile Manifesto values and principles, coaching and leadership, strategies, self-organizations, and sales management. It utilizes an established cycle of receiving feedback from the client, continuous hypothesis testing, cooperation with marketing, short Sprints, and rapid improvement events.

Another great example of a people-centric approach is a company called Menlo Innovations, described by its CEO and Chief Storyteller Richard Sheridan [15].

Agile Finance and Budget Management

The fundamental business question "How much will it cost?" applies equally to Agile or Waterfall project management. However, **budget management in Agile is fundamentally different** from traditional (Waterfall) project management. In Agile, budgeting is happening in Sprints, either monthly or quarterly. Based on the team composition and compensation by role and location, the cost of each Sprint is calculated per team and multiplied by the number of teams, with all the necessary adjustments: loaded compensations (including benefits and other expenses) as well as other costs, such as hardware, software, licenses, supplies, and anything else required to complete the deliverables.

Who manages a budget in an Agile environment? There are several approaches to this:

1. Business or Functional Manager who is responsible for the overall deliverable

2. Product Manager responsible for the product overall, including P&L, in collaboration with the Product Owners for Agile teams who drive prioritization and road mapping

3. Agile Project Manager, a separate role responsible for the project management aspects of Agile delivery, such as external dependency management, coordination, resourcing requests, procurement, and multiple other functions, which may include budget management and dependency management

In Waterfall, a project budget is defined as the total projected costs needed to complete a project over a defined period of time. It's used to estimate what the costs of the project will be for every phase of the project. The most fundamental difference between Agile and Waterfall is that in Waterfall, the budget is fully allocated at the beginning of a project, and during subsequent delivery, assessments are made whether a project is on budget, is below budget, or exceeds the budget, which requires an immediate course correction. PMBOK defines Project Cost Management as a group of processes involved in planning, estimating, budgeting, and controlling costs so that the project can be completed within the approved budget. According to PMBOK Sixth Edition, "the cost management planning effort occurs early in project planning and sets the framework for each of the cost management processes so that performance of the processes will be efficient and coordinated" [16, p. 236]. In Waterfall, it is hard to estimate whether a project is on budget during the analysis, design, and even coding because none of the features have been tested or delivered to users for their feedback. This is the reason why Waterfall project managers need to add a significant "contingency margin," usually starting at 20–25% for complex deliverables.

In both instances, the following five sources of information are considered when performing budget estimations:

1. High-level estimations from the people doing the work

2. Historical data from similar deliverables/goals

3. Lessons learned from prior initiatives

4. Expert opinion from subject matter experts known within the organization and in the field

5. Baselines – organizational and industry-wise

Agile puts emphasis on decomposing the work to be done into features and performing high-level feature estimations, while Waterfall relies on similar work performed within the organization and the estimations provided by line managers.

In addition, in Agile, the validation of deliverables is performed throughout the process by delivering working software to the customer and replanning based on customer and business feedback. If additional features are requested, the team does a high-level estimation of the work required to deliver these features and provides a cost estimate to the sponsor or requestor. At this post, their sponsor can make an informed decision whether it is worth investing in based on the Sprint cost and duration, or they prefer to descope less important functionality to stay within the originally allocated budget.

This makes all calculations in Agile very simple compared to the complexity of budget calculations in Waterfall, where the phase of the project defines the value that is being delivered. In Agile, there are two major parameters:

1. Stable dedicated Agile teams

2. Timeboxed iterations

Let's review an example. Four Scrum teams are allocated to deliver an application that has a set number of features. Upon high-level estimation, the teams forecasted that they would need six Sprints to deliver all the features. Each team has nine team members. Based on the organizational data, the average loaded rate (i.e., a "blended rate") per employee is $150/hour. The total cost calculation becomes very simple:

1. Employees per Sprint: 10 FTE team members × 4 teams = 40 employees per Sprint

2. Cost per employee per a two-week Sprint: $150/hour × 80 hours = $12,000 (fixed burn rate per person per Sprint)

3. Cost per Sprint: $480,000

4. Cost for 6 Sprints: $480,000 × 6 = $2,880,000

5. Additional costs (licenses, equipment), not including vendor costs: $120,000

6. Total estimated cost: $2,880,000 + $120,000 = $3,000,000

It is important to understand that in Agile, **an estimate is not a commitment; it's a forecast**, which will be adjusted Sprint by Sprint, by validation with the customers and business and based on incremental deliverables, learnings, and feedback loop. This calculation is an example of top-down planning, rather than bottom-up estimation done in Waterfall, where a project manager creates a top-down description of work, known as a Work Breakdown Structure (WBS), all the way down to each task, which is estimated by Subject Matter Experts (SMEs). The comparison of Agile and Waterfall cost management is presented in Table 9-1.

Table 9-1. Comparison of Agile and Waterfall cost management

Agile	Waterfall
Iterative	Full scope
Top-down	Bottom-up
Forecast	Commitment
Flexible	Fixed
Provided by the team	Provided by managers/Subject Matter Experts (SMEs)

Once the budget is established, the following strategies allow Agile teams to continuously refine the budget:

1.   High-quality product backlog reflecting MVP and subsequent feature set

2.   Continuous product backlog refinement along with the consistent estimation

3.   Short feedback loops via demos to the customers

4.   Agile planning to implement the value of iterative delivery

---

Topic for a Group Discussion   In groups, discuss the difference between Agile and Waterfall cost management. How do you handle budget overruns in Agile and traditional project management? How would you handle budget estimations in Kanban vs. Scrum?

As an ultimate approach to Agile budgeting in a modern knowledge-oriented world, the principle of "beyond budgeting" has been implemented in some Agile organizations due to its revolutionary nature. This approach represents a new management philosophy that is more Agile and adaptable, aiming at eliminating bureaucracy and rigid control mechanisms, empowering people, and promoting transparency. Instead of focusing on long-term, complex budgets, which become obsolete as soon as they are published, beyond-budgeting organizations focus their budgets on short-term financial performance.

According to the co-creators of this framework, "the traditional annual budgeting process–characterized by fixed targets and performance incentives–is time-consuming, overcentralized, and outdated. Worse, it often causes dysfunctional and unethical managerial behavior. Based on an intensive, international study into pioneering companies, Beyond Budgeting offers an alternative, coherent management model that overcomes the limitations of traditional budgeting. Focused around achieving sustained improvement relative to competitors, it provides a guiding framework for managing in the twenty-first century" [17]. "Beyond budgeting" framework is not in scope of this book; however, it is important to be aware of the fact that more Agile and flexible approaches to budgeting are already in place in modern project management.

 Five key questions to review:

1. What is the difference between top-down and bottom-up cost estimation?

2. What is the difference between Agile and Waterfall cost management?

3. What is the difference between budget commitment and forecast?

4. What would happen If some of the team members are consultants?

5. What does the "burn rate" mean for a team?

Agile Risk Management

A risk is anything that could prevent or marginalize project success. When a risk materializes, it becomes an issue. Agile practices provide a built-in mechanism to manage a wide range of risks usually encountered in software development.

Agile neither offers a universal definition of risk nor provides a standardized approach to risk management. Risk management in Agile is built into the cadence in such a way that Agile provides a framework to manage risks early and proactively. Based on continuous improvement and a short feedback cycle, any potential issues are exposed early and triaged within a short time frame. In addition, the transparency of Agile culture contributes to exposing risks early and being able to address them without blame.

"All projects are risky since they are unique undertakings with varying degrees of complexity that aim to deliver benefits. They do this in a context of constraints and assumptions, while responding to stakeholder expectations that may be conflicting and changing. Organizations should choose to take project risk in an controlled and intentional manner in order to create value while balancing risk and reward."

— PMBOK, 6th edition, p. 397 [16]

PMBOK distinguishes between **individual project risks** (uncertain event or condition that, if it occurs, has a positive or negative effect on one or more project objectives) and **overall project risks** (the effect of uncertainty on the project as a whole, arising from all sources of uncertainty including individual risks, representing the exposure of stakeholders to the implications of variation in project outcome).

In Agile, risks are not structured the same way: they are **built into** an execution cadence. As an example, in a daily Scrum meeting, team members have to answer the question "Which impediments am I having?" and the whole team gets engaged in unblocking their peers. In Waterfall projects, team members are mostly focused on their individual tasks, so there are no similar mechanisms to expose the risks daily, triage the risks immediately after they arise, and support team members in resolving them based on severity.

These built-in mechanisms are the reason why most Agile frameworks do not specify how they manage risks. Risks are managed via early feedback, the collaboration between business and technology, test-driven development where quality is "built into" the delivery process, and many other mechanisms that mitigate risks up front.

For external risks and dependencies in Agile, there are still multiple mechanisms and tools available for risk management. Some Agile practitioners still maintain a list of risks for their team, which includes primarily external dependencies, especially ones outside of IT: legal, vendor, compliances, regulatory, licensing, and other risks. For more complex scaled deliverables, some companies hire project coordinators who maintain risk logs and follow up on the status.

In sum, while there is no predefined approach to risk management in Agile, sometimes, traditional risk management tools and techniques are leveraged for high-risk and high-complexity deliverables.

-ʘ́- **Tip** In Waterfall, risk identification usually happens when a project kicks off. In Agile, risk assessment and analysis are continuous and are performed at least once per iteration and updated throughout execution. Risks are identified and logged into Agile tools such as Jira to ensure that the risk is being assessed and actioned upon.

There are some techniques adopted from traditional project management, frequently used in scaled Agile environments to classify and prioritize external risks, such as **impact** vs. **probability** matrix. According to this model, risk is defined as a function of probability and impact. The probability is the likelihood of an event occurring, and the consequences, to which extent the project is affected by an event, are the impacts of risk. Based on this assessment, the following matrix gets created (see Figure 9-2).

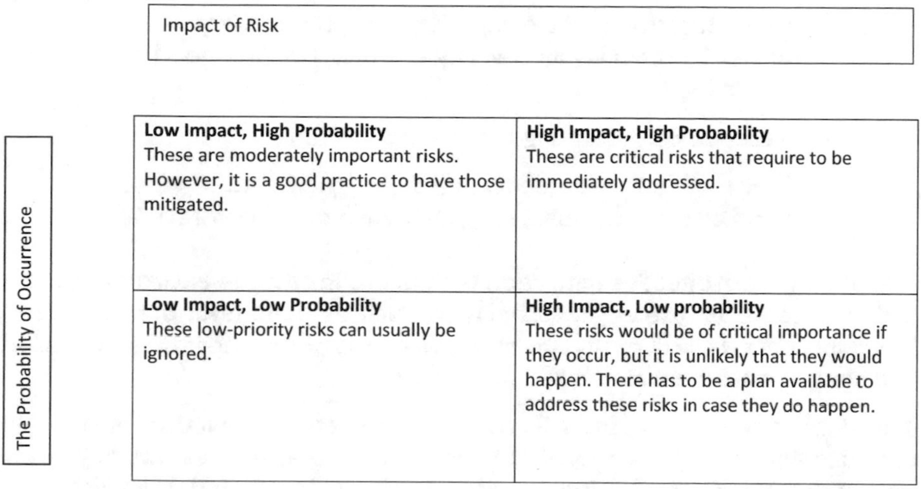

Impact of Risk

The Probability of Occurrence	**Low Impact, High Probability** These are moderately important risks. However, it is a good practice to have those mitigated.	**High Impact, High Probability** These are critical risks that require to be immediately addressed.
	Low Impact, Low Probability These low-priority risks can usually be ignored.	**High Impact, Low probability** These risks would be of critical importance if they occur, but it is unlikely that they would happen. There has to be a plan available to address these risks in case they do happen.

Figure 9-2. Risk matrix

The same technique is used sometimes with the Risk index where probability and impact are assessed on a scale of 1 through 5, and the product is used for Risk prioritization as a Risk Rating (see Table 9-2).

Table 9-2. Risk prioritization sample

Risk ID	Risk Category	Risk Description	Impact (1 lowest to 5 highest)	Probability (1 lowest to 5 highest)	Rating (Sort DESC)
B3	Budget	Funds are not available	10	8	80
A2	Skills	Security engineer SME not available	5	8	40
A4	Skills	DevOps engineer not available	2	6	12

It is helpful to categorize risks to ensure successful mitigation. Some categories include resourcing, security, compliance, business continuity, financial, fraud/theft, and multiple other categories depending on the nature of work being performed. In addition, there are several primary risk response strategies, with the primary ones being the following:

1. Risk avoidance: Eliminating the thread of risk by eliminating the cause

2. Risk mitigation (controlling): Reducing the consequences of risk by reducing its severity of impact or likelihood of occurring

3. Acceptance: Accepting the risk if it occurs

4. Share of transfer (allocation): Assigning the risk to another party by purchasing insurance or subcontracting

To come up with effective mitigation techniques in an Agile environment, it is highly effective to use Agile techniques, such as team-level brainstorming, Retrospectives, daily Scrums, and other forums for discussing the information and aligning on dependencies and next steps.

The integration of traditional risk management techniques into Agile environments requires a thoughtful approach so that it does not negatively impact team self-organization, efficient feedback loops, and Lean decision-making. The following Agile built-in mechanisms allow for efficient risk management:

1. Transparency via Kanban board

2. Effective prioritization via product backlog

3. Daily alignment via Scrum meetings

Topic for a Group Discussion   Review 12 Agile principles. Which of these principles address risk mitigation and in what way?

A final consideration in selecting the risk management strategy for an Agile initiative and making the decision whether to combine it with the traditional risk management practices lies in the major components of decision-making as shown in Table 9-3.

Table 9-3. Criteria for selecting risk management strategy

Select Traditional Risk Management	Focus on Agile Built-In Risk Management
A large scope new product or feature	Continuous feature release of an existing product
Highly scaled long-term deliverable (e.g., seven to nine or more teams for more than six Sprints)	Smaller-scale deliverable (less than seven teams for less than six Sprints)
Compliance and other regulatory requirements	No specific compliance or regulatory requirements outside of the organization's environment

Procurement Management in an Agile Organization

The final area of traditional project management that we are discussing from an Agile point of view is procurement management. According to PMBOK, project procurement management includes the processes required to purchase or acquire the products, services, or results needed from outside the project team to perform the work [16]. There are usually multiple processes involved in procurement management: request for proposals coordination, vendor interviews, negotiations, legal and contract considerations, execution, payments, and so forth. This is a complex endeavor, and it needs to be thoroughly coordinated in any environment, Agile or not.

One of the values of the Agile Manifesto is "customer collaboration over contract negotiation." This does not mean that Agile does not take procurement management very seriously; rather, it pays special attention to the collaborative nature of this process. Vendors and contractors are part of the Agile delivery ecosystem and the contract services as a guide for value delivery. The positive value-driven nature of contract negotiations is the most important part of Agile delivery.

From the procurement activities perspective, though, there is not much difference between the traditional project management's procurement and Agile procurement. There is still a need to plan purchases for products and services, then select the right vendor, negotiate, contract, and, finally, execute the contracts and close them once complete.

Usually, there are several standard steps in the procurement process:

1. **Identify the need**. This includes making "build vs. buy" decisions, considering multiple options, existing products, and a flexible approach to problem-solving.

2. **Perform a comparative analysis** of the available options in the market and make the vendor selection.

3. **Negotiate with the vendor** for pricing, timelines, deliverables, and delivery frameworks. While it is possible to work with a non-Agile vendor, the preference is always for the vendor who practices Agile delivery. Usually, Vendor Management, Legal, and other relevant company functions are involved.

4. **Vendor selection.** In Agile, this happens early in project delivery so that the vendor can co-create the product together with the Agile team(s). They get involved in early discovery, MVP definition, and scope brainstorming sessions as relevant.

5. **Collaboration with the vendor is an important part of the Agile delivery process.** No matter what the procurement is for, it is important to ensure that the vendor understands the product objectives, customer needs, and the value of the product being created. This will provide motivation and alignment opportunities, and ensure that the relationship with the vendor is mutually beneficial and positive.

The major difference between traditional and Agile procurement is that in traditional procurement management, the scope is fixed while in Agile, change is welcome. While legacy contract models reflect the "iron triangle," Agile welcomes change.

"In Agile projects, the research into criteria for buying decisions is often expanded to include the team. Teams are empowered to investigate and share knowledge whenever possible. The creation of a "learning culture" in Agile teams is valuable from a purchasing perspective in that there is grassroots involvement in both the research and selection of items of purchase."

— Michele Sliger and Stacia Broderick, The Software Project Manger's Bridge to Agility, p 190 [18]

There are four major types of standard contracts:

1. A firm fixed price (fixed price, fixed date, and fixed specification)

2. Target price (fixed specification, fixed date, and target price)

3. Cost-plus (target specification, target date, the customer pays the supplier's cost plus profit margin)

4. Time and materials (no complete specification, price based on rate)

Neither of them fully addresses the flexibility of Agile delivery. For example, a fixed price presents a risk to the supplier in case the deliverable is more complex than originally envisioned. The Time and Materials type is more Agile, but it presents a risk to a customer in case the value is not delivered as fast as expected.

As a result, in Agile, the goal is to establish a value-driven partnership between the supplier and the customer through the following:

- Optimize delivery against value, not the time or the original scope.

- Provide flexibility in response to newly validated requirements.

- Provide transparency to the supplier into the funding pipeline.

- Motivate both supplier and customer to build the best solution to address customer problems within agreed-upon constraints established at negotiation.

Topic for a Group Discussion   What are the benefits of Agile procurement management? How to make it mutually beneficial to customers and suppliers?

Five key questions to review:

1. What is procurement?

2. How is Agile procurement similar to the traditional one?

3. How is Agile procurement different from the traditional one?

4. Why is it so important to build Agile procurement around value delivery vs. "the iron triangle"?

5. What are the ways of making the procurement relationship collaborative in Agile?

Quality Management in Agile

Quality management in Agile and Waterfall is equally important. In Agile, however, quality control and quality management are an inherent part of product delivery. As stated in Lean manufacturing, quality is "built-in" since Agile teams have a focus on early and ongoing testing throughout the sprint, followed by integration testing either in the end of each sprint or at equal iterations. It is no longer a group of testers who are responsible for quality in Agile. The whole team is responsible for high quality and for ensuring the needs of the customer are being met with high quality and high customer satisfaction levels. Technical excellence and test automation are important proactive ways of ensuring high quality of deliverables.

Communications Management in Agile

Communications management is also important in Agile as well as Waterfall. However, Agile has communication mechanisms built into its cadence – from daily standup and planning sessions between team members to demos to the customers. Immediate, transparent, and honest communication is the key to Agile success. A significant difference from Waterfall communications is stated in the Agile Manifesto. Agile puts less emphasis on detailed documentation and communication in favor of immediate face-to-face communication. Agile advocates for co-locating team members, whenever feasible.

To summarize this chapter, it is as important to manage budgets, risks, vendors, quality, and communication in Agile as in Waterfall. However, the nature of those activities differs – it is built on collaboration, teamwork, value delivery, and continuous improvement.

Key Points

1. The Agile concept of incremental and iterative delivery of value to the customer, internal or external, applies to almost any industry, company, or professional. As a result, Agile and Lean concepts are used in many areas: from executives running their companies to sales, marketing, or human capital organizations, and even in personal life.

2. Agile for HR looks at how Human Resource professionals can apply an Agile mindset and various working methods within their own teams and products, as well as across the whole organization. Agile for HR has the potential to reinvent human capital organizations' operational model and modernize HR as a profession. Any organization can realize the benefits of applying some basic concepts in their everyday work. This includes focus on outcomes vs. processes, focus on the team vs. individuals, and continuous improvement to achieve efficiency and alignment. Agile includes Agile mindset, Agile ways of working, organizational design of Agile (cross-functional teams), and the establishment of psychologically safe organizations via collaboration and team empowerment.

3. The recruiting function needs to look for people with a Lean-Agile mindset – the ones who are customer oriented and team driven, the ones who have had a chance to work in a similar environment. Too often, the hiring process at any level becomes heavily based on referrals and behavioral interviews to reveal the servant/ leader nature of the individual, in addition to job-specific competencies. Within the Agile and Lean framework, a good topic for a behavioral interview is job dynamics and team-level collaboration.

4. There are two fundamental changes in the Lean-Agile approach to employee recognition: First, recognition comes from peers and customers rather than managers. Second, awards are no longer individual and depend on the team's success.

5. In the learning culture, there is no shame for failure – mistakes are seen as a learning opportunity; hence, "fail fast, succeed faster" approach to failure is taken. Some companies even establish "failure walls" where employees share their failures to allow others to learn from their mistakes.

6. Lean-Agile culture requires different thinking about organization hierarchy and the role of management. Managers are no longer assigning work or evaluating performance; rather, their role is to support employee development and growth and provide tools for issue resolution and team-based delivery. In most instances, midlevel managers are "playing coaches" on their teams. This philosophy goes all the way to C-level management.

7. HR is the backbone of the Lean and Agile ecosystem – empowering employees and teams and providing all the underlying functions, from employee hiring development to team enablement and recognition, is the key to a Lean enterprise. This is one of the reasons why the success of Lean-Agile transformation for a modern enterprise is measured by two sets of parameters: The first set is in relation to business objectives and product delivery metrics, such as time to market, quality, and customer satisfaction; the second set is employee driven and is represented as "employee happiness," collaboration within the teams, and employee retention rate.

8. Business Agility demands new ways of organizing businesses – from startups to multithousand-employee corporations. It is imperative for businesses nowadays to be flexible and respond quickly to shifts and changes in the market environment. Agile organizations are able to rapidly change their business processes to satisfy customer needs.

9. Budget, risk, and procurement management apply to the Agile environment as well as the traditional project management. However, these areas in Agile are fundamentally different from the traditional (Waterfall) project management.

10. The major difference between traditional and Agile cost, risk, or procurement management is that in traditional project management, these parameters are fixed while in Agile, any change is welcome.

Scaling Agile Delivery

This chapter covers project management at an organizational level, referred to as Scaled Delivery. It compares project and portfolio management with scaled Agile approaches, including Scaled Agile Framework (SAFe), Large-Scale Scrum (LeSS), and Scrum@Scale. We discuss the complexities of large-scale project delivery, including enterprise-level prioritization, project and product portfolio management, organizational alignment, and related organizational structures, as well as organizational culture and mindset. We also cover the concept of organizational Agile transformation and successful patterns (pilots, change management models, communities of practice), as well as teamwork and innovation at the enterprise level.

In Chapter 9, we covered the topic of delivery beyond software products. We demonstrated that project management covers all areas of work, including marketing and finance, human capital management, the service industry, and beyond. It covers cultural aspects of project management and organizational change management, leadership, and influence without authority. It also addresses traditional management areas, such as budget management ("beyond budgeting" principle), risk management via impediment resolution, and procurement management.

© Mariya Breyter 2022
M. Breyter, *Agile Product and Project Management*,
https://doi.org/10.1007/978-1-4842-8200-7_10

In this chapter, we will describe Agile at scale. So far, we've primarily spoken about Agile mindset and Agile implementation at a team level or in specific organizational functions, such as IT, marketing, HR, Finance, and so on. This final chapter of this book is focused on organizational agility. It covers organizational culture, organizational alignment, dependency management, and the role of leaders in Agile organizations. It also describes primary Agile frameworks, such as Scaled Agile Framework (SAFe), Large-Scale Scrum (LeSS), Disciplined Agile (DA), Nexus, Spotify model, and Scrum@Scale.

What Does Agile at Scale Mean?

Software development teams have proven that implementing Agile frameworks, like Scrum and Kanban, lets them deliver solutions to customers faster, with more predictability and higher quality, and gives them the ability to react quickly based on customer feedback. Implementing Agile at the individual team level is relatively easy, but it is much more challenging to implement Agile across multiple teams in a large organization.

Agile at scale is defined as the ability to drive Agile at the organizational level by creating Agile culture and mindset and applying Agile principles, practices, and outcomes throughout the whole organization. This is extremely important because in large organizations, it is almost impossible to succeed in Agile implementation without scaling agility. Let's review the following example.

Agile Scaling Case Study ("Transformers"). A software delivery team decided to implement Scrum at the team level in their company, a large bank. In their previous organizations, three out of seven members worked on Scrum teams, and they were excited about team empowerment and collaboration with their customers in an Agile environment. They shared their experience with other team members and introduced them to the Agile Manifesto and Scrum Guide. Initially, other team members were skeptical and did not think that team self-organization would work in a large financial services company. However, they decided to be open-minded and try it out. The first thing they did was to get support from their functional managers, who did not mind them trying some Agile practices as long as the team members delivered high-quality software on time and kept them in the loop. They asked for weekly updates and offered help and advice to the team members. This was a helpful first step.

Next, team members selected one of the developers, Anthony, as their part-time Scrum Master. Anthony was excited because he was always curious about the whole end-to-end process of software delivery, was people-oriented, and was interested in customer outcomes. He immediately set up the basic Scrum cadence every two weeks: Sprint planning for two hours on the first day of a Sprint with their stakeholders and customer representatives, daily Scrum meetings for 15 minutes every day, Sprint Review session for an hour at the end of the Sprint, and a Retrospective to finish the Sprint by discussing the opportunities for the team to improve their practices. He also added weekly product backlog refinements sessions for an hour each so that the team focuses on creating a high-quality product backlog with the user stories and technical tasks defined at least one Sprint in advance.

At that point, it was clear to the team that they needed a dedicated Product Owner. They had a business analyst on the team, Anna, whom they asked to become a Product Owner. However, Anna did not feel that she was ready for this role. The Product Owner needs to own the product working with multiple stakeholders, including most senior ones. This person needs to be empowered to make product decisions, work with marketing and sales to promote this product, and realize commercial benefits. Anna suggested during their Scrum meeting to reach out to their business stakeholders to find someone with the right level of experience.

To remove this blocker, Anthony reached out to their internal business stakeholders, and they delegated one of the subject matter experts, Lena, to join the team as the Product Owner. Lena did a great job making herself available to the team members, and they together established a consistent and successful delivery pipeline. They invited stakeholders and their functional managers to the Sprint Review sessions, where they discussed the outcomes of the Sprint and demoed working software that they were able to deliver during the Sprint. The stakeholders provided immediate responses and suggestions, which Lena frequently prioritized for the upcoming Sprint so that when the stakeholders came back in two weeks, they saw that their suggestions and ideas were already implemented. This created a short feedback loop and built a lot of trust with the business.

The team, which selected the team name "Transformers" because they were transforming the way of working and delivering software to their customers, was providing weekly updates about the number of user stories and tasks completed, bugs resolved vs. created, and functionality delivered to their managers. In four Sprints, functional managers said they did not need those reports because they could see all up-to-date information in Jira, the tool that the team selected to manage their work. Without this overhead, the team became even more productive. This did not mean that everything was perfect. Sometimes, they would get a blocker that they did not expect with a new tool, the solution that had to be tweaked based on security review, and other reasons, and miss on their Sprint commitment. They learned not to get upset with it and turn every challenge into an opportunity and to discuss these concerns and inefficiencies in their Retrospective to find ways to do it better next time.

As a side product of this transition, team members were happy and committed. They felt that rather than getting tasks, they were given a direction and the freedom to make their choice in terms of implementation details, sequencing and planning their work, and self-organizing their team delivery. They also felt that there was almost no overhead in the way they managed their work compared to their prior experience of weekly management reports with RAG (red-amber-green) project status and a lot of explanations they had to provide. They worked at a sustainable pace vs. their prior weekend heroics and were motivated by showing their work to the users and hearing their direct appreciation and feedback. Compared to high attrition on other teams within the organization, no team member has left since their Agile adoption started, and on the opposite, multiple people within the company heard about their team and were reaching out to them, indicating that they'd like to join.

However, things were not all smooth and easy. Anthony's team was not alone in the organization. They depended on many other teams for infrastructure, solutions, software integration, data backup, legal and compliance reviews, and so forth. They did not work in a vacuum, and it was becoming more and more apparent to them that other groups do not have the same level of flexibility and customer-centricity as they do. Within a few months, multiple challenges transpired. These three were the most impactful:

1. Management required long-term plans with every activity detailed out, with timelines and deliverables listed up front with their red, amber, or green (RAG) status. The Transformers team's iterative delivery reports listing features delivered and planned for one full quarter ahead were not seen as sufficient or informative, as management struggled with interpreting burndown charts and roadmaps.

2. Legal and compliance departments were hard to engage with less than four-to-eight-week notice, so many features, while they were delivered within a short time frame, were not being released awaiting legal or compliance review. Once reviews were provided, there were frequent changes requested, at which point a set of user stories would go back into the upcoming Sprint, disrupting Sprint structure and challenging incremental delivery.

3. There was a similar pattern with software dependencies on other teams that did not practice Agile delivery. Even though Transformers did their best to decouple features they delivered from a software architecture standpoint, they did not build software in a vacuum. Whenever there were integration requirements, shared data structures, or other consumer services

delivered by their peers, they had to be part of the long-term (over one quarter) planning efforts and engage in multihour planning discussions while committing to deliverables they would have to produce months ahead. Those efforts were rarely fruitful, in their experience, as these plans would change within weeks after planning based on things they learned as they engaged in writing code.

In addition to all these challenges, the attitude toward Transformers within the organization was not that positive. Some of their peers thought they were just trying to stand out and make life more difficult for others around them. Some of the managers were clearly annoyed by their lack of enthusiasm related to advance planning. It was easy to understand – the managers had to plan a year ahead based on the annual budget cycle, so incremental planning was seen by them as an impediment. The Chief Software Architect was taking Transformers' newfound agility almost personally because she saw it as a threat to the Architecture Board that she chaired. The concept of emergent design in an Agile environment challenged the whole existence of this group and all related processes, as she thought. Their organization's CTO used to say that "perception is reality," and the perception was that there is no planning in Agile, no architecture, and no collaboration outside of the team. Everyone felt that Agile was the wrong way for their organization to go, and the Transformers team was restructured with team members individually assigned to different projects.

Agile at scale is seen as the organizational approach to agility, which allows to maximize benefits of Agile delivery and avoid challenges, similar to the one experienced by the Transformers. Scaled Agile implementations changed the whole company culture to support the value of the Agile Manifesto: focus on people, business outcomes, being comfortable with iterative planning and iterative delivery, business and technology working together to delight their customers, prioritizing value delivered over reporting about the work being done, including team-level collaboration between cross-functional teams, and others. This can be achieved in many different ways, which have been summarized in several well-known Agile scaling frameworks. Let's review those frameworks one by one and then compare them based on the type of organization those are most suitable for.

Topic for a Group Discussion   In groups, discuss the challenges that Transformers faced in their company. What could they have done to overcome those challenges? What possible scenarios do you see for the future of this team and the whole organization? Which of those scenarios are most likely?

Summarize your discussion in the following format and order your list by probability from the most probable outcome to the least one:

Scenario ID	Description	Driving Factors	Impact	Probability (%)

The set of most popular Agile scaling frameworks includes the following:

1. Scaled Agile Framework (SAFe)

    SAFe is the world's leading framework for scaling Agile across the enterprise. Used by hundreds of the world's largest organizations, SAFe sustains and drives faster time to market, dramatic increases in productivity and quality, and improvement in employee engagement. SAFe is designed to help businesses continuously and more efficiently deliver value on a regular and predictable schedule. It provides a knowledge base of proven, integrated principles and practices to support enterprise agility [1].

    Dean Leffingwell and Drew Jemilo released SAFe in 2011 to help organizations design better systems and software that meet customers' changing needs in large organizations. Since the need to respond to changing market conditions increased rapidly, new frameworks such as SAFe emerged to help businesses improve solution delivery across their enterprises. SAFe is currently one of the most popular scaled Agile delivery frameworks and continues to evolve. The case studies include American Express, FedEx, Chevron, MetLife, Lockheed Martin, PepsiCo, Bosch, Cisco, Capital One, NHS, Intel, Vantiv, Philips, and many others [2].

2. Large-Scale Scrum (LeSS)

    According to its creator, Craig Larman, Large-Scale Scrum (LeSS) isn't new and improved Scrum. And it's not Scrum at the bottom for each team, and something different layered on top. Rather, it's about figuring out how to apply the principles, purpose, elements, and elegance of Scrum in a large-scale context, as simply as possible. Like Scrum and other truly Agile frameworks, LeSS is a "barely sufficient methodology" for high-impact reasons. This framework is based on the 2002 Craig Larman's book *Agile and Iterative Development* [3].

LeSS was invented in 2005 by Craig Larman and Bas Vodde, who worked with clients to apply their framework for scaling Scrum, Lean, and Agile development to big product groups. Their case studies include JPMorgan Chase, Ericsson, BMW Group, Bank of America Merrill Lynch, Nokia Networks, John Deere, Alcatel-Lucent, and many other large companies in multiple industries across the world [4].

3. Disciplined Agile Delivery (DAD)

DAD enables teams to make simplified process decisions around incremental and iterative solution delivery. DAD builds on the many practices invented by advocates of Agile software development, including Scrum, Agile modeling, Lean software development, and others. DAD evolves the enterprise way of working (WoW) in a context-sensitive manner with this people-first, learning-oriented hybrid Agile approach [5].

The primary reference for Disciplined Agile Delivery is the 2012 book *Disciplined Agile Delivery: A Practitioner's Guide to Agile Software Delivery in the Enterprise* written by Scott Ambler and Mark Lines [6]. In particular, DAD has been identified as a means of moving beyond Scrum. It provides a mechanism that not only streamlines IT work but, more importantly, enables scaling. Since 2012, DAD has been redefined as a "toolkit" to help teams make context-appropriate decisions. This toolkit could be considered a super of all other available frameworks, including Lean, Scrum, Kanban, and even parts of scaled ones, such as LeSS and SAFe. It includes techniques, such as Agile modeling and test-driven development. Some analysts do not even consider it a separate scaled approach, more of a comprehensive set of tools and techniques [14].

4.   Spotify Scaling Model

The Spotify model isn't a framework, as Spotify coach Henrik Kniberg noted since it represents Spotify's view on scaling from both a technical and a cultural perspective. The Spotify model champions team autonomy so that each team (or Squad) selects their framework (e.g., Scrum, Kanban, Scrumban, etc.) This model was made popular by Henrik Kniberg and Anders Ivarsson [9].

The secret to the popularity of this model lies in two primary factors: First, organizational topology is one of the most confusing aspects of scaling Agile, and the concepts of tribes, squads, chapters, and guilds provide a scaled repeatable solution to it. Second, the model preserves an Agile mindset with team self-organization, collaboration across the organization, the bottom-up mindset, and team empowerment. It introduces continuous improvement without constraints, which other, more prescriptive frameworks do not offer.

5.   Nexus

The Nexus model developed by Scrum Alliance is becoming increasingly popular. Nexus is a simple framework that implements Scrum at scale across multiple teams to deliver a single integrated product. It can be applied to three to nine Scrum teams that are working in a common development environment and are focused on producing a combined increment every Sprint with minimal dependencies.

"Nexus promotes value instead of expansion. It is a scaling framework that does not say that much about stakeholders. It guides the Scrum teams on how to prosper and resolve coordination issues."

A cross-functional Scrum team is the prerequisite of Nexus. Possessing knowledge and having worked in a Scrum environment gives you an edge to work with Nexus. It promotes and ensures transparency, continuous integration, and relentless improvement.

"Working in a shared environment where work is constantly being integrated into one final product guarantees continuous integration." This eliminates the need for a Scrum of Scrums meeting, which is an essential part of other scaling frameworks [12].

6.   Scrum@Scale

Scrum@Scale framework developed by Scrum Alliance is a natural extension of the Scrum framework. Its goal is to empower organizations to achieve business agility and deliver value to their customers. It is a framework within which networks of Scrum teams operating consistently with the Scrum Guide can address complex problems while creatively delivering products of the highest possible value. These "products" may be hardware, software, complex integrated systems, processes, services, etc., depending upon the domain of the Scrum teams.

Scrum@Scale enables the transformation of every division, department, and service in any organization and can efficiently coordinate an unlimited number of Scrum teams through its use of a "scale-free" architecture. Scrum@Scale naturally extends the core Scrum framework and was created by Jeff Sutherland, the co-creator of Scrum [15].

The following is a detailed review of each of these frameworks.

Scaled Agile Framework (SAFe)

According to the 14th State of Agile Report by CollabNet [10], the Scaled Agile Framework (SAFe) continues to be the most popular scaling method cited by respondents, increasing 5% over last year and outpacing the number two choice, Scrum@Scale, by 19%.

SAFe provides guidance for all the levels of the enterprise that are actively engaged in solution development: Team, Program, Large Solution, and Portfolio. The result is greater alignment and visibility across the organization, connecting the business strategy to execution, enabling better business results faster and with a higher degree of predictability and quality.

The Scaled Agile Framework (SAFe) is a set of organization and workflow patterns intended to guide enterprises in scaling Lean and Agile practices. SAFe is made freely available by Scaled Agile, Inc., which retains the copyrights and registered trademarks.

SAFe promotes alignment, collaboration, and delivery across large numbers of Agile teams. It was developed by and for practitioners by leveraging three primary bodies of knowledge: Agile software development, Lean product development, and systems thinking.

According to its authors, SAFe is based upon ten underlying concepts, which are derived from existing Lean and Agile principles, as well as observations:

1. Take an economic view.

2. Apply systems thinking.

3. Assume variability; preserve options.

4. Build incrementally with fast integrated learning cycles.

5. Base milestones on an objective evaluation of working systems.

6. Visualize and limit work in progress, reduce batch sizes, and manage queue lengths.

7. Apply cadence (timing); synchronize with cross-domain planning.

8. Unlock the intrinsic motivation of knowledge workers.

9. Decentralize decision-making.

10. Organize around value.

The primary reference for the scaled Agile framework was originally the development of a "big picture" view of how work flowed from product management through governance, program, and development teams, out to customers. With the collaboration of others in the Agile community, SAFe is progressively refined. The framework continues to be developed and shared publicly, with an academy and an accreditation scheme supporting those who seek to implement, support, or train others in the adoption of SAFe. The SAFe framework website features the "big picture" graphic [11]. It provides a visual model of the framework and is the primary user interface to the knowledge base. Each icon of the image is clickable and offers access to extensive SAFe guidance. The configurations support a full range of development and business environments and the foundational principles, values, mindset, roles, artifacts, and implementation elements that make up the SAFe framework.

Starting from its first release in 2011, already five major versions have been released [10]. While SAFe continues to be recognized as the most common approach to scaling Agile practices (at 30% and growing), it also has received criticism for being top-down and implementing enterprise-level governance that limits team self-organization.

Large-Scale Scrum

LeSS consists of the LeSS Principles, the Framework, the Guides, and a set of experiments. All of these are also available on the following website: http://less.works. LeSS is different from other scaling frameworks in the sense that it provides a very minimalistic framework that enables empiricism on a large scale, which enables the teams and organizations to inspect-adapt their implementation based on their experiences and context. LeSS is based on the idea that providing many rules, roles, and artifacts and asking the organization to tailor it down is a fundamentally flawed approach, and instead, scaling frameworks should be minimalistic and allow organizations to fill them in.

LeSS defines ten principles for applying the value, elements, and overall purpose of Scrum across an enterprise. They help create more responsible teams with greater customer focus and collaboration. Teams focus on learning, transparency, and delivering customer-centric values that product organizations need to remain competitive and responsive. Here's the complete list:

- Large-Scale Scrum is Scrum
- Empirical process control
- Transparency
- More with less
- Whole product focus
- Customer-centric
- Continuous improvement toward perfection
- Systems thinking
- Lean thinking
- Queuing theory

LeSS offers two configurations: Basic LeSS for two to eight teams (10–50 people) and LeSS Huge for more than eight teams (50–6000+ people).

LeSS Huge starts with the Basic LeSS foundation in place and adds a key role – the Area Product Owner (APO) – and additional artifacts and meeting changes. It's recommended to start with Basic LeSS in an organization – to experiment, experience, and get feedback – before jumping straight into LeSS Huge. There are two suggested approaches to LeSS Huge adoption:

1. One requirement area at a time focused on a requirement area within the larger product

2. Gradually expanding the scope of work of the team, Definition of Done, and the product definition

This allows an organization to build team experience with LeSS, expand throughout a product area, and gain management support before scaling LeSS throughout the whole organization [12].

Basic LeSS focuses on the team and the key Scrum roles: the Scrum product owner who is responsible for the product vision and direction, Scrum development teams who are responsible for product creation and delivery, and Scrum Master who helps the team with continuous improvement and coaching. One area that LeSS expands upon is the role of the manager and how they assist the team with removing barriers for continuous improvement and autonomy.

The Area Product Owner of LeSS Huge assists and coordinates with the overall Product Owner and is critical to bridging the business needs with the technical team. The Area Product Owner does the same work as the Product Owner, but with a more focused and limited scope for the team they support. The Area Product Owner specializes in customer-focused tasks and acts as Product Owner for product-focused feature teams.

Disciplined Agile Delivery (DAD)

According to the Project Management Institute, "Disciplined Agile Delivery (DAD) is a people-first, learning-oriented hybrid Agile approach to IT solution delivery. It has a risk-value delivery life cycle, is goal-driven, is enterprise aware, and is scalable. Its features include the following:

1. **DAD picks up where Scrum leaves off**. DAD describes how all Agile techniques fit together, going far beyond Scrum, to define a full Agile solution delivery life cycle. Like Scrum, the DAD addresses leadership, roles & responsibilities, and requirements change management. Unlike Scrum, DAD doesn't stop there; it also addresses other important aspects of software development such as architecture, design, testing, programming, documentation, deployment, and many more. In short, DAD provides a much broader understanding of how Agile development works in practice, doing a lot of the "heavy process lifting."

2. **DAD is pragmatic**. The DA toolkit provides choices, not prescriptions, enabling teams to easily tailor a strategy that reflects the situation. To do this effectively, teams need to understand the process-oriented choices they have and what the trade-offs are. DAD makes these choices explicit through its process-goal-driven approach.

3. **DAD supports both Lean and Agile ways of working (WoW)**. DAD supports several delivery life cycles including a Scrum-based Agile life cycle, a Kanban-based Lean life cycle, two continuous delivery life cycles, a Lean Startup-based exploratory life cycle, and a Program "team of teams" life cycle. Teams find themselves in unique situations, and as a result, one process size does not fit all. Even in small companies, some teams are taking an Agile approach, some a Lean approach, and some combinations thereof.

4. **DAD is based on empiricism**. For several years Scott Ambler, Mark Lines, and many other contributors to DAD worked in or visited hundreds of enterprises around the world in a wide range of industries and environments. DAD, and the DA toolkit in general, captures the proven strategies adopted by these organizations, describing the strengths and weaknesses of each strategy, and providing guidance for when and when not to apply them.

5. **DAD provides a solid foundation from which to scale Agile**. DAD supports the successful scaling of Agile and Lean techniques in several ways. First, its full delivery lifecycles and breadth of software development advice answers how to successfully apply Agile in practice. Second, its goal-driven approach provides the required flexibility for tailoring your Agile process to meet the challenges faced by Agile teams working at scale. Third, DAD builds in many foundational concepts required at scale, including DevOps, explicit Agile governance, and enterprise awareness.

6. **DAD describes strategies for organizing large and distributed teams**. DAD describes several strategies for organizing large or geographically distributed teams. It describes a range of options for scaling the approach to Agile and Lean software development.

7. **DAD teams deliver solutions, not just software**. DAD recognizes that the software we develop runs on hardware, which may need upgrades, and is supported by documentation. The stakeholders may also need to evolve their business processes, and sometimes even their organizational structures, to address the new needs of the situation that they face. DAD teams deliver

solutions that comprise software, hardware changes, supporting documentation, improved business processes, and even organizational changes.

8. **DAD is evolving**. DAD practitioners are continuously learning about and experimenting with new Agile and Lean strategies. These learnings are constantly being applied to evolve DAD" [7].

DAD promotes the "Shu-ha-ri" Agile learning strategy originating from martial arts and starting by building a strong foundation (Shu – learn). As people's knowledge deepens, they progress to a stage where they can demonstrate a deeper understanding of the range of strategies available to them (Ha – reflect). Finally, once they've achieved a proficiency (Ri – transcend) in disciplined Agile, they can extend and improve upon disciplined Agile techniques by sharing their earnings with others.

Disciplined Agile Delivery (DAD) is a people-first, learning-oriented hybrid Agile approach to IT solution delivery. It has a risk-value delivery life cycle, is goal-driven, is enterprise aware, and is scalable. DAD benefits include the following:

- **"Discover A Goal-Driven Approach to process-related Decisions**

  Disciplined Agile teams are guided through choosing their way of working (WoW) via straightforward process goal diagrams. Better process decisions lead to better outcomes. Because each Agile team is unique, the DA toolkit helps organizations find a way to effectively tailor the way that they work to best face that situation.

- **Adapt for Each Situation: Guided Continuous Improvement (GCI)**

  By understanding that every practice has trade-offs and works well in some situations and poorly in others, the DA toolkit helps organizations identify the right process for the moment at hand.

- **Unlock the Capacity to Scale Agility as an Enterprise**

  A Disciplined Agile Enterprise (DAE) can sense and respond swiftly to changes in the marketplace with organizational culture and structure that facilitates change within the context of the situation that it faces" [8].

Spotify Scaling Model

The model, described previously in Chapter 6, is called by the company's name (Spotify), where Agile coach Henrik Kniberg and his colleagues came up with several groundbreaking ideas [9]. They were very clear in stating that they did not invent this model. Spotify, like any other company, was evolving fast, and this article provided a snapshot of their current way of working. This model allowed Spotify to become a fascinating company that transformed the music industry. In its first six years, the company generated 15 million active users and over 4 million playings. They referred to this product as a "magical music player in which you can instantly find and play every song in the world." When Alistair Cockburn, one of the signatories of the Agile Manifesto, visited Spotify, he's reported to say: "Nice – I've been looking for someone to implement this matrix format since 1992 :) so it is really welcome to see" [9, p. 1]. So what was this model that allowed Spotify to grow exponentially while disrupting the global music industry?

Spotify matrix organizational model included four structures shown in Figure 10-1:

1. **Squad:** A squad is similar to a Scrum team and is designed to feel like a mini-startup. They are a cross-functional team; that is, they have all the required skills to design, develop, test, integrate, deploy, and release to production. Similar to Scrum, they are a self-organizing team. At Spotify, it was not prescribed whether a squad should use Scrum, Kanban, or any other framework; this was up to the team members to decide. Each squad includes a Product Owner who makes prioritization decisions and serves as the voice of the customer and an Agile Coach who helps them identify impediments and coaches them to continuously improve their processes.

2. **Tribe:** A tribe is a collection of squads that work in related areas, such as the music player or back-end infrastructure. The tribe is seen as the "incubator" for the squad mini-startups. Tribes have a large degree of freedom and autonomy. Each tribe has a tribe lead who is responsible for providing the environment for the squads within the tribe so that the collaboration is successful and all squad-level dependencies are coordinated. Tribes are sized based on the concept of the "Dunbar number," which says that most people cannot maintain a social relationship with more than 100 people or so. When groups get too big, there are more bureaucracy, constraints, and management overhead – everything that is referred to as "waste" in Lean.

3. **Chapters:** Chapters and Guilds are created to avoid the loss of "economies of scale." This includes two categories: reusability when several squads need the same tool or build similar functionality (e.g., a payment system for all Spotify products) and best practices sharing between professional groups, for example, test automation or new programming languages and technology stacks. This challenge is resolved by having Chapters and Guilds, which serve as a glue of keeping the company together. A Chapter is a group of people having similar skills and working within the same general competency area who meet regularly to discuss their area of expertise and their specific challenges, for example, the testing chapter, web developers, or the back-end chapter. The chapter lead is the line manager for their chapter members, who are responsible for professional development, compensation, and promotions.

4. **Guilds:** A guild is a more organic and wide-reaching community of interest, a group of people that want to share knowledge, tools, code, and practices across the whole organization, for example, an Agile Coach guild. This allows for company-wide cross-pollination in building the best practices between different tribes.

In sum, squads and tribes provide autonomy, while chapters and guilds provide economies of scale. The Spotify model is shown in Figure 10-1.

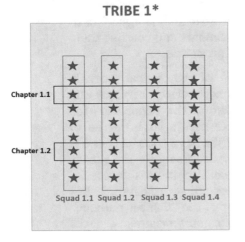

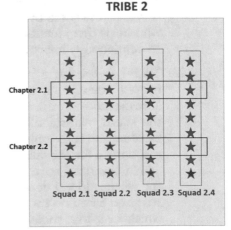

* Legend: ★   - employee (red color shows employees belonging to one guild, e.g. DevOps Guild)

Figure 10-1. Spotify Scaling Model

Many analysts, including the creators of this model, do not consider Spotify an Agile scaling model. Spotify implemented a scalable matrix organizational structure well suited for Agile companies; however, this does not cover the "ways of working," which are described in the "Spotify Engineering Culture" videos reviewed in Chapter 9. Together, this would create a framework; however, it was never described comprehensively and has not been positioned as one. This was not the intent of Henrik Kniberg and his colleagues, who wanted to share Spotify's best practices rather than building a prescriptive model. They made it very clear that while this is the way Spotify worked at the time this was shared, it was relevant to a specific company at a specific point in time, and others should use it as an inspiration for building an Agile mindset and Agile culture, rather than a prescriptive framework.

Nexus

The Nexus Agile scaling model created by Scrum Alliance is designed for a combination of three to nine Scrum development teams working off a single product backlog used by all of the teams, and it builds on the foundations of Scrum. The core of the Nexus framework is the integration team that consists of a Product Owner, a Scrum Master, and one or more members from each team. The purpose of the integration team is to coordinate the work of all the Scrum teams to be sure their completed work intermeshes together and is in harmony and not in conflict. The need for an integration team becomes even more essential the larger the number of Scrum teams all working on the same project using the same product backlog. The stated goal of Nexus is to minimize cross-term dependencies and integration issues [17].

Nexus is a framework for developing and sustaining scaled product delivery initiatives. It builds upon Scrum, extending it only where absolutely necessary to minimize and manage dependencies between multiple Scrum teams while promoting empiricism and the Scrum values.

The Nexus framework inherits the purpose and intent of the Scrum framework as documented in the Scrum Guide (www.Scrumguides.org). Scaled Scrum is still Scrum. Nexus does not change the core design or ideas of Scrum, leave out elements, or negate the rules of Scrum.

Nexus adds to or extends the events and artifacts defined by Scrum. The duration of Nexus events is guided by the length of the corresponding events in the Scrum Guide. They are timeboxed in addition to their corresponding Scrum events. Nexus events are attended by whichever members of the Nexus are needed to achieve the intended outcome of the event most effectively. A Sprint in Nexus is the same as in Scrum. The Scrum teams in a Nexus produce a single Integrated Increment.

In addition to Sprints, Nexus adds an ongoing Cross-Team Refinement. Cross-Team Refinement of the product backlog reduces or eliminates cross-team dependencies within a Nexus. The product backlog must be decomposed so that dependencies are transparent, identified across teams, and removed or minimized. Product backlog items pass through different levels of decomposition from very large and vague requests to actionable work that a single Scrum team could deliver inside a Sprint. Cross-Team Refinement of the product backlog at scale serves a dual purpose:

- It helps the Scrum teams forecast which team will deliver which product backlog items.
- It identifies dependencies across those teams.

Where needed, each Scrum team will continue their own refinement in order for the product backlog items to be ready for selection in a Nexus Sprint Planning event. An adequately refined product backlog will minimize the emergence of new dependencies during Nexus Sprint Planning.

The purpose of Nexus Sprint Planning is to coordinate the activities of all Scrum teams within a Nexus for a single Sprint. Appropriate representatives from each Scrum team and the Product Owner meet to plan the Sprint. Nexus retains the Daily Scrum to identify any integration issues and inspect progress toward the Nexus Sprint Goal. Appropriate representatives from the Scrum teams attend the Nexus Daily Scrum, inspect the current state of the integrated Increment, and identify integration issues and newly discovered cross-team dependencies or impacts. Each Scrum team's Daily Scrum complements the Nexus Daily Scrum by creating plans for the day, focused primarily on addressing the integration issues raised during the Nexus Daily Scrum.

The Nexus Sprint Review is held at the end of the Sprint to provide feedback on the done Integrated Increment that the Nexus has built over the Sprint and determine future adaptations.

Since the entire Integrated Increment is the focus for capturing feedback from stakeholders, a Nexus Sprint Review replaces individual Scrum team Sprint Reviews. Nexus Sprint Retrospective is held to plan ways to increase quality and effectiveness across the whole Nexus. The Nexus inspects how the last Sprint went with regard to individuals, teams, interactions, processes, tools, and its Definition of Done. In addition to individual team improvements, the Scrum teams' Sprint Retrospectives complement the Nexus Sprint Retrospective by using bottom-up intelligence to focus on issues that affect the Nexus as a whole. The Nexus Sprint Retrospective concludes the Sprint [18].

Scrum@Scale

Scrum, as originally outlined in the Scrum Guide, is a framework for developing, delivering, and sustaining complex products by a single team. Since its inception, its usage has extended to the creation of products, processes, services, and systems that require the efforts of multiple teams. Scrum@Scale was created to efficiently coordinate this new ecosystem of teams. It achieves this goal by setting up a "minimum viable bureaucracy" via a "scale-free" architecture. Dr. Jeff Sutherland, co-creator of Scrum, developed Scrum@Scale based on the fundamental principles of Scrum, Complex Adaptive Systems theory, game theory, and object-oriented technology.

Scrum@Scale is described in the Scrum@Scale Guide [15]. According to the Guide, "Scrum, as originally outlined in the Scrum Guide, is focused on a single Scrum Team being able to deliver optimal value while maintaining a sustainable pace. Since its inception, the usage of Scrum has extended to the creation of products, processes, and services that require the efforts of multiple teams. In the field, it was repeatedly observed that as the number of Scrum Teams within an organization grew, two major issues emerged:

The volume, speed, and quality of their output (working product) per team began to fall, due to issues such as cross-team dependencies, duplication of work, and communication overhead

The original management structure was ineffective for achieving business agility. Issues arose like competing priorities and the inability to quickly shift teams around to respond to dynamic market conditions

To counteract these issues, a framework for effectively coordinating multiple Scrum Teams was clearly needed, which would aim for the following:

- Linear scalability: A corresponding percentage increase in delivery of working product with an increase in the number of teams

- Business agility: The ability to rapidly respond to change by adapting the initial stable configuration

Scrum@Scale helps an organization to focus multiple networks of Scrum Teams on prioritized goals. It aims to achieve this by setting up a structure which naturally extends the way a single Scrum Team functions across a network and whose managerial function exists within a minimum viable bureaucracy (MVB)" [15].

Scrum@Scale introduces two cycles, Scrum Master Cycle and the Product Owner Cycle, and brings them together to establish successful delivery of value. It is a lightweight organizational framework based on a network of teams. This framework addressed the complex adaptive problems of a large organization while creatively delivering products of high value to the customer. These products could be physical, digital, complex integrated systems, processes, services, and any others.

According to Agile Alliance, Scrum@Scale has been successfully implemented at implementing these concepts at GE, 3M, Toyota, Spotify, Maersk, Comcast, AT&T, and many other companies [16].

Other Frameworks

There are multiple other Agile proprietary frameworks, such as Crystal Clear, cPrime's Solutions for Agile Governance in the Enterprise (SAGE^SM) [13], Agile Portfolio Management (APM), Enterprise Scrum, Lean Management, and others. Each of them is adopted by 4% or less of all companies scaling Agile.

Comparison of Scaled Agile Frameworks

In the 14th State of Agile Report, the following statistics are provided for Agile scaling methods and approaches: "The Scaled Agile Framework® continues to be the most popular scaling method cited by respondents (35% this year compared to 30% last year). As a percentage of all responses, SAFe® outdistances the next nearest response, Scrum of Scrums, by 19%" [10, page 14].

The details are provided in Figure 10-2.

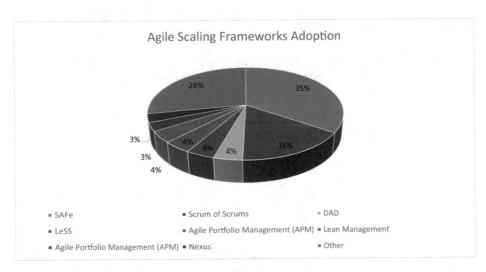

Figure 10-2. Agile scaling frameworks, methods, and approaches according to the 14th State of Agile Report [10]

The primary challenges experienced with Agile scaling include the following:

- General organizational resistance to change
- Not enough leadership participation
- Inconsistent processes and practices across teams
- Organizational culture at odds with Agile values
- Inadequate management support and sponsorship
- Lack of skills and experience with Agile methods
- Insufficient training and education
- Lack of business/customer/Product Owner availability
- The pervasiveness of traditional development methods
- Fragmented tooling and project-related data/ measurements
- Minimal collaboration and knowledge sharing
- Regulatory compliance or government issues

The following table provides a comparative overview of Agile scaling frameworks:

Table 10-1. Comparative Overview of Agile Scaling Frameworks

	Type and size of the organization	Methods and practices adopted	Specifies portfolio management and business prioritization	Establishes a collaborative dependency management mechanism	Professional association that endorsed the framework
Scaled Agile Framework (SAFe)	50–124 people in an Agile Release Train, scaling indefinitely	Scrum, Kanban, Lean, DevOps, XP Practices	In detail: Lean portfolio management and business prioritization based on Value Stream Mapping (VSM)	Advanced dependency management starting with long-term planning	Scaled Agile Academy
Large-Scale Scrum (LeSS)	LeSS Huge allowed for thousands of people	Scrum primarily	By scaling product management	Via structured ongoing collaboration	LeSS practitioner groups

(continued)

Table 10-1. *(continued)*

	Type and size of the organization	Methods and practices adopted	Specifies portfolio management and business prioritization	Establishes a collaborative dependency management mechanism	Professional association that endorsed the framework
Disciplined Agile Delivery (DAD)	200 people or more	Full toolbox: Scrum, Agile modeling, Unified Process, XP, TDD, Agile	Focuses on technical practices	Via collaboration	Project Management Institute
Spotify Scaling Model	Around 300 people	Allows the team to make a choice of any Agile framework	Via Tribe-specific accountability and the role of product management	Organic	N/A
Scrum@Scale	No limitations imposed; however, successes are limited to several hundred	Scrum	Product Owner collaboration	Via Scrum of Scrums	Agile Alliance
Nexus	Three to nine Scrum teams	Scrum	Product Owner collaboration	Advanced dependency management via an Integration Team	Scrum Alliance

 Five key questions to review:

1. What are the most popular Agile scaling frameworks?

2. Which framework resonates with you and why?

3. Why do you think SAFe is the most popular Agile scaling framework at this time?

4. What is the benefit of using an Agile scaling framework vs. implementing Scrum or Kanban?

5. Which Agile scaling framework is best suited for a medium-size company with ten Agile teams? For a large company with 100+ employees and multiple product lines?

"Scaling Agile is a cultural transformation, where the business' people, practices, and tools are committed to improving collaboration and the organization's ability to execute against its strategy.

Ultimately, changes across these areas will help decentralize decision-making, create greater transparency and alignment around work, and increase speed to market, all while hard coding the values of Agile into the DNA of the organization."

— Atlassian Agile Coaching blog [19]

Organizational-Level Agile Transformation

No matter which Agile scaling strategy is being used, there are some principles that need to be always maintained. Those include the following:

1. Implement organizational-level Agile transformation as a **change management** activity, in accordance with John Kotter's organizational change principles [20]:

    ✓ Create a sense of urgency

    ✓ Build a guiding coalition

    ✓ Form a strategic vision and initiatives

    ✓ Enlist a volunteer army

    ✓ Enable action by removing barriers

    ✓ Generate short-term wins

    ✓ Sustain acceleration

    ✓ Institute change

2. Start by defining clear drivers for change and measurements of success with the organizational leadership. Agree to the Agile scaling roadmap, and define timelines and expected outcomes. OKR framework is a helpful mechanism in defining success.

3. Get people within the organization excited about scaling Agile. Explain the value of self-organization and cross-functional teams. Share experiences from other companies of similar size in their Agile transformation at scale and set up Scaled Agile training for the model of your choice that fits the organization best.

4. Start initiatives that address major pain points. This is easy to do with a value stream. Show the business impact of scaling agility is faster incremental delivery, business and technology collaboration, team ownership, and positive outcomes.

5. Show success of these initiatives. Be vocal and communicate on multiple levels. Create internal case studies. Launch metrics and make progress at scale transparent to everyone. Celebrate successes and build Champions groups and communities of practice, which organically support the scaling efforts.

6. Sustain acceleration via expanding scaled Agile practices throughout the organization, with the help of the Champions team. Ensure there is a well-defined career path and career progression for all Agile roles (Scrum Master, Product Owner, any other new role, such as Agile Product Manager or Agile Coach) and define the learning path for people in these roles.

7. Enhance and continuously improve Agile scaling culture and practices via Retrospectives, a short feedback loop with your customers, metrics review with Agile organizations, continuous contact with the leadership, and an Agile mindset.

Topic for a Group Discussion   Based on what you know, which Agile scaling framework would the Transformers team from the case study in this chapter use most effectively and how would their Agile scaling roadmap look like?

To summarize this chapter, Agile is mostly impactful at scale, that is, in large organizations. However, special mechanisms are required to build and sustain Agile implementation at scale, such as dependency management between teams, consistent prioritization mechanisms, alignment of value streams and Agile delivery teams, and many others. Agile scaling frameworks discussed in this chapter provide different ways of accomplishing this goal while maintaining team-level agility.

Key Points

1. Agile at scale is defined as the ability to drive Agile at the organizational level by creating Agile culture and mindset and applying Agile principles, practices, and outcomes throughout the whole organization.

2. Agile at scale is seen as the organizational approach to agility, which allows to maximize benefits of Agile delivery and avoid challenges, similar to the one experienced by the Transformers. Scaled Agile implementations change the whole company culture to support the value of Agile Manifesto: focus on people, business outcomes, being comfortable with iterative planning and iterative delivery, and business and technology working together to delight their customers. This also includes prioritizing value delivered over reporting about the work being done, team-level collaboration with cross-functional teams, and others. This can be achieved in many different ways, which have been summarized in several well-known Agile scaling frameworks.

3. SAFe is the leading framework for scaling Agile across the enterprise. Used by hundreds of the world's largest organizations, SAFe sustains and drives faster time to market, dramatic increases in productivity and quality, and improvement in employee engagement. SAFe is designed to help businesses continuously and more efficiently deliver value on a regular and predictable schedule. It provides a knowledge base of proven, integrated principles and practices to support enterprise agility

4. According to its creator, Craig Larman, Large-Scale Scrum (LeSS) is about figuring out how to apply the principles, purpose, elements, and elegance of Scrum in a large-scale context, as simply as possible. Like Scrum and other truly Agile frameworks, LeSS is a "barely sufficient methodology" for high-impact reasons and provides a toolbox for scaling Agile delivery.

5. Disciplined Agile Delivery (DAD) enables teams to make simplified process decisions around incremental and iterative solution delivery. DAD builds on the many practices espoused by advocates of Agile software development, including Scrum, Agile modeling, Lean software development, and others. DAD allows to evolve the enterprise way of working (WoW) in a context-sensitive manner with this people-first, learning-oriented hybrid Agile approach.

6. The Spotify Scaling Model was not invented by Spotify and was never defined as a model; however, Spotify built practices that allowed for rapid scaling based on value delivery. This model is being implemented by many organizations of different sizes, based on the organizational matrix of squads and tribes that allow scaling Agile delivery while maintaining autonomy. In the Spotify model, squads and tribes provide autonomy, while chapters and guilds provide economies of scale.

7. The Nexus Agile scaling model created by Scrum Alliance is designed for a combination of three to nine Scrum development teams working off a single product backlog used by all of the teams, and it builds on the foundations of Scrum. The core of the Nexus framework is the integration team that consists of a Product Owner, a Scrum Master, and one or more members from each team. The purpose of the integration team is to coordinate the work of all the Scrum teams to be sure their completed work intermeshes together and is in harmony and not in conflict. The need for an integration team becomes even more essential the larger the number of Scrum teams all working on the same project using the same product backlog. The stated goal of Nexus is to minimize cross-term dependencies and integration issues.

8. Scrum@Scale was created to efficiently coordinate this new ecosystem of teams. It achieves this goal by setting up a "minimum viable bureaucracy" via a "scale-free" architecture. Dr. Jeff Sutherland, co-creator of Scrum, developed Scrum@Scale based on the fundamental principles of Scrum, Complex Adaptive Systems theory, game theory, and object-oriented technology.

9. In the 14th State of Agile Report, the following statistics are provided for Agile scaling methods and approaches: "The Scaled Agile Framework® continues to be the most popular scaling method cited by respondents (35% this year compared to 30% last year). As a percentage of all responses, SAFe® outdistances the next nearest response, Scrum of Scrums, by 19%."

10. No matter which Agile scaling strategy is being used, there are some principles that need to be always maintained. These include leadership buy-in, defining metrics and success criteria up front, continuous improvement via organizational-level Retrospectives, and focus on dependency management and Agile culture.

Final Project, Agile Career Progression, and Interview Tips

The Goal

The goal of the final project is to give a chance to the students and the teams they are part of to present the project they have been working on throughout this course in a cohesive and informative way. Students work on this project starting from their first class. The project is a simulation of an Agile product delivery in a compressed way. In the first class, students split into groups of five to nine team members and come up with an idea of a product or service. It does not have to be an original idea but it has to have a deliverable with clear success criteria defined. In my teaching experience, students came up with ideas of wearable software, shopping and learning apps, party planning

© Mariya Breyter 2022
M. Breyter, *Agile Product and Project Management*,
https://doi.org/10.1007/978-1-4842-8200-7_11

business, international job fair, and many others. The goal of the project is to supplement teaching materials lesson by lesson: product concept, OKRs, product vision, customer research and prototyping, backlog creation, estimation and planning, risk analysis, budget and vendor management, and, finally, the product pitch that combines all this information. If you are not in a classroom, work on this project yourself or with your friends. In either case, this project can be used as an Agile experience on your resume, especially if it ends up as a successful business. The goal is to simulate (or to live through) the Agile experience end-to-end until delivery (which can be actual or just a plan). The topics to cover in the final pitch include the following:

1. The product/idea that the team has chosen.

2. Market research is done to validate the idea and any pivots done along the way.

3. Product vision, its customers, competition and differentiating factors, go-to-market strategy (done in an incremental way).

4. Any prototypes (optional).

5. Which framework was selected and why? What are the expected benefits?

6. Product backlog description and samples of user stories.

7. Planning: Release plan, high-level Sprint planning, estimation techniques used.

8. Risk analysis and mitigation techniques.

9. Product pricing strategy. Basic budget analysis.

10. Product pitch (summary).

The Format

The format for the final pitch in a classroom (physical or virtual) is usually a presentation. The project is presented as an artifact in a ten-minute presentation to the instructor, peers, and any relevant invitees, such as students in other courses interested in the topic or relevant faculty. There are two steps in this process:

1. Presentation artifact: The default format is a slide deck (10–15 slides maximum, with unlimited appendices); however, any other format is allowed.

2. Verbal presentation by each team of three to seven team members working together on this project incrementally during the course. The length of the presentation is ten minutes, followed by a five-minute Q&A from an instructor and the participants.

Appendices are expected to contain details related to the project, such as the product backlog, release plan, cost-benefit analysis, risk log, budget registry, pricing document, and any other relevant information. A sample product backlog appendix format is provided below:

Story Number	Story Name	Details	Acceptance Criteria	Story Type (User Story, Task, Spike)	Release	Story Points	Epic	Status	MoSCcoW
				Sprint 1					
				Sprint 2					

The Grading Rubric

There are two grades assigned to each student for the final project:

Individual score based on this student's contribution to the team project, their presentation skills, coverage and understanding of Agile product and project management, and their contribution to the Q&A session at the end of the team's presentation

Team score (which is the same for all members of each team) based on the overall cohesiveness, content, and presentation of the team project, team members' understanding of Agile product and project management, and the Q&A session at the end of the team's presentation

ASSESSMENT SCORING SHEET & RUBRIC

Name	Team	Timing/Story (1-5)	Style (non-verbal) (1-5)	Style (verbal) (1-5)	Content (1-5)	Presentation (1-5)	Agile Concepts Team (1-5)	Agile Concepts Individual (1-5)

The individual grade is based on the overall content, understanding of the material, creativity, logic, and thoughtfulness of the presentation, style (verbal and nonverbal), and the timebox. Each of these is rated on a scale of 1–5. The coverage of Agile concepts is graded separately with a score of 1–5 and contributes to 50% of the overall student's grade.

The team grade is based on how seamlessly each individual's presentation and content combine to create an effective overall description of an Agile delivery process and the product the team is presenting. The coverage of Agile concepts is graded separately with a score of 1–5 and contributes to 50% of the overall team grade.

This is a proposed rubric; however, each instructor should target it to their higher institution's standards, templates, expectations, and grading techniques.

Agile Roles

There are a number of roles for Agile professionals at all levels. They are specific to the level of experience, type of responsibilities, and subject matter areas. There is no standard approach, but for each company, it is important to define titles and roles for Agile professionals in a consistent way and set up related expectations. It is also important to have the interview process, job descriptions, and hiring decisions aligned based on the Agile titles' nomenclature.

There are two primary tracks: Agile project and product management. The structure and organizational hierarchy are presented in the following comprehensive table:

	Project		Product		Number of years of experience in this role
	Scrum	Agile	Scrum/Agile	Traditional	
Entry Level	Jr Scrum Master	Jr Agile Project Manager	Jr Product Owner	Business Analyst, Product Management Apprentice	1-3
Experienced Level	Scrum Master	Agile Project Manager	Product Owner	Product Manager	4-6
Senior Level	Sr Scrum Master/Lead Scrum Master/Agile Coach	Sr Agile Project Manager, Agile Program Manager	Sr Product Owner	Sr Product Manager	7-10
Executive Level	Head of Agile Delivery (Director or VP-level)		Chief Product Owner	Principal Product Manager/Chief Product Manager	10+
Consulting Level	Enterprise Agile Coach/Agile Trainer		Product Management Consultant		10+

The titles presented in this table differ for each organization. Standards are still being established. This is one of the reasons why you need a comprehensive job description while making your choice of which Agile position to apply for. Many companies do not distinguish between the level of experience and seniority for Scrum Masters, so this role can be quite junior or fairly senior for different employers. Job description, including the number of required years of experience, is a good indication of the seniority of the role. In some companies, additional mechanisms are used to convey this information, such as levels (e.g., Scrum Master I, Scrum Master II, Scrum Master III).

What are the standard expectations for a Scrum Master? According to the Scrum Guide:

"The Scrum Master is accountable for establishing Scrum as defined in the Scrum Guide. They do this by helping everyone understand Scrum theory and practice, both within the Scrum Team and the organization.

The Scrum Master is accountable for the Scrum Team's effectiveness. They do this by enabling the Scrum Team to improve its practices within the Scrum framework.

Scrum Masters are true leaders who serve the Scrum Team and the larger organization.

The Scrum Master serves the Scrum Team in several ways, including:

- Coaching the team members in self-management and cross-functionality;

- Helping the Scrum Team focus on creating high-value Increments that meet the Definition of Done;

- Causing the removal of impediments to the Scrum Team's progress; and,

- Ensuring that all Scrum events take place and are positive, productive, and kept within the timebox.

The Scrum Master serves the Product Owner in several ways, including:

- Helping find techniques for effective Product Goal definition and Product Backlog management;

- Helping the Scrum Team understand the need for clear and concise Product Backlog items;

- Helping establish empirical product planning for a complex environment; and,

- Facilitating stakeholder collaboration as requested or needed.

The Scrum Master serves the organization in several ways, including:

- Leading, training, and coaching the organization in its Scrum adoption;

- Planning and advising Scrum implementations within the organization;

- Helping employees and stakeholders understand and enact an empirical approach for complex work; and,

- Removing barriers between stakeholders and Scrum Teams."

(Source: Scrum Guide 2020 https://Scrumguides.org/docs/Scrumguide/v2020/2020-Scrum-Guide-US.pdf)

The number of concurrent teams differs by Scrum Master and depends on their experience. Usually, it varies between two and three. If a Scrum Master is responsible for more than three teams, they start acting in an Agile Coach capacity.

Sample Scrum Master Job Description

<Company> is looking for an experienced Scrum Master with 3–5 years of experience on globally distributed Scrum teams, who will support one to two teams in building software products that delight our customers. Excellent knowledge of the Scrum framework and Agile mindset is required, as well as the ability to facilitate change and support the team in producing meaningful outcomes. Strong communication and leadership skills are a must.

Responsibilities include the following:

- Lead the Scrum team in using Agile methodology and Scrum practices

- Help the Product Owner and development team to achieve customer satisfaction

- Lead the Scrum and development teams in self-organization

- Remove impediments and coach the Scrum team on removing impediments

- Help the Scrum and development teams to identify and fill in blanks in the Agile framework

- Resolve conflicts and issues that occur

- Help the Scrum team achieve higher levels of Scrum maturity

- Support the product owner and provide education where needed

Qualifications:

- Prior experience on a Scrum team as a Scrum Master (3–5 years)

- Ability to analyze and think quickly and to resolve conflict

- Knowledgeable in techniques to fill in gaps in the Scrum

- Ability to determine what is Scrum and what is not

- Experience with successful Agile techniques

- Ability to work with and lead a team

- Strong communication, interpersonal, and mentoring skills

- Ability to adapt to a changing environment

- Self-motivation and the ability to stay focused in the middle of distraction

Source: Glassdoor. www.glassdoor.com/Job-Descriptions/
Scrum-Master.htm

The goal of an Agile Coach is to teach the team "how to fish" rather than fish for them. This person leads by asking questions, challenging the performance to be better, and delivering a high-quality product with better outcomes. Usually, Agile Coaches have significant Agile/Scrum experience and a good understanding of trends and patterns in Agile adoption.

Agile Project Managers may be required to perform some traditional project management functions, such as budget management, dependency coordination, management reporting, and others. Many of them also act as Scrum Masters or Agile Coaches.

Agile Program Managers are usually responsible for a larger program, usually spanning dozens of teams and hundreds of people.

The **Product track** is significantly different. It focuses on "what" instead of "how" and is responsible for the prioritization of requirements, alignment with business needs, and stakeholder communications. At the end of the day, the Product Owner is responsible for product success. The following is the Scrum Guide definition of the Product Owner role:

"The Product Owner is accountable for maximizing the value of the product resulting from the work of the Scrum Team. How this is done may vary widely across organizations, Scrum Teams, and individuals.

The Product Owner is also accountable for effective Product Backlog management, which includes:

- Developing and explicitly communicating the Product Goal;
- Creating and clearly communicating Product Backlog items;
- Ordering Product Backlog items; and,
- Ensuring that the Product Backlog is transparent, visible, and understood.

The Product Owner may do the above work or may delegate the responsibility to others. Regardless, the Product Owner remains accountable.

For Product Owners to succeed, the entire organization must respect their decisions. These decisions are visible in the content and ordering of the Product Backlog and through the inspectable Increment at the Sprint Review.

The Product Owner is one person, not a committee. The Product Owner may represent the needs of many stakeholders in the Product Backlog. Those wanting to change the Product Backlog can do so by trying to convince the Product Owner."

(Source: Scrum Guide 2020. https://Scrumguides.org/docs/Scrumguide/v2020/2020-Scrum-Guide-US.pdf)

It is important that the Product Owner is empowered to prioritize requirements and make product decisions. Otherwise, the Product Owner role becomes similar to a Business Analyst who captures the requirements provided by the stakeholders without ownership over outcomes.

As for the Product Manager, this role is customer and external facing. Product Managers own the business strategy behind a product, specify its functional requirements, and generally manage the launch of features. There are Product Managers in Agile organizations as well. A model product manager is Steve Jobs. This role has been described in detail in Marty Cagan's books, *Inspired* and *Empowered*.

Sample Product Owner Job Description

<Company> is looking for an experienced Product Owner with 4–5 years of experience managing customer-facing products in a Scrum environment. Strong communication and leadership skills are a must.

Responsibilities include the following:

- Responsible for innovation and end-to-end launch of products

- Collaborates with global commercial services partners and customers to codevelop a roadmap and drive products and features from concept to launch in a fast-paced environment

- Works with cross-functional teams and various stakeholders, including analytics, design/user experience, engineering, and user enablement

- Turns data insights into products with actionable outcomes to the ultimate customer

- Works in an Agile environment and continuously reviews the business needs, refines priorities, outlines milestones and deliverables, and identifies opportunities and risks

- Partners with stakeholders and customers across the organization to inform the product vision, strategy, features, and prioritization

- Develops, owns, and executes product roadmap

- Works with user-focused departments to define the self-service user experience, support, and monitoring for customers

- Partners with sales departments to define the user experience for internal GCS users, including support and monitoring

- Translates product roadmap features into well-defined product requirements, including features, user stories, and acceptance test criteria

- Prioritizes and maintains the Sprint backlog for assigned products, balancing the requirements of stakeholders

- Leads the product functional design process based on an intimate knowledge of the users and technology

- Defines and executes the go-to-market plan, working to ensure that product management, marketing, and sales have what they need to be successful.

- Develops and maintains appropriate tracking and reporting of product performance postlaunch to evaluate the future investment

Qualifications:

- Master's in Business Administration preferred

- Minimum two years of experience as a product owner in the industry

- Strong knowledge of Agile principles and processes

- In-depth understanding of industry market conditions and trends

- Outstanding verbal and written communication skills

- Successful track record of developing products within deadlines

- Excellent attention to detail

- Sharp analytical and problem-solving skills

- Creative and innovative thinking

- Customer-centric mindset

- A high degree of organization, individual initiative, and personal accountability

Education, Experience, and Licensing Requirements:

- Bachelor's degree and four years of product or project development experience

- At least one year of experience in product management and/or product development

- Proven track record of delivering data-driven solutions with a customer-first mindset

- Established background in launching software or services in partnership with engineering teams and a high degree of proficiency in prototyping, iterative development, and understanding of Agile principles

- Experience in successfully driving end-to-end delivery of data and intelligence solutions, including a wide variety of mechanisms, for example, dashboards, APIs, real-time alerts, etc.

- Experience with procurement, expense management, and treasury businesses and processes

Source: Glassdoor (`www.glassdoor.com/Job-Descriptions/Product-Owner.htm`)

and Moster.com (`https://hiring.moster.com/employer-resources/job-description-templates/product-owner-job-description-sample/`)

Agile Career Progression

In the prior section, we described hierarchical levels for each profession. Once you join an organization in a specific role, it makes sense to find out almost immediately what the criteria are to grow to the next level. In larger corporate organizations, there are formal criteria for growing to the next level, and there is no reason to delay this growth.

At the same time, "ladder" (hierarchical) career progression nowadays is not a choice for every professional, especially in a collaborative Agile environment. Many Agile professionals prefer "lattice" (horizontal) career progression whether they get a chance to learn both project and product management skills within the same organization. The best way of defining your path is to reach out to mentors and career coaches without your work environment, who will provide targeted advice, in addition to formal promotion rules.

The best way to grow in an Agile role is to practice, learn, and share with other professionals. The Agile community is very welcoming, and knowledge sharing is encouraged. Meetup (`https://www.meetup.com/`) is a helpful source of free meetups, and other gatherings of Agile professionals in each geographic area or online provide a great way of building your Agile network. In May 2022, there were a total of 86 Agile meetups in the United States, including 21 in the New York Area, or two sessions every three days. The topics ranged from "Scrum Master Interview Prep" to "What you always wanted to know about enterprise agility." There are 10–20 people in each meetup on average, so there is always an opportunity to ask questions and meet other Agile practitioners. Besides meetups, there are LinkedIn Forums and other communities of practice.

Finally, there are professional associations, such as Agile Alliance, Scrum Alliance, Agile Groups within the Project Management Institute (PMI), and numerous Agile and product management conferences. Agile Alliance holds an annual Agile Conference. **Agile Alliance's annual conference** is dedicated to exploring, innovating, and advancing Agile values and principles and creating a space for people and ideas to flourish. The Agile20XX conference brings Agile communities together year after year to share experiences and make new connections. Join passionate agilists from around the world to learn about the latest practices, ideas, and strategies in Agile software development from the world's leading experts, change agents, and innovators.

Besides large conferences, there are many regional and topic-specific Agile conferences, such as Agile DevOps, LeanAgileUS, Agile Open, Scrum Days, Scrum Gatherings, Path to Agility, Agile Coach Camp, Agile Play, XP Conference, Agile Testing Days, regional Agile conferences, and many others where you can build your network and learn new skills.

Agile Certification is a controversial topic. Since Agile is team and people oriented, certifications primarily attest to a person's theoretical knowledge but do not guarantee that a certified person is a mature professional. However, many companies are considering Agile certifications a must when they hire Agile professionals.

While selecting certifications, focus on the one that is right for you. Prior to choosing the course, answer the following questions:

1. Am I interested in "what" (Product track) or "how" (Scrum Master track)?

2. Am I interested in Scrum (timeboxed iterations) or how (continuous delivery)?

3. Am I interested in working at the team level or the organizational level (scaled Agile)?

4. Am I coming from a traditional project management background or environment?

Then, depending on your answer, select the certification that is right for you:

1. Product track vs. Scrum Master track

   There are two most established certification providers on these tracks: Scrum Alliance and Scrum.org. The details are provided as follows:

	Product Track	Scrum Master Track
Scrum Alliance www.Scrumalliance.org/get-certified	There are three levels, from most basic to most experienced: Certified Scrum Product Owner (CSPO) Advanced Certified Scrum Product Owner (A-CSPO) Certified Scrum Professional Product Owner (CSP-PO)	There are three levels, from most basic to most experienced: Certified ScrumMaster (CSM) Advanced Certified ScrumMaster (A-CSM) Certified Scrum Professional Scrum Master (CSP-SM)
Scrum.org www.Scrum.org/professional-Scrum-certifications	There are three levels, from most basic to most experienced: Professional Scrum Master (PSM I, PSM II, PSM III)	There are three levels, from most basic to most experienced: Professional Product Owner (PSPO I, PSPO II, PSPO III)

Scrum Master certification is the most requested Agile certification in the world, and the CSM by Scrum Alliance is considered the most widely adopted Agile certification. CSM course covers the framework, principles, and values that make Scrum work. In addition, as a Scrum Alliance CSM, you can tap into a community network that extends far beyond the classroom through events, resources, education, and coaching. This certification has no prerequisites except for attending a two-day training and passing a basic multiple-choice test.

For those who would like to go deeper and diversify their Agile skills, the following certifications are available.

2. For those interested in **Kanban**, there is a set of certifications offered by Kanban University.(https://Kanban.university/#certifiedKanban) There are four levels of offers:

   - Foundation (Team Kanban Practitioner (TKP), Kanban System Design (KSD), and Kanban System Improvement for Kanban Management Professionals (KMP I and KMP II))

   - Trainer (for those interested in becoming an accredited Kanban Trainer and teaching others)

- Advanced (coaching, leadership, maturity model at the organizational level)

- Strategic (enterprise services planning to fit for purpose) for Kanban consultants

3. For those interested in **scaled Agile**, classes differ depending on the scaled framework. The most popular framework is the Scaled Agile Framework (SAFe). Related certifications are provided by the Scaled Agile Academy, the most basic being the Certified SAFe Agilist. There are multiple specializations and levels of SAFe certifications, including Agile DevOps, Lean Portfolio Management, and many others. More information is provided at the Scaled Agile website: www.scaledAgile.com/certifications/about-safe-certification/

    Other scaled Agile certifications include Scrum@Scale certification provided by Scrum Inc. (www.Scruminc.com/Scrum-at-scale-certification), Certified LeSS Practitioner (https://less.works/courses/less-practitioner), and others.

4. If you are transitioning from the traditional project management into an Agile environment, no matter what your role is on the team, the recommended certification is PMI-ACP from the Project Management Institute (PMI) (www.pmi.org/certifications/Agile-acp). The PMI-ACP certification provides assurance that the certification holder has real-world experience managing Agile projects and is familiar with multiple Agile frameworks and methodologies, including Scrum, Kanban, Lean, and others.

No matter which certification you choose, there are several things to keep in mind:

1. Agile certifications are costly; usually, the cost for basic certifications ranges from $500 to $1,200, so it is important to do careful research before investing in each of them.

2. Agile certifications differ in terms of the complexity and level of assessments. Most of them have a prerequisite training course by a certified provider, and the advanced certifications usually have the basic ones as a prerequisite. Assessment tests also differ.

For example, the CSM certification test contains 50 multiple-choice questions, and candidates have one hour to complete it. It requires a two-day CSM course before the test can be taken. The passing score is 74%. The PMI-ACP certification exam has 120 multiple-choice questions, and you have three hours to complete it. It does not require attending a specific class; however, prerequisites include the following:

- Secondary degree.

- 21 contact hours of training in Agile practices.

- 12 months of general project experience within the last five years. Traditional PMP or PgMP certifications satisfy this requirement but are not required to apply for the PMI-ACP.

- Eight months of Agile project experience within the last three years.

  Do your research using each of the registered provider sites (not the private sites advertising specific certifications) to make your choice based on the provider, content, and certification type.

3. Another important consideration is that there are usually fees and prerequisites to maintain each of the certifications. Scrum Alliance, PMI, and most other organizations require you to collect Professional Development Units (PDUs or SDUs) that show that you continue learning and practicing in the field and charge a renewal fee every one to three years. Usually, the fees are around $100–$200, but for the advanced certifications, these can go up to thousands of dollars annually. Make sure to check the provider site for renewal criteria before applying for certification.

4. **Membership in professional associations** and access to their resources, communities of practice, as well as relevant discounts on professional publications and conferences are a big part of the professional certifications. For example, CSM certification includes a membership fee for Scrum Alliance. All certificate holders are listed on the Scrum Alliance website, participate in communities of practice available to members only, get discounts on participation in the Scrum Gathering conference globally,

and take advantage of multiple perks provided by the organization. Similarly, other certifications provide an opportunity to take advantage of their resources.

To summarize, Agile certifications are highly valuable to anyone in an Agile environment – from a developer to a Scrum Master and to the CEO of the organization. Do your research, choose the right certification for you, prepare diligently, achieve certification, and take advantage of all the opportunities it provides to you.

Agile Job Interviews

I hope you found this course highly practical. Anyone who successfully completes this course should be ready to apply for an entry-level Scrum Master or product manager role. This final section of the book will help you start preparing for a Scrum Master interview and share multiple sources for feeling confident as you apply for your Agile roles.

Scrum Master is one of the most in-demand positions now and has been such for the last 10+ years. As Agile development becomes the mainstream development framework replacing traditional project management, the demand for Agile professionals of any level is continuously growing. In the following, we will address the interview process for the entry-level Scrum Master role as an example of preparing and succeeding in your interview process.

The interview preparation process consists of the following:

> **Getting an interview.** To get an interview, ensure that your resume reflects your Agile knowledge and experience. List any professional certifications discussed before and training courses you have completed. Ensure that you list any adequate professional experience. If you do not have any, no worries: describe the project you've done in this class from an iterative delivery perspective. If you have developed working prototypes as part of this project, make them available online and provide a link to them. Describe the methodology you used and your role on the team. List any tools that you used, such as Jira and Trello. Any collaboration and productivity tools, such as Mural, Miro, Freehand, and similar ones, are also highly relevant.

If you do not have any experience besides this course, do not give up. Try "personal Kanban" and describe this experience in your resume. Personal Kanban refers to using the Kanban board and other Scrum practices, such as timeboxed iterations in your personal life. This allows for clear focus, deliberate actions, fast delivery, and purpose. Write a blog on LinkedIn about your experience and include this online publication in your resume. This all provides a solid foundation to prove your Agile mindset.

Step 1. Research the Company and Analyze the Fit

There are two parts to your research:

1. Research the company

    - Mission, vision, goals, culture, employee experience (in general and in a similar role)

    - State of agility, Agile frameworks, expectations, potential peers

2. Analyze the fit (and the gaps)

    - Memorize the job description.

    - Ensure full accuracy of your resume.

    - Re-create your own elevator pitch; be explicit about the gaps.

    - Rehearse in front of the mirror and with a friend.

    - Prepare the questions.

Sample questions may include the following:

1. What do you know about <company>? Why are you interested in working here?

2. What is your Scrum Master experience? Why do you think you are a fit for this position?

3. Are you aware of our company's values? Do they resonate with you?

4. Why are you making this career move? What are your long-term career objectives?

5. What is your work experience? Why did you choose Agile as your profession?

6. What are your professional strengths/weaknesses? What makes you happy/frustrates you?

7. Do you prefer to work individually or as part of a team? Why?

8. What questions do you have for the interviewer(s)?

Step 2. Refresh Your Basic Agile Knowledge

1. Read the Scrum Guide (www.Scrumguides.org/Scrum-guide.html):

   - Definition of Scrum, Scrum values

   - Scrum roles (Product Owner, the development team, the Scrum Master)

   - Scrum events (Sprint, Spring Planning, Daily Scrum, Sprint Review, Sprint Retrospective)

   - Scrum artifacts (Product Backlog, Sprint Backlog, Increment)

   - Artifact transparency (Definition of Ready, Definition of Done)

2. Beyond Scrum Guide

   - Agile values and principles, Agile mindset, value, and impact of Scrum (https://Agilemanifesto.org/)

   - Other Agile frameworks (e.g., https://en.wikipedia.org/wiki/Kanban_(development))

   - Product development practices (sample: www.jpattonassociates.com/user-story-mapping/)

   - Scaling Agile (sample: www.scaledAgileframework.com, www.Scrumatscale.com/Scrum-at-scale-guide)

Sample questions may include the following:

1. What are Agile values and principles?

2. What is Scrum? What are Scrum values? What other Agile frameworks are you aware of?

3. Why Scrum? What value does it bring? How different is it from other Agile frameworks?

4. What are Scrum roles? Who owns the product backlog? What is a cross-functional team?

5. What is your experience working with a distributed team? What is your experience with a scaled Agile framework?

6. What are Scrum events? Who can cancel a Sprint, and why? What are the Sprint planning techniques? What happens at a Sprint Review? What is the purpose of a Sprint Retrospective?

7. What are Scrum artifacts? Which metrics do you track? What is the Definition of Ready and Definition of Done? What are the major challenges in implementing Scrum? When do you use Scrum vs. Kanban?

Step 3. Prepare to Describe Your Experience

1. Prepare your story.

   - Enhance your elevator pitch and rehearse it multiple times.

   - Tell a story; do not list bullet points.

   - Be concise; make a compelling statement.

   - Select relevant information based on the job description.

2. Be clear about what you need to convey.

   - What are the one to three things you want the interviewer to take away?

   - What was your role in the event/approach/artifact you describe?

   - Be aware of your nonverbal communication.

Sample Interview Question/Answer

I. Good Example

Have you had a challenge as a Scrum Master, and how did you overcome it?

When I worked as a Scrum Master on the Claims team in a large health insurance company, we used Scaled Agile Framework and did our Program Increment (PI) planning as part of an eight-team Agile Release Train. First, I coached my team in getting an accurate long-term forecast based on an established velocity and a consistent story point estimation. However, there was still a challenge with my peer's team - they were failing their forecast and were not able to deliver on the dependencies, thus slowing us down. I worked with their Scrum Master to help establish the predictability of their delivery by encouraging a thorough analysis of misestimated user stories they had in their backlog. As a result, our joint predictability rate went to over 90% across the release train.

Comment: *As you can see, in this story, the Scrum Master emphasizes experience in working in a scaled Agile environment, exposure to other frameworks, and the ability to work with peers successfully to achieve a win-win solution.*

II. Improvement Opportunity

How do you do planning in Scrum?

Sprint planning is an event in the Scrum framework where the team determines the product backlog items they will work on during that Sprint and discusses their initial plan for completing those product backlog items.

Teams may find it helpful to establish a Sprint goal and use that as the basis by which they determine which product backlog items they work on during that Sprint.

Comment: *This is the correct answer "by the book." However, it does not speak to your own experience, the challenges you had, or the lessons you learned. It does not provide any information about the toolbox you have as a Scrum Master that enables you to make your Sprint planning successful and predictable. It does not reflect why it is important to provide an accurate estimation.*

Step 4. Demonstrate Your Soft Skills

Soft skills are a combination of people skills, social skills, communication skills, character or personality traits, attitudes, mindsets, career attributes, social intelligence, and emotional intelligence. Soft skills are very important for anyone and especially for a Scrum Master. This is usually assessed through behavioral questions when hypothetical situations are presented by interviewers, and the candidates are expected to suggest their course of action if they face a situation similar to the one presented to them.

1. Be flexible and authentic and at the same time

    - Show that you are a servant leader

    - Show your effective communication and facilitation skills, including conflict resolution

    - Prove that you are open to continuous improvement

2. Respond to the challenge.

    - How to handle a situational question/case study

    - How to handle role play

    - How to handle ethical questions

Sample Interview Question/Answer

I. Improvement Opportunity

Standup Situation

On your team, there is a tech lead. During the daily standup, every team member provides an update directly to the tech lead, and the tech lead is asking the follow-up questions. They do not communicate with each other; they are just doing the update to their lead. To make matters worse, team members are all quite junior; they respect the team lead, and they see nothing wrong with these dynamics. What would you do as a Scrum Master?

Answer: *I will tell them that as described in the Scrum Guide, the Daily Scrum is a 15-minute timeboxed event for the development team to synchronize activities and create a plan for the next 24 hours. The Daily Scrum is held every day of the Sprint. At the Daily Scrum, the development team plans work for the next 24 hours.*

II. How to Improve This Answer?

Standup Situation

On your team, there is a tech lead. During the daily standup, every team member provides an update directly to the tech lead, and the tech lead is asking follow-up questions. They do not communicate with each other; they are just doing the update to their lead. To make matters worse, team members are all quite junior; they respect the team lead, and they see nothing wrong with these dynamics. What would you do as a Scrum Master?

Answer: *It is a common situation, especially when the tech lead is knowledgeable and respected by the team. When I face this situation, I start by understanding why they are acting this way: Is this something the tech lead is asking them to do or is it that they do not understand the goal for the Daily Scrum? First, I will speak with the tech lead one-on-one and explain that the Daily Scrum is for the Scrum team to* *synchronize activities with each other and create a plan for the next 24 hours. Once I get support from the tech lead, I will speak to the team and explain that this event is for them to align; it is not a status update to their tech lead. Once everyone is in consensus, I will use my facilitation skills to confirm that the team members are making their Daily Scrums collaborative, informative, and productive.*

Compare answers I and II. As you can see, in the first version, Scrum Master is coming top-down at the team. Rather than coaching them in best practice, the Scrum Master is telling them what to do. The instruction is provided "by the books" without explaining why their approach is not effective and how they would benefit from the one suggested to them. This behavior does not create trust between the Scrum Master and the team and usually results in the team ignoring the Scrum Master instructions. In the second answer, the Scrum Master acts as a coach trying to understand the root cause of the unwanted behavior pattern and takes ownership of resolving the issue in a collaborative people-oriented way.

On the Day of the Interview

Ensure that you are fully prepared for the interview at least the day before: test the proposed online meeting platform for the online interview or, in case of an in-person interview, research your commute for a face-to-face one, refresh the information about the company and the group you are interviewing with, write down the names of the interviewers and check out their background on LinkedIn, memorize job description, print out your resume, and prepare the questions for your interviewers. Now you are all set for success!

Now you are well equipped for your Agile journey, no matter which capacity you choose for yourself. The sky is the limit! Keep in mind that the Agile body of knowledge is continuously evolving, and we all contribute to it. To stay informed, join Agile meetups on Meetup, Agile forums on LinkedIn, and professional associations, such as Scrum Alliance or Agile Alliance; connect with other Agile professionals; and continue to learn and grow while elevating others along your journey. At the end of the day, Agile is all about continuous improvement!

C

Conclusion

This course is highly pragmatic. As you have engaged on the journey to understand agility and learn the foundations of Agile software delivery and beyond, you expanded your delivery horizons, no matter which role you hold now or will hold in the future: software developer, business executive, Scrum Master, or Product Owner. The foundations of Agile' product and project management are applicable to value delivery at any level of the organization and in every role. As a result, in this conclusion, we are going to provide an overview of the Agile professions and related certifications: from identifying relevant career paths to getting a job and then advancing in your career.

© Mariya Breyter 2022
M. Breyter, *Agile Product and Project Management*,
https://doi.org/10.1007/978-1-4842-8200-7

Homework

Chapter 1

Write a short two to three-page essay on one of the following topics:

1. Suggest a graphic representation of the "Waterfall" sequence-based methodology vs. Agile framework (repeatable delivery of outcomes to the customers). Compare feedback loops (the process and timelines of receiving customer feedback) in each of the approaches.

2. From a project management perspective, any major change to timelines or key deliverables is a major event in "Waterfall" project management. It requires a special process referred to as "change management" for the key stakeholders to review the impact and sign off on the next steps. In Agile, change is built into execution and is managed by the process itself. Since work is implemented iteratively, change happens in Agile on an ongoing basis and does not require any separate reviews and approvals. Imagine that the team found out that there is a new feature required by their customers that they were not aware of previously. Walk through what happens in this case in traditional and Agile project management.

© Mariya Breyter 2022
M. Breyter, *Agile Product and Project Management*,
https://doi.org/10.1007/978-1-4842-8200-7

3. In companies practicing traditional project management, there are usually separate teams of business analysts who write requirements documents, software developers who develop software, QA testers who test the software, and so forth. In Agile organizations, there are product-based teams. For example, in a health insurance company, there is a claims team, customer portal team, provider support team, and so forth. On each team, there are business stakeholders and IT professionals who are focused on providing products and services to each customer group. How do you explain this difference in their organizational structure?

4. Which project management framework resonates with you more and why? Why do traditional projects take years while Agile teams frequently deliver the first iteration of their software (referred to as MVP – minimum viable product) within months, if not weeks, since inception?

Chapter 2

Review the following OKR examples and provide critique based on the information in Chapter 2. Pay attention to the following:

- Are objectives inspirational and compelling?
- Are key results measurable?
- Are key results based on outcomes vs. tasks?
- Is the number of key results below six for each objective?
- Are key results directly reflecting the stated objective?
- Are key results specific, concise, and unambiguous?

Example 1:

OBJECTIVE – We will increase the efficiency of QA processes by

KEY RESULT 1 – Test cases for all P1, P2 stories are completed and handed over to dev before development starts (compliance to be measured every Sprint)

KEY RESULT 2 – One week before the release date, no blocker and critical bugs should be open

KEY RESULT 3 – Bug leakage to production for critical issues is less than 1%

KEY RESULT 4 – Less than three bugs reported by end users per release

KEY RESULT 5 – Hire two testers

KEY RESULT 6 – Achieve QA certification from the Quality Institute

KEY RESULT 7 – Log all defects in Jira and provide weekly reporting

Example 2:

OBJECTIVE - We will deliver working software to the customer regularly with high quality by

KEY RESULT 1 – Delivering to production every week (no single release is more than one day late)

KEY RESULT 2 - Achieving over 80% regression test automation

KEY RESULT 3 - Increasing unit test coverage to 75 % from current 45%

KEY RESULT 4 - Implementing a continuous monitoring tool to ensure "six nines" uptime for lower environments

KEY RESULT 5 - Enabling engineers to manage lower environments within required SLAs

Example 3:

OBJECTIVE - We will achieve higher operational availability and lower operational costs as measured by

KEY RESULT 1 – Zero DevOps-owned services in AWS (move everything to the cloud)

KEY RESULT 2 - 10% reduction in AWS operational cost

KEY RESULT 3 – Zero single points of failure

KEY RESULT 4 – 10% increase in employee satisfaction

KEY RESULT 5 – Implementing two new tracking and monitoring reports

Simulation Project

Split into teams of five to seven and brainstorm on establishing a mock startup that will provide software development or IT products to institutional or retail customers. Choose the area you are passionate about that addresses a known customer problem. For your company, select a company name and create a mission and vision statement for both the company and the product that it will build. It could be any online product (online store, childcare portal, a learning management system, collaboration software, or any other product addressing customer needs) or an IT initiative related to infrastructure, technology-based service, data center, communications and collaboration platform, or network technology, or any other product or service of your choice. Start defining first-year OKRs for your company.

Please note that this will be an ongoing simulation project throughout the whole course, so everyone on your team has to be supportive of the product you have selected and familiar with the subject matter area. The teams will be persistent throughout the duration of this course, in accordance with best practices.

Chapter 3

Homework

Select one consumer and one corporate IT product (hardware or software) that all your team members are familiar with. Create a customer journey for each of those products and describe the difference.

Simulation Project

Use product techniques described in Chapter 3 to create a Business Model Canvas for your simulation project. Present this artifact to other teams as a five-minute summary of your product, its features, market positioning, and distribution channels.

Chapter 4

Homework

Describe a famous pivot based on your own research. Identify all the considerations that went into the "pivot or persevere" decision. Suggested examples include Pixar, which started as an animation tool development company, Graphics Group. For nine years, their business was targeted at developing the Menv (Modeling Environment) animation system. After the platform was developed, Pixar leadership team made a decision to move into film creation. Other examples include Intel's shift from chips to microprocessors and Netflix's shift from a mail-order business to streaming content and then to creating content. You can also use any of the examples from this chapter that you have discussed in class or come up with your own example.

Simulation Project

As a team, use a Validation Canvas to record your riskiest assumption and get ready to validate it with customers.

Chapter 5
Homework

Write three to five user stories for software that you use on a regular basis, such as your calendar, car sharing app, or an e-mail app. Once you wrote the use stories, decompose each of them into multiple smaller-scope user stories based on the criteria discussed in Chapter 5.

Simulation Project

For the project you selected as a team, create a story map and a skeleton for your product backlog with all relevant epics and draft 10–15 user stories in it (for one to two epics, as applicable). While it is recommended to conduct the story map session together as a team, you can "divide and conquer" the rest of the product backlog work to create user stories and specify acceptance criteria for each one. You can also use any relevant metadata; for example, create categories or specific components.

You can use a free tool, such as Trello, for this exercise or do it in a spreadsheet.

Chapter 6
Homework

Discuss the following three topics as a group and then document individually:

1. Describe the limitations and benefits of each type of organizational structure depending on the software delivery life cycle (SDLC).

2. Explain roles in Scrum. How do those map to traditional project management roles?

3. Read the article about why product management is a bad idea (www.infoq.com/news/2020/09/product-owner-good-bad-complex/) - Do you agree with it? Why?

Simulation Project

Use product techniques described in Chapter 6 to define the framework that your team will use to deliver your product MVP.

Chapter 7

Homework

Create a backlog of tasks to implement your favorite dish recipe, starting from procuring all ingredients and finishing with serving this dish to your guests. Prioritize, sequence, and estimate backlog items and create a roadmap for this initiative. As step 2, imagine that you deliver this dish in three iterations, equal in their duration. Plan these iterations and update the roadmap to reflect this plan.

Simulation Project

Use product delivery techniques described in Chapter 7 to estimate the product backlog for your project. How many Sprints are required for your team to complete this project? Create a roadmap based on your backlog and the estimation you provided.

Chapter 8

Homework

Create a roadmap for the product you are building. Define milestones and timelines based on relative estimation.

Simulation Project

Using the Retrospective techniques described in Chapter 8, discuss how your simulation project is progressing. What is going well? What would you like to do better? Come up with three to five action items that you as a group would like to commit to and work on improving during the upcoming two weeks.

Chapter 9

Homework

Review Agile Manifesto and list Agile principles that are relevant to the purchase of services or goods needed to deliver the product's scope. For each of the principles, compare how Agile and traditional approaches are different. The following is an example of one of the principles:

Principle	Traditional Project Management	Agile Delivery
Welcome changing requirements; even late in development, Agile processes harness change for the customer's competitive advantage.	The scope is fixed, and any change has to be separately discussed and agreed upon. Change management is time-consuming and requires to renegotiate the contract.	Agile assumes flexibility in delivery and welcomes change. It creates mechanisms for the vendor and the customer to collaborate in delivering value to the end user.

Simulation Project

Create a Risk Log for your simulation project. Use brainstorming and other Agile techniques while working on this project. Ensure the Risk Log allows for flexibility. What allows to establish transparency into delivery and risk management in an Agile environment?

Chapter 10

Homework

Based on videos and materials of Lesson 10, list two strong sides and two inefficiencies related to each of the Agile scaling frameworks discussed in Lesson 10.

Simulation Project

For your simulation project, imagine that it is highly successful, and after the initial launch, you have to rapidly scale it 10x within six months. Which framework would you select and why? Create an overview and a roadmap of your scaled Agile implementation, and present to your peers.

Self-Review Quizzes

Chapter 1

1. When did project management form as a profession?

   A. 2570 BC when the Great Pyramid of Giza was completed

   B. In the 20th century

   C. Starting from 2001, when the Agile Manifesto was created

   D. None of the above

2. Which is NOT an example of a project management method or technique?

   A. Gantt chart

   B. Work breakdown structure

   C. Agile Manifesto

   D. PERT analysis

© Mariya Breyter 2022
M. Breyter, *Agile Product and Project Management*,
https://doi.org/10.1007/978-1-4842-8200-7

3. In which industry did Lean practices originate?

    A. Car manufacturing

    B. Pharmaceuticals

    C. Software development

    D. None of the above

4. Which company is known for introducing modern Lean practices?

    A. General Motors

    B. GE

    C. Google

    D. Toyota

5. Which is NOT a value from the Agile Manifesto?

    A. Individuals and interactions over processes and tools

    B. Working software over comprehensive documentation

    C. Self-organizing teams over top-down management

    D. Responding to change over following a plan

6. What is applicable to Agile teams?

    A. Agile teams are collaborative

    B. Agile teams are cross-functional

    C. Agile teams are self-organizing

    D. All of the above

7. Which statement is true?

    A. Agile, Lean, and Waterfall are all project management methodologies

    B. The major difference between Agile and Waterfall is that in Agile, there is no planning

    C. Agile is based on incremental and iterative delivery, while Waterfall delivers the product when it is completed

    D. In Lean, project managers use Gantt charts to manage delivery

8. What is a scaled Agile framework?

    A. It refers to a large number of teams in one organization or division

    B. It means that each team includes more than 20 IT professionals

    C. It means that the resulting product has more than one million users

    D. It means that there are more rules and processes defined

9. What is a product manager?

    A. A person responsible for marketing

    B. A person responsible for product pricing

    C. A person responsible for guiding the success of a product and leading the cross-functional team that is responsible for improving it

    D. A business analyst who writes requirements

10. What is a project manager?

    A. Project managers have the responsibility for the planning, procurement, and execution of a project

    B. Project managers manage people on the team

    C. Project managers are responsible for hiring the execution team

    D. All of the above

Answer key: 1-B, 2-C, 3-A, 4-D, 5-C, 6-D, 7-C, 8-A, 9-C, 10-A

Chapter 2

1. What is the difference between product and project?

    A. There is no difference

    B. Products have a life cycle that consists of multiple stages. First, the product is conceived, then developed, then introduced and managed in the market, and finally, the product is retired when the need for it diminishes. A project is a temporary endeavor that is undertaken to create a unique product or service

    C. Projects may include multiple products, but products may not include multiple projects

    D. Projects are managed by product managers

2. What is the purpose of the company's vision and mission statements?

    A. Mission and vision statements provide a statement of the company's purpose, goals, and values

    B. Mission and vision statements are required by IRS as part of corporate tax withholding

    C. Mission and vision statements are a bureaucratic activity that some companies engage in

    D. Mission and vision statements are no longer used by modern technology companies

3. When is achieving a score 0.6-0.7 out of 1 does not indicate that the Objectives has been successfully achieved?

    A. When there is a mandatory (compliance- or dependency-related) timeline for delivering the feature or the product

    B. This depends on management decision

    C. This depends on the team's decision

    D. It's never considered a success. OKR has to always be achieved at 100%

4. "To put people at the center of enterprise software." Which company does this mission belong to?

   A. Microsoft

   B. Workday

   C. Intuit

   D. Intel

5. What is a product elevator pitch?

   A. Brief description of the market landscape for your product

   B. Product design technique aligned with the enterprise pricing strategy

   C. A product flyer displayed in a corporate elevator

   D. A short, snappy, easy-to-grasp product statement

6. What is the recommended time frame to review the company's OKRs?

   A. Weekly

   B. Monthly

   C. Quarterly

   D. Annually

7. Which is NOT one of the five categories that are recommended for DevOps OKRs?

   A. Continuous delivery

   B. Lean management and monitoring

   C. Requirements management

   D. Product and process

8. When should an organization start using OKRs?

   A. When it has more than 1,000 employees

   B. When the CEO announces organizational-level OKRs

   C. When a tool, such as Workboard or Betterworks, is procured by the company

   D. At any time – there are hardly any prerequisites to start OKR adoption

9. Which is the most accurate definition of OKRs?

    A. OKRs are a management framework to manage by objectives

    B. OKRs are rarely graded because this may decrease team motivation

    C. OKRs are an effective goal-setting framework

    D. OKRs were popular in the 1970s

10. Which is NOT a benefit of OKRs?

    A. OKRs establish transparency throughout the company

    B. OKRs help define promotions and compensation

    C. OKRs reduce ambiguity in defining success criteria

    D. OKRs provide alignment in prioritization

Answer key: 1-B, 2-A, 3-A, 4-B, 5-D, 6-C, 7-C, 8-D, 9-C, 10-B

Chapter 3
Self-Review Quiz

1. What is the relationship between product discovery and execution?

    A. It is sequential: once business analysts complete their research and document their findings, IT professionals start execution

    B. Execution happens first, and once the product is ready, the user research team conducts discovery, collecting customer feedback

    C. Discovery and execution happen in parallel; one process does not affect the other

    D. Discovery and execution are interconnected – once a feature is developed, feedback from customers helps shape further product development

2. Products, as opposed to services, always have a physical shape or form.

    A. True

    B. False

3. What does the "Job-to-Be-Done" (JTBD) concept reflect?

   A. It reflects McDonald's product consumption as related to milkshakes

   B. It reflects a list of tasks that need to be completed

   C. It reflects underlying user needs

   D. None of the above

4. What is a user persona in product analysis?

   A. It is a customer type represented as a fictional character – with a made-up biography, demographics, characteristics, and a clear representation of their need

   B. It is not described as a type; it is described as a specific person

   C. User personas change over time based on market changes, new product demands, or new information that becomes available to the product teams

   D. All of the above

5. Which is NOT a component of a business model canvas?

   A. Empathy maps

   B. Customer segments

   C. Customer relationships

   D. Revenue streams

6. Which aspect of the Business Model Canvas covers vendors, suppliers, and external dependencies for product development?

   A. Key resources

   B. Customer relationships

   C. Key partners

   D. Key activities

7. Which is NOT a valid customer segmentation category?

   A. Economic segmentation

   B. Brand segmentation

   C. Geographic segmentation

   D. Behavioral segmentation

8. According to Geoffrey Moore, technology products differ by their level of customer adoption.

   A. True

   B. False

9. In the Technology Adoption Life Cycle, Geoffrey Moore identifies four types of customers in terms of their IT product adoption.

   A. Early adopters, late adopters, majority customers, and decreasing customers

   B. Early adopters, early majority, late majority, and laggards

   C. Visionaries, early adopters, majority customers, and laggards

   D. Visionaries, early adopters, late majority, and followers

10. For IT professionals, the topic of building the right product is as important as building the product right.

    A. The topic of building the right product is more important

    B. The topic of building the product right is more important

    C. Neither one is relevant to IT professionals since their job is to code, design, and execute requirements.

    D. Both are equally important

Answer key: 1-D, 2-B, 3-C, 4-D, 5-A, 6-C, 7-A, 8-A, 9-B, 10-D

Chapter 4

Self-Review Quiz

1. What does it mean to "fail fast, succeed faster" in the context of the Lean startup?

   A. In order to succeed, one has to practice a lot

   B. Failures cause resilience in the future

   C. By invalidating a hypothesis, we are able to define successful products before building them

   D. None of the above

2. What is Lean startup?

    A. A framework that is relevant for startups only

    B. A framework to make product decisions quickly and accurately

    C. A synonym for "Agile product management"

    D. A "build-measure-learn" iteration

3. Why does the Lean startup approach minimize risks?

    A. Because it is iterative

    B. Because it establishes customer feedback loops

    C. Because it validates assumptions early in the product development

    D. All of the above

4. Which company has customer obsession as its #1 leadership principle?

    A. IDEO

    B. Stanford Design School

    C. Google

    D. Amazon

5. Which is NOT a step to validate a customer hypothesis?

    A. State the hypothesis

    B. Come up with a list of assumptions

    C. Run the experiment and compare metrics against expectations

    D. Get management approval

6. What are the four steps of user research according to Chapter 4?

    A. Identify target personas, define the way of collecting customer feedback, conduct the research, aggregate, and interpret the data

    B. Recruit customers, identify target personas, draft questions, and collect and interpret customer feedback

    C. Identify customers, validate assumptions, suggest solutions, and get customer feedback

    D. Recruit participants, ask questions, record responses, aggregate, and present results

7. What is the Lean Validation Canvas used for?

    A. To validate user hypotheses

    B. To structure and record data throughout hypotheses validation and user research

    C. To record customer responses

    D. To provide a report to the management

8. Which is NOT an example of a pivot?

    A. Customer feedback pivot

    B. Channel pivot

    C. Platform pivot

    D. Zoom-in pivot

9. What is a design Sprint?

    A. Google Ventures' customer research technique

    B. A fixed duration iteration of Agile product delivery

    C. A design document is provided in a quick and efficient way

    D. A Lean technique is used to deliver prototypes

10. What is the purpose of MVP?

    A. Establish a fast user feedback loop

    B. Minimize risks by refining product solutions

    C. Build a minimal valuable deliverable for the customer

    D. All of the above

Answer key: 1-C, 2-B, 3-D, 4-D, 5-D, 6-A, 7-B, 8-A, 9-A, 10-D

Chapter 5
Self-Review Quiz

1. Which is NOT part of requirements management in traditional project management?

   A. Requirements elicitation

   B. Stakeholder analysis

   C. Requirements analysis

   D. Change control

2. What does UML stand for?

   A. United Master Ledger

   B. Unique Method of Learning

   C. Unified Modeling Language

   D. Unique Modeling Language

3. What is the most accurate description of a product backlog?

   A. Collection of user stories

   B. Prioritized collection of user stories

   C. Prioritized list of product features, which may be expressed as user stories

   D. Requirement in Agile

4. What is the difference between a product backlog and a software requirements specification (SRS) document?

   A. The product backlog is not prioritized

   B. The product backlog is more comprehensive

   C. The product backlog is iterative, while SRS has to be finalized and signed off before development starts

   D. The team writes SRS, while the product backlog is created by users

5. What does INVEST mean as related to a user story?

    A. It means that it's important to invest a budget in creating user stories

    B. It is a design thinking principle used to create a user story

    C. It's a requirement in Agile

    D. It's a mnemonic to remember features of a user story

6. Which is NOT a valid method of a user story decomposition?

    A. CRUD (Create, Read, Update, Delete)

    B. Based on stakeholders who requested this user story

    C. Business rules

    D. Based on workflow steps

7. Which is NOT true about epics?

    A. Epics are used to capture a feature

    B. Epics cannot contain spikes

    C. Epics have a parent/child relationship to user stories

    D. Epics may contain risks and defects if an organization uses those elements in its backlog

8. This is a good quality story: As a team member, I want to develop logon functionality so that users can log onto the site.

    A. True

    B. False

9. User story mapping is used to create a "big picture" of the product features and sequence them for delivery.

    A. True

    B. False

10. The benefits of story mapping do NOT include:

    A. Ability to prioritize and sequence features

    B. Specifying features based on personas

    C. Providing an opportunity for the team to align and collaborate

    D. Creating a comprehensive software requirements specification

Answer key: 1-B, 2-C, 3-C, 4-C, 5-D, 6-B, 7-B, 8-B, 9-A, 10-D

Chapter 6
Self-Review Quiz

1. Which is NOT a standard Scrum role?

   A. Scrum Team

   B. Tech Lead

   C. Scrum Master

   D. Product Owner

2. Which type of organizational structure has been adopted by Spotify?

   A. Traditional

   B. Flexible

   C. Hierarchical

   D. Matrix

3. Which one is NOT a standard project management process group as defined by PMBOK?

   A. Initiation

   B. Executing

   C. Testing

   D. Closing

4. Which is NOT true about traditional project management and Agile?

   A. There is a need for change management and approval processes in Agile

   B. Agile works for small projects; traditional project management works more for small enhancements

   C. Traditional project management has longer planning horizons

   D. Agile project management is more flexible than Waterfall

5.   What is a tribe in Spotify?

   A.   It's an equivalent of a team in Scrum

   B.   It is a community of practice

   C.   It is a collection of teams working on the same product or product line

   D.   It is a group of people who have the same cultural habits and beliefs

6.   Which one is not a team type according to the Team Topologies book?

   A.   Stream-aligned team

   B.   Scrum team

   C.   Enabling team

   D.   Complicated-subsystem team

7.   What is the Definition of Ready?

   A.   It defines whether a feature is ready

   B.   It marks the end of a project

   C.   It contains a list of criteria that have to be met for a product backlog item before it is taken into delivery

   D.   It is related to an employee's exit from the organization when they have to meet the Definition of Ready

8.   What is the Conway Law about?

   A.   In any organization, three types of communication channels exist: formal, informal, and unofficial

   B.   There is a cognitive limit to the number of people with whom one can maintain stable social relationships

   C.   The primary reason projects fail is due to communication mishaps, not for technical reasons

   D.   Organizational design systems mirror their own communication structure

9.   What is an optimal size for a Scrum team?

   A.   No more than 5 people

   B.   5–9 people

   C.   10–15

   D.   More than 15 people

10. What is the purpose of Kanban?

    A. To remove bottlenecks every step of the way, visualizing any bottleneck in the flow

    B. To deliver faster than in Scrum

    C. To attract more students next year to this course

    D. To promote itself in order to move all Agile teams to Kanban over five years

Answer key: 1-B, 2-D, 3-C, 4-A, 5-C, 6-B, 7-C, 8-D, 9-B, 10-A

Chapter 7
Self-Review Quiz

1. Which one is not a planning horizon in Agile?

    A. Short term

    B. Near term

    C. Medium term

    D. Long term

2. Which one is the correct set of categories in the Johari matrix?

    A. Known and unknown events

    B. Known knowns and unknown unknowns

    C. Known events, unknown events, predictable events, and unpredictable events

    D. Known knowns, known unknowns, unknown knowns, and unknown unknowns

3. What is the unit of estimating effort in Agile?

    A. Day

    B. Hour

    C. Story point

    D. Effort point

4. Which is an important prerequisite for Sprint planning?

    A. Product backlog refinement

    B. User acceptance testing

    C. Team Retrospective

    D. Sponsor approval based on the Definition of Ready

5. Who facilitates Sprint planning?

    A. Development team

    B. Product Owner

    C. Scrum Master

    D. No one – the team self-organizes for Sprint planning

6. What is a product roadmap?

    A. A list of milestones

    B. A plan of action that aligns the organization around product goals and how they will be achieved

    C. Customer expectations for product delivery

    D. A product delivery calendar outlining all tasks and activities

7. Which metaphor is used to show multiple concurrent levels of planning in Agile?

    A. Parent-child hierarchical relationship

    B. Tree structure

    C. Planning onion

    D. Customer-vendor interaction

8. Who provides estimations during Sprint planning?

    A. Everyone in the meeting

    B. Product Owner

    C. Scrum Master

    D. Development team

9. What happens if a team has a velocity of 16 and then planned their Sprint up to 15 points already and the next item on their backlog is estimated at three story points?

   A. The team takes in the next item hoping to complete it within the Sprint

   B. The team takes the next item in the backlog that is estimated at one story point

   C. The team stops their planning

   D. The team comes up with an idea of a small enhancement they can complete in the remaining time

10. Why is incremental planning narrowing the cone of uncertainty in every iteration?

    A. Planning for shorter intervals is more accurate

    B. At the end of each iteration, the roadmap can be adjusted based on customer feedback

    C. Based on the outcome of each iteration, planning can be revisited based on the outcome

    D. All of the above

Answer key: 1-B, 2-D, 3-C, 4-A, 5-C, 6-B, 7-C, 8-D, 9-B, 10-D

Chapter 8
Self-Review Quiz

1. What is the difference between incremental and iterative delivery?

   A. There is no difference

   B. Incremental means adding features one by one, while iterative means gradually building up functionality for each feature

   C. Incremental means adding more users, while iterative means adding more functionality

   D. Iterative means integration software, while incremental means that the product backlog is defined top to bottom as a continuous effort

2. What is release planning in Agile?

   A. Planning for the dates when software is going to be released to customers

   B. Short-term planning for the releases that are scheduled once per Sprint

   C. Planning when to release software from the production environment to the customers

   D. Longer-term (usually one quarter and longer) planning that enabled delivery teams to answer the questions when specific features or new products are going to be delivered, or released, to the customer

3. What is true about the product roadmap?

   A. A product roadmap is a shared source of reference for a product that outlines the vision, direction, priorities, and feature delivery of a product over time

   B. Multiple Agile teams may share a single product roadmap if they work on the same product

   C. Both A and B

   D. Neither A nor B

4. What does RAG reporting status stand for?

   A. Red, Amber, Green

   B. Role, Analysis, Goal

   C. Retrospective, Action, Goal

   D. Role, Assumption, Goal

5. What are vanity metrics?

   A. Inaccurate metrics

   B. Inflated metrics

   C. Useless metrics, which are not informative and do not provide any value

   D. There is no such term in Agile

6. What is a lead time in Kanban?

   A. The total amount of time a task spends from the start of work to delivery in the system

   B. The total amount of time a task spends from order to delivery in the system

   C. The time required to lead a roadmapping session

   D. The amount of time for a leader to present their ideas

7. Which framework recommends burndown charts to measure team progress within a Sprint?

   A. Kanban

   B. Waterfall

   C. Scrum

   D. XP (extreme programming)

8. What is a Retrospective?

   A. An artifact in Kanban

   B. A process in Scrum to generate high-quality code

   C. A team that is responsible for continuous improvement

   D. A Scrum event where team members prioritize areas of improvement, analyze root causes, and agree on a small number of action items that they want to commit to as a team during the upcoming Sprint

9. Which one is not a standard step of a Retrospective?

   A. Set the stage

   B. Assign action items

   C. Gather data

   D. Close the Retrospective

10. What are the phases of the product life cycle?

    A. Development, introduction, growth, maturity, and decline

    B. Development, growth, maturity, and decline

    C. Development and design, introduction, growth, and maintenance

    D. Design and development, growth, delivery, maintenance, and decline

Answer key: 1-B, 2-D, 3-C, 4-A, 5-C, 6-B, 7-C, 8-D, 9-B, 10-A

Chapter 9
Self-Review Quiz

1. True or false: Agile is specific to IT.

    A. True

    B. False

2. Finish the sentence: the concept of extending Agile implementation beyond IT and engaging the whole organization to be able to quickly and flexibly respond to customer and market needs is known as_____.

    A. Scrum

    B. Kanban

    C. Business agility

    D. Value stream mapping

3. In the Moonpig case study, the teams are referred to as "cross-functional" because ...

    A. Each of the teams contained product function, marketing function, creative function, and engineering function

    B. The teams work on different product functionality

    C. The teams collaborate with functional managers

    D. The features that teams developed addressed multiple product functions

4. Why is the traditional performance review not applicable in an Agile company?

   A. Because it focuses on individuals rather than teams

   B. Because it promotes silos rather than value delivery

   C. Because it does not reflect the collaborative nature of an Agile mindset

   D. All of the above

5. True or false: in Agile, budget estimations are usually done bottom-up.

   A. True

   B. False

6. What are the two major parameters influencing Agile budget management?

   A. Stable dedicated Agile teams and value delivery

   B. Customer needs and timeboxed iterations

   C. Stable dedicated Agile teams and timeboxed iterations

   D. Product backlog and estimations

7. What is the principle of beyond budgeting?

   A. This approach aligns additional budget with Agile teams

   B. The Beyond Budgeting framework considers cost management obsolete

   C. This approach relies on team composition and capacity management

   D. This approach represents a new management philosophy that is more Agile and adaptable, aiming at eliminating bureaucracy and rigid control mechanisms, empowering people, and promoting transparency

8. Which built-in Agile mechanisms allow for transparency in risk management?

    A. Transparency via Kanban board, effective prioritization via product backlog, and daily alignment via Scrum meetings

    B. Budget management via beyond budgeting, procurement management via fixed cost contracts, and capacity management via bottom-up planning

    C. Backlog management via Sprint planning, product backlog prioritization, and team collaboration

    D. Risk management, budget management, and procurement management

9. Which of the traditional contracts is suitable for Agile procurement?

    A. Firm fixed price

    B. Target price

    C. Cost plus

    D. None of the above

Answer key: 1-B, 2-C, 3-A, 4-D, 5-B, 6-C, 7-D, 8-A, 9-D

Chapter 10
Self-Review Quiz

1. What does it mean to scale Agile?

    A. Increase the number of Agile teams

    B. Expand Agile to program, portfolio, or organizational level

    C. Train more people in Agile delivery

    D. Provide metrics to show the growth rate of Agile adoption

2. Which Agile framework uses Lean portfolio management to scale Agility?

    A. LeSS

    B. DAD

    C. SAFe

    D. Nexus

3. Which framework is primarily applied to three to nine Scrum teams that are working in a common development environment?

    A.   LeSS

    B.   DAD

    C.   SAFe

    D.   Nexus

4. What is a Squad in Spotify model similar to?

    A.   A division

    B.   A Scrum team

    C.   A community of practice

    D.   A group reporting to a single manager

5. Which is NOT one of the SAFe principles?

    A.   Take an economic view

    B.   Apply systems thinking

    C.   Assume variability; preserve options

    D.   Create Agile Release Trains (ARTs) for cross-functional teams

6. Which Agile scaling framework advocates for the "Shu-ha-ri" approach?

    A.   DAD

    B.   Scrum@Scale

    C.   SAFe

    D.   Spotify Scaling Model

7. Which framework introduces two cycles, Scrum Master Cycle and the Product Owner Cycle?

    A.   LeSS

    B.   Scrum@Scale

    C.   SAFe

    D.   Spotify Scaling Model

8. Which is the most popular scaled Agile framework?

    A.   Nexus

    B.   Scrum@Scale

    C.   SAFe

    D.   LeSS

9. Which is NOT a step in John Kotter's change management model?

    A.   Create a sense of urgency

    B.   Launch Communities of Practice

    C.   Sustain acceleration

    D.   Generate short-term wins

10. Which step of the John Kotter model is addressed by launching multiple pilots within an organization?

    A.   Enable action by removing barriers

    B.   Generate short-term wins

    C.   Sustain acceleration

    D.   Institute change

Answer key: 1-B, 2-C, 3-D, 4-B, 5-D, 6-A, 7-B, 8-C, 9-B, 10-B

Videos, Books, and Online Sources for In-Depth Learning

Chapter 1

References

[1] Gartner Press Release. Gartner Survey Finds that 45% of Product Launches Are Delayed by at Least One Month. September 9, 2019

© Mariya Breyter 2022
M. Breyter, *Agile Product and Project Management*,
https://doi.org/10.1007/978-1-4842-8200-7

[2] George Castellion & Stephen K. Markham. Myths About New Product Failure Rates. Journal of Product Innovation & Management, 2013, pp. 976-979

[3] Charles Duhigg. Smarter Faster Better: The Transformative Power of Real Productivity. Random House. March 7, 2017

[4] Mary Poppendieck, Tom Poppendieck. Lean Software Development: An Agile Toolkit. Addison Wesley, 2003

[5] Y.H. Kwak, Brief history of project management, 2003

[6] Scaled Agile customer stories. `https://scaledagile.com/insights-customer-stories/`, as retrieved on March 13, 2022

Videos, Books, and Online Sources for In-Depth Learning

(1) Fred Brooks. The Mythical Man-Month: Essays on Software Engineering. Addison-Wesley, 1975

(2) James P. Womack, Daniel Roos, Daniel T. Jones. The Machine That Changed the World. Free Press, April 1990

(3) Eliyahu M. Goldratt. The Goal: A Process of Ongoing Improvement, 1984

(4) Agile Manifesto, 2001. `https://Agilemanifesto.org`

(5) Project Management Body of Knowledge by Project Management Institute and Software Extension to the PMBOK® by Project Management Institute (latest edition)

Chapter 2

References

[1] John Kotter. Leading Change: Why Transformation Efforts Fail. Harvard Business Review, 1995

[2] Southwest Airlines: Purpose, Vision, and The SouthWest Way. `http://investors.southwest.com/our-company/purpose-vision-and-the-southwest-way` as retrieved on August 18, 2020

[3] Peter Drucker. The Practice of Management. Harper & Row, 1954

[4] Gene Kim, Jez Humble, Nicole Forsgren. Accelerate: The Science of Lean Software and DevOps: Building and Scaling High Performing Technology Organizations. IT Revolution, 2018

Videos, Books, and Online Sources
for In-Depth Learning

(1) Simon Sinek. Start with Why: How Great Leaders Inspire Everyone to Take Action. Penguin Group, 2009

(2) Geoffrey Moore. Crossing the Chasm: Marketing and Selling High-Tech Products to Mainstream Customers. HarperCollins, 1991

(3) John Doerr. Measure What Matters: How Google, Bono, and the Gates Foundation Rock the World with OKRs. Penguin Random House, 2018

(4) Christina Wodtke. Radical Focus: Achieving Your Most Important Goals with Objectives and Key Results. 2014

(5) Why the secret to success is setting the right goals | John Doerr. https://www.youtube.com/watch?v=L4N1q4RNi9I

(6) Paul R. Niven, Ben Lamorte. Objectives and Key Results: Driving Focus, Alignment, and Engagement with OKRs. Wiley, 2016

Chapter 3
References

[1] Clayton M. Christensen, Taddy Hall, Karen Dillon, David S. Duncan. Know Your Customers' "Jobs to Be Done." Harvard Business Review, September 2016

[2] Peter Drucker. Managing for Results. First edition: 1964

[3] Tony Ulwick. Jobs-to-be-Done Case Study: Beware of Lead Users. August 4, 2017. https://jobs-to-be-done.com/jtbd-case-study-beware-of-lead-users-1c25329e63f5 as retrieved on August 20, 2020

[4] Alan Cooper. The Inmates are Running the Asylum: Why High-Tech Products Drive Us Crazy and How to Restore the Sanity". 2004, p. 123

[5] Dave Grey, James Macanufo, Sunni Brown. Gamestorming: A Playbook for Innovators, Rulebreakers, and Changemakers. O'Reilley, August 10, 2010

[6] Alex Osterwalder, Yves Pigneur. Business Model Generation: A Handbook for Visionaries, Game Changers, and Challengers. Thesis, 2010

Videos, Books, and Online Sources for In-Depth Learning

(1) Prof. Clayton Christensen. Jobs-to-Be-Done. March 13, 2017. www.youtube.com/watch?v=Q63PZR7mG70 as retrieved on August 20, 2020

(2) Dave Gray. Updated Empathy Map Canvas. Medium, July 15, 2017. https://medium.com/the-xplane-collection/updated-empathy-map-canvas-46df22df3c8a as retrieved on August 21, 2020

(3) Geoffrey Moore. Crossing the Chasm: Marketing and Selling Disruptive Products to Mainstream Customers. HarperBusiness Essentials, 1991. Recommended: 3rd edition, 2014

(4) Jeff Gothelf, Josh Seiden. Lean UX. Applying Lean Principles to Improve User Experience. O'Reilly, 2013, pp. 59–71

(5) Colin Bryar, Bill Carr. Working Backwards: Insights, Stories, and Secrets from Inside Amazon. St. Martin's Publishing Group, February, 2021

Chapter 4

References

[1] Eric Ries. The Lean Startup: How Today's Entrepreneurs Use Continuous Innovation to Create Radically Successful Businesses. Crown Business, New York, 2011

[2] Steve Blank. Why the Lean Start-Up Changes Everything. Harvard Business Review, May 2013

[3] Leander Kahney, Jony Ive: The Genius Behind Apple's Greatest Products. Penguin Group, November 14, 2013

[4] Jim Johnson, Chairman of The Standish Group, Keynote "ROI, It's Your Job." Third International Conference on Extreme Programming, Alghero, Italy, May 26–29, 2002

[5] Charles Arthur. Amazon has Sold No More than 35,000 Fire Phones, Data Suggests. The Guardian, August 26, 2014

[6] Eric Schonfeld. Grockit Gets a $7 Million Venture Infusion and Launches Video Q&A Site Grockit Answers. TechCrunch, October 17, 2011. https://techcrunch.com/2011/10/17/grockit-7-million-answers/ as retrieved on May 17, 2020

[7] Vince Barabba. The Decision Loom: A Design for Interactive Decision-Making in Organizations. Triarchy Press, 2011

[8] Jay Yarow. Jeff Bezos with a Super Awesome Explanation of Why He's Not Scared of Failure at Amazon. Business Insider, June 7, 2011. www.businessinsider.com/jeff-bezos-on-failure-2011-6 as retrieved on May 17, 2020

[9] Brad Stone. Jeff Bezos and the Age of Amazon. Little, Brown, and Company, October 2013, pp. 182–183

[10] MG Siegler. A Pivotal Pivot. TechCrunch, November 8, 2010. https://techcrunch.com/2010/11/08/instagram-a-pivotal-pivot/ as retrieved on May 17, 2020

[11] David Travis. The 7 Deadly Sins of User Research. December 1. 2014. www.youtube.com/watch?v=sS81W1xHuVw

[12] Jake Knapp with John Zeratsky and Braden Kowitz. Sprint. How to Solve Big Problems and Test New Ideas in Just Five Days. Simon & Schuster, 2016, pp. 228–229

[13] Jeff Gothelf, Josh Seiden. Lean UX. Applying Lean Principles to Improve User Experience. O'Reilly, 2013, pp. 59–71

Videos, Books, and Online Sources for In-Depth Learning

(1) Eric Ries. The Lean Startup: How Today's Entrepreneurs Use Continuous Innovation to Create Radically Successful Businesses. Crown Business, New York, 2011

(2) Steve Blank. Why the Lean Start-Up Changes Everything. Harvard Business Review, May 2013

(3) Tomer Sharon. Validating Product Ideas through Lean User Research. Rosenfeld Media, 2016

(4) Jeff Gothelf, Josh Seiden. Lean UX. Applying Lean Principles to Improve User Experience. O'Reilly, 2013

(5) Jake Knapp with John Zeratsky and Braden Kowitz. Sprint. How to Solve Big Problems and Test New Ideas in Just Five Days. Simon & Schuster, 2016

Chapter 5
References

[1] IEEE Standard 29148-2018 - ISO/IEC/IEEE International Standard — Systems and software engineering — Life cycle processes — Requirements engineering, 2018

[2] A Guide to the Project Management Body of Knowledge (PMBOK® Guide), Sixth Edition. Project Management Institute, 2017

[3] Software Engineering Body of Knowledge (SWEBOK Guide). IEEE, 2016

[3a] Jacob Bell. Alternatives to Object-Oriented Programming. November 2019. https://medium.com/@Jacob_Bell/alternatives-to-object-oriented-programming-13b28a12492 as retrieved on August 23, 2020

[4] Ron Jeffries. Essential XP: Card, Conversation, Confirmation. August 30, 2001. https://ronjeffries.com/xprog/articles/expcardconversationconfirmation/ as retrieved on August 23, 2020

[5] Agile Alliance Glossary. Product Backlog. www.Agilealliance.org/glossary/backlog as retrieved on August 23, 2020

[6] Jeff Patton. Blog. www.jpattonassociates.com/user-story-mapping/ as retrieved on August 24, 2020

Videos, Books, and Online Sources for In-Depth Learning

(1) UML Use Case Diagram Examples. www.uml-diagrams.org/examples/online-shopping-use-case-diagram-example.html?context=uc-examples as retrieved on August 23, 2020

(2) Henrik Kniberg. ATDD from the Trenches. Info!, October 17, 2013. www.infoq.com/articles/atdd-from-the-trenches/ as retrieved on August 23, 2020

(3) Jeff Patton. User Story Mapping: Discover the Whole Story, Build the Right Product. O'Reilly, 2014

(4) Jeff Patton. Story Essentials. www.jpattonassociates.com/wp-content/uploads/2015/03/story_essentials_quickref.pdf as retrieved on August 24, 2020

(5) Mike Cohn. User Stories Applied: For Agile Software Development. Addison-Wesley, 2004

Chapter 6
References

[1] Software Extension to PMBOK Guide Fifth Edition. Project Management Institute, 2013, p. 13

[2] Bruce Tuckman. Developmental Sequence in Small Groups. *Psychological Bulletin, 63*(6), 384–399. https://doi.org/10.1037/h0022100

[3] Gil Broza. Agile Mindset: Making Agile Processes Work. 3P Vantage Media, 2015

[4] Robert K. Greenleaf. Servant Leadership: A Journey into the Nature of Legitimate Power & Greatness. 1977

[5] Agile Manifesto. www.Agilemanifesto.org

[6] 14th State of Agile Report. Published by Digital.ai 2020, p. 19

[7] 14th State of Agile Report. Published by Digital.ai 2020, p. 10

[8] Scrum Guide. www.Scrumguides.org/. Licensed under the Attribution Share-Alike license of Creative Commons, accessible at http://creativecommons.org/licenses/by-sa/4.0/legal code. The latest revision was done in 2020. Please note that the information in this chapter reflects some of the prior version concepts.

[9] Eliyahu M. Goldratt, Jeff Cox. The Goal: A Process of Ongoing Improvement. First edition, North River Press, 1984

[10] Kent Beck. Extreme Programming Explained. Second Edition. Personal Education, 2005

[11] Melvin E. Conway. How do Committees Invent? Datamation, April 1968

[12] Matthew Skelton, Manual Pais. Team Topologies. IT Revolution, 2019

[13] Marty Cagan. Inspired: How to Create Tech Products Customers Love. John Wiley & Sons, 2017

[14] Richard L. Brandt. Birth of a Salesman. The Wall Street Journal, October 15, 2011

[15] Lyssa Adkins. Coaching Agile Teams: A Companion for ScrumMasters, Agile Coaches, and Project Managers in Transition. Addison-Wesley, 2010

Videos, Books, and Online Sources for In-Depth Learning

(1) Agile Practice Guide published by Project Management Institute and Agile Alliance, 2017

(2) Agile Manifesto. www.Agilemanifesto.org

(3) Scrum Guide. www.Scrumguides.org/

(4) Jeff Sutherland. Scrum: The Art of Doing Twice the Work in Half the Time. Crown Business, 2014

(5) Donald G. Reinertsen. The Principles of Product Development Flow: Second Generation Lean Product Development. Celeritas Publishing, 2009

(6) Gene Kim, Kevin Behr, George Spafford. The Phoenix Project: A Novel about IT, DevOps, and Helping Your Business Win. IT Revolution, 2013

(7) David J. Anderson. Kanban: Successful Evolutionary Change for Your Technology Business. Blue Hole Press, 2010

(8) How Spotify Balances Employee Autonomy and Accountability. Harvard Business Review, February 2017

(9) Henrik Kniberg, Anders Ivarsson. Scaling Agile @ Spotify with Tribes, Squads, Chapters, and Guilds. Whitepaper. October 2013. https://blog.crisp.se/wp-content/uploads/2012/11/SpotifyScaling.pdf as retrieved on September 5, 2020

(10) Michael Spayd. The Tao of Scrum. April 8, 2010. http://collectiveedgecoaching.com/2010/04/the-tao-of-Scrum-complete/ as retrieved on September 9, 2020

(11) Douglas Talbot. Product Owner Is a Bad Idea. InfoQ, September 7, 2020.

www.infoq.com/news/2020/09/product-owner-good-bad-complex/ as retrieved on September 9, 2020

Chapter 7
References

[1] Project Management Institute. PMI's Pulse of the Profession: 10th Global Project Management Survey. PMI, 2019.

[2] Luft, J.; Ingham, H. The Johari window, a graphic model of interpersonal awareness. Proceedings of the Western Training Laboratory in Group Development. University of California, Los Angeles, 1955

[3] Donald Rumsfeld. U.S. Secretary of Defense. News briefing, February 12, 2002

[4] Pradeep Ittycheria, Is Agile Failing Long-Term Planning, Forbes Technology, October 10, 2019, as retrieved on November 3, 2020. www.forbes.com/sites/forbestechcouncil/2019/10/10/is-Agile-failing-long-term-planning/?sh=764b4270619f

Videos, Books, and Online Sources for In-Depth Learning:

(1) Agile Practice Guide published by Project Management Institute and Agile Alliance, 2017

(2) Scaled Agile Framework. PI Planning: www.scaledAgileframework.com/pi-planning/ as retrieved on November 3, 2020

(3) Mike Cohn. Agile Estimating and Planning. Prentice Hall, November 2005

(4) PI (Program Increment) planning in Scaled Agile Framework (SAFe). www.scaledAgileframework.com/pi-planning/ as retrieved on November 5, 2020

Chapter 8
References

[1] Jeff Patton. I don't Know What I Want, But I Know How to Get It. www.jpattonassociates.com/dont_know_what_i_want/   as retrieved on 1/3/2021

[2] iPhone 13: All of the rumors we've heard about Apple's upcoming 2021 iPhones so far. www.macrumors.com/roundup/iphone-13 by MacRumors Staff, December 18, 2020, as retrieved on January 3, 2021

[3] CNBC: Here's everything Apply Just Announced. www.cnbc.com/2020/09/15/apple-event-live-updates.html by Kif Leswing, Jessica Bursztynsky, Todd Haselton, September 16, 2020, as retrieved on January 3, 2021

[4] Top Roadmap Software. www.getapp.com/p/sem/product-roadmap-software as retrieved on January 4, 2021

[5] John Bonini. The 10 Most-Tracked Google Analytics Metrics. https://databox.com/the-most-tracked-google-analytics-metrics as retrieved on April 25, 2021

[6] Kanban Metrics. www.digite.com/Kanban/Kanban-metrics/ as retrieved on April 25, 2021

[7] David Anderson. Kanban: Successful Evolutionary Change for Your Technology Business. Blue Hole Press, April 2010

[8] Accelerate Building Digital Talent and Enabling Enterprise Agility. https://agilityhealthradar.com/

[9] Katrin Morales, Sarah Goff-Dupont. How to run a remote Retrospective and have fun doing it. www.atlassian.com/blog/teamwork/run-Retrospective-distributed-team-fun as retrieved on April 25, 2021

[10] Diana Larsen, Esther Derby, Ken Schwaber. Agile Retrospectives: Making Good Teams Great. The Pragmatic Bookshelf, August 2006

Videos, Books, and Online Sources for In-Depth Learning

(1) The Amazon Roadmap: How Innovative Brands are Reinventing the Path to Market by Betsy McGinn, Philip Segal, March 7, 2019

(2) The ART of Avoiding a Train Wreck: Practical Tips and Tricks for Launching and Operating SAFe Agile Release Trains by Em Campbell-Pretty, Adrienne L. Wilson et al., Sep 28, 2019

(3) Strategize Product Strategy and Product Roadmap Practices for the Digital Age by Roman Pichler. Pichler Consulting, 2016

Chapter 9
References

[1] Business Agility Institute. https://businessagility. institute/about-us as retrieved on 5/2/2021

[2] The Business Agility Reports 2020 and 2021 by the Business Agility Institute. https://api.businessagility.institute/storage/ files/download-research/bai-business-agility-report-2020c.pdf and https://api.businessagility. institute/storage/files/download-research/BAI-Business-Agility-Report-2021.pdf as retrieved on January 8, 2022. Materials and graphics are licensed under a Creative Commons Attribution-ShareAlike 4.0 International License and allowed for sharing.

[3] SolutionsIQ (acquired by Accenture) What is Business Agility? April 1, 2019. www.solutionsiq.com/resource/blog-post/ what-is-business-agility/ as retrieved on 5/2/2021

[4] Amanda Colpoys. Case Study: Adopting Business Agility at Moonpig. www.Agilebusiness.org/page/Resource_ casestudy_Moonpig as retrieved on 5/2/2021

[5] Daniel Pink Drive: The Surprising Truth About What Motivates Us. Canongate Books Ltd, 2010

[6] Jurgen Appelo. Managing for Happiness: Games, Tools, and Practices to Motivate Any Team. John Wiley and Sons, 2016

[7] Mariya Breyter, Darshana Z. Narayanan. Lean Enterprise: Using Agile and Lean Practices to Transform Organizations. Workplace Solutions Review, December 2017

[8] Dana Pylayeva. Self-selection for Resilience and Better Culture. InfoQ blog, April 2019. www.infoq.com/presentations/teams-self-selection/ as retrieved on May 3, 2021

[9] David Green. Diane Gherson on How IBM is Reinventing HR with AI and People Analytics. LinkedIn, September 8, 2020. www. linkedin.com/pulse/diane-gherson-how-ibm-reinventing-hr-ai-people-analytics-david-green/ as retrieved on May 3, 2021

[10] Encyclopedia Britannica. Frederick W. Taylor. www.britannica. com/biography/Frederick-W-Taylor as retrieved on May 3, 2021

[11] Wouter Aghina, Karin Ahlback, Aaron De Smet, Gerald Lackey, Michael Lurie, Monica Murarka, and Christopher Handscomb. The five trademarks of Agile organizations. McKinsey & Company. January 22, 2018. www.mckinsey.com/business-functions/organization/our-insights/the-five-trademarks-of-Agile-organizations as retrieved on May 3, 2021

[12] Brian J. Robertson. Holacracy: The New Management System for a Rapidly Changing World. Henry Holt and Company, March 2015

[13] Holacracy.org website. www.holacracy.org/explore/why-practice-holacracy as retrieved on May 4, 2021

[14] Agile in Sales, website by Marina Alex. http://Agileinsales.org/ as retrieved on May 4, 2021

[15] Richard Sheridan. Joy, Inc.: How We Built a Workplace People Love. Penguin Group, January 2015

[16] A Guide to the Project Management Body of Knowledge. PMBOK Guide, Sixth Edition. Project Management Institute, 2017

[17] Jeremy Hope, Robin Fraser. Beyond Budgeting: How Managers Can Break Free from the Annual Performance Trap. Harvard Business School Press, 2003

[18] Michele Sliger, Stacia Broderick. The Software Project Manager's Bridge to Agility. Addison-Wesley, 2008

Videos, Books, and Online Sources for In-Depth Learning

(1) Peter Cappelli and Anna Tavis. HR Goes Agile: Agile isn't just for tech anymore. HBR Magazine, March–April 2018

(2) Agilest. Agile Budgeting: How much will it cost? www.Agilest.org/Agile-project-management/budgeting/ as retrieved on 5/9/2021

(3) Rick Yvanovich. What Is Beyond Budgeting and How Is It Reinventing Management? July 23, 2019. https://blog.trginternational.com/what-is-beyond-budgeting as retrieved on 5/9/2021

(4) Managing Risk in an Agile Organization. www.protiviti.com/US-en/insights/managing-risk-Agile-organization as retrieved on 5/9/2021

(5) Alberto S. Silveira Jr. Building and Managing High-Performance Distributed Teams: Navigating the Future of Work. Apress, 2021

Chapter 10
References

[1] SAFe: Framework for Scaling Agile. Source: www.scaledAgile. com/enterprise-solutions/what-is-safe/ as retrieved on May 15, 2021

[2] SAFe Customer Stories: how some of the world's most successful brands are using SAFe. https://less.works/case-studies/index as retrieved on May 15, 2021

[3] LeSS Case Studies. https://less.works/case-studies/index as retrieved on May 15, 2021

[4] Craig Larman. Agile and Iterative Development: A Manager's Guide 1st Edition. Addison Wesley, 2004

[5] Success Story: Disciplined Agile Changes Everything. www.pmi. org/disciplined-Agile as retrieved on May 15. 2021

[6] Scott Ambler and Mark Lines. Disciplined Agile Delivery: A Practitioner's Guide to Agile Software Delivery in the Enterprise, 1st Edition. IBM Press/Pearson plc, 2012

[7] Why Disciplined Agile Delivery (DAD)? www.pmi.org/ disciplined-Agile/process/introduction-to-dad/why-dad-introduction as retrieved on May 15, 2021

[8] Streamline How You Work with the Industry-Leading Process-Decision Toolkit. www.pmi.org/disciplined-Agile as retrieved on May 15, 2021

[9] Henrik Kniberg & Anders Ivarsson. Scaling Agile @Spotify with Tribes, Squads, Chapters & Guilds. October 2012. https://blog. crisp.se/wp-content/uploads/2012/11/SpotifyScaling. pdf as retrieved on May 15, 2021

[10] 14th Annual State of Agile Report. www.collab.net/news/ press/14th-annual-state-Agile-report-shows-60-respondents-have-increased-speed-market-and-55   as retrieved on May 15. 2021

[11] SAFe 5.1 Big Picture. www.scaledAgileframework.com/safe-for-Lean-enterprises/ as of May 15, 2015. © Scaled Agile, Inc.

[12] The Nexus Framework by Scrum.org for Scaling Agile, October 2, 2018. https://kendis-io.medium.com/the-nexus-framework-by-Scrum-org-for-scaling-Agile-c4a82b94bbb8# as retrieved on May 15, 2021

[13] Solutions for Agile Governance in the Enterprise (SAGE^{SM}). www.cprime.com/sage/ as retrieved on May 15, 2021

[14] Anthony Mersino. Beyond SAFe – Trends in Agile Scaling Approaches 2020. Vitality Chicago, June 30, 2020. https://vitalitychicago.com/blog/beyond-safe-trends-in-Agile-scaling-approaches-2020/ as retrieved on May 15, 2021

[15] Scrum Alliance. The Definitive Guide to Scrum@Scale: Scaling that Works. www.Scrumatscale.com/wp-content/uploads/2020/12/official-Scrum-at-scale-guide.pdf as retrieved on May 15, 2021

[16] The Scrum @ Scale ® Guide. www.Scrumatscale.com/Scrum-at-scale-guide-online/#People-and-Organizations as retrieved on May 15, 2021

[17] Kurt Bittner, Patricia Kong, Eric Naiburg, Dave West. The Nexus Framework for Scaling Scrum: Continuously Delivering an Integrated Product with Multiple Scrum Teams. 1st Edition. The Professional Scrum Series, Scrum.org. Prentice Hall, 2018

[18] Nexus Guide. www.Scrum.org/resources/online-nexus-guide as retrieved on May 15, 2021

[19] Atlassian Agile Coaching blog. Agile at Scale: Movin' on up: scaling Agile in large organizations. www.atlassian.com/Agile/Agile-at-scale#:~:text=Agile%20at%20scale%20is%20the,other%20layers%20of%20the%20organization as retrieved on May 15, 2021

[20] John Kotter. The 8-step process for leading change. www.kotterinc.com/8-steps-process-for-leading-change/ as retrieved on May 15, 2021

Videos, Books, and Online Sources for In-Depth Learning

(1) Dean Leffingwell. What is SAFe? www.youtube.com/watch?v=0r4GIFPTFQs as retrieved on May 15, 2021

G

Glossary

A

Acceptance criteria are product characteristics specified in the user story or task that need to be satisfied before they are accepted by the Product Owner or directly by the customer. Acceptance criteria are used as standards to measure and compare the characteristics of the final product with specified parameters.

Agile is a group of iterative and incremental methods originating in software development. It encourages flexibility and speed in responding to change. Agile delivery values and principles are defined in the Agile Manifesto.

Agile Manifesto is a set of values and principles defining Agile software development.

Agile Product Delivery is a customer-centric approach to defining, building, and releasing a continuous flow of valuable products and services to the customer.

Agile Release Train (ART) in Scaled Agile Framework (SAFe) is a long-lived team of Agile teams, which, along with other stakeholders, incrementally develops, delivers, and, where applicable, operates one or more solutions in a value stream.

Agile Release Train (ART) in Scaled Agile Framework (SAFe) consists of the existing code, components, and technical infrastructure needed to implement near-term features without excessive redesign and delay.

M. Breyter, *Agile Product and Project Management*,
https://doi.org/10.1007/978-1-4842-8200-7

B

Backlog (see product backlog).

Built-in quality practices originate in Lean manufacturing. These proactive quality practices ensure that the solution meets quality expectations upfront.

Burndown chart is a graphical representation of the amount of work completed vs. the elapsed time period. Burndown charts are used to estimate the time needed to complete the project. The vertical axis represents the planned work, and the horizontal axis represents the time. The general trend in the graph is to "burn down" to a zero where no work remains.

Business agility takes Agile outside of software development and refers to the ability to compete and thrive in the digital age by quickly responding to market changes and emerging opportunities with innovative, customer-centric, and digitally enabled business solutions.

C

Cadence is the approach to achieving commitment and reliability with a system. Sprints of regular duration establish a cadence for a development effort.

Certified Scrum Master (CSM) is the most popular and basic Scrum Master certification from Scrum Alliance, which is perfect for aspiring Scrum Masters.

Continuous delivery means delivering the product or a product feature to its users immediately after it is integrated and tested, without further manual steps.

Continuous improvement – Agile aims to continuously learn and apply lessons learned right away. There are multiple tools and techniques to enable continuous improvement in Agile, including Retrospectives, experience sharing sessions, and many others.

Cross-functional team - A team that has expertise from different fields, for example, designers, developers, and testers who have the skills required to complete the work end to end effectively and efficiently.

Customers are the ultimate beneficiaries of the value provided.

D

Daily Scrum (Daily Standup) is a 15-minute timeboxed Scrum event held each day for the Scrum team. In this meeting, the team plans to work for the next 24 hours. This optimizes team collaboration and performance by inspecting the work since the last Daily Scrum and forecasting upcoming Sprint work. The Daily Scrum is held at the same time and place each day to reduce complexity.

Definition of Done refers to the criteria of accepting work once it is completed within the required quality standards. These criteria are defined by the entire team in collaboration with the business stakeholders. This includes, by default, delivering potentially releasable software at the end of every iteration.

Definition of Ready refers to a shared understanding by the Product Owner and the Scrum Team regarding the level of description of the product backlog items introduced at Sprint planning.

Demo is an opportunity for a team to show their production-ready product to the customer for their feedback. A demo is part of a Sprint Review (see Sprint Review).

Design thinking is a customer-centric development process that creates desirable products that are profitable and sustainable over their life cycle

DevOps refers to technical practices as well as a mindset where software development, integration, automation, and deployment are done in collaboration by a group of people who plan, develop, deploy, and release software.

E

Epic is a feature represented by a collection of user stories. Epics are often used as placeholders for new ideas or for lower-priority features on the bottom of the backlog.

Estimation is a process of agreeing on a size measurement of the user stories and tasks in a product backlog. Estimation measurements may differ, most frequently being story points (see story point).

Extreme programming – see XP

F

Feature is a function or attribute of a software product or service. Features are large requirements delivering incremental value to the customer. Frequently, a feature is represented by one or multiple epics (see epic).

Fibonacci sequence is a sequence of numbers in which the next number is derived by the sum of the previous two (1, 2, 3, 5, 8, 13, etc.). Fibonacci sequence in Agile is frequently used for story point estimation.

Five levels of Agile planning include vision, roadmap, release, iteration (Sprint), and daily standup.

Flow is the continuous delivery of value to the customer.

Forecast is the selection of items from the product backlog the team deems feasible for implementation within a Sprint.

I

Increment is a Scrum artifact that defines the complete and valuable work produced by the team during a Sprint. The sum of all increments forms a product.

Impediment in Scrum is any blocker or challenge that prevents the team from performing their work as efficiently as possible. Impediments are usually announced during the Daily Scrum meeting (see Daily Scrum).

Inspect and adapt is a concept in Scrum that captures the idea of discovering emerging requirements over the course of development as well as ways to improve the overall performance of the team as part of the short ongoing feedback loop.

INVEST is an acronym introduced by Bill Wake that defines a simple set of rules used in creating high-quality user stories: independent, negotiable, valuable, estimable, small, and testable.

Iteration is a standard, fixed-length timebox, during which Agile team delivers incremental value in the form of working, tested software and systems. The recommended duration of this timebox is two weeks; however, one to four weeks is acceptable, as long as this duration is consistent.

K

Kanban is a method that originated from Lean manufacturing, which allows to manage knowledge work. Kanban provides techniques to visualize the work and how it moves through the workflow in order to effectively operate and deliver, including understanding and managing risks in delivering products and services to the customers. Using a task board ("Kanban board"), Kanban visually represents the state of work in process (WIP). It also constraints how much work can happen at any specific point in time (WIP limits).

L

Lean refers to a set of principles and practices that maximize customer value while minimizing waste and reducing time to market (TTM).

Lean startup is a business methodology designed to apply Lean manufacturing principles to delivering products and services.

M

Milestone – Milestones are used to track progress toward a specific goal or event.

Minimum viable product (MVP) is a version of a product with just enough features to be usable by early customers who can then provide feedback for future product development. A focus on releasing an MVP means that Agile teams can potentially avoid lengthy and unnecessary work before they receive customer feedback.

MoSCoW is a mnemonic describing a prioritization technique used in management, business analysis, project management, and software development to reach a common understanding with stakeholders on the importance they place on the delivery of each requirement. It stands for Must Have, Should Have, Could Have, and Won't Have this time.

N

Nonfunctional requirements (NFR) describe system attributes, such as security, reliability, scalability, and usability (also referred to as "-ilities"). They represent persistent qualities and constraints and usually are part of the Definition of Done (see Definition of Done).

P

Pair programming is a programming technique in which two programmers work together on a single system, part of XP practices (see XP). As studies have shown, pair programmers are more than twice as efficient as one single programmer.

Persona represents an archetypical user of a system, based on the knowledge about the actual users.

Planning Poker is an Agile estimation practice based on consensus-based sizing. It is used to estimate the effort or relative size of user stories by assigning story points to each user story (see story points).

Product refers to a collection of tangible and intangible features that are integrated and packaged into software releases that offer value to a customer or to a market.

Product backlog is a Scrum artifact that consists of a prioritized list of the work to be done in order to create, maintain, and sustain a product. Product backlog is owned and managed by the Product Owner.

Product backlog refinement is the activity in a Sprint through which the Product Owner and the Scrum Team add details to the product backlog.

Product Goal describes a future state of the product that can serve as a target for the Scrum team to plan against.

Product manager is a role that is responsible for the development of products for the customer. Product managers own the business strategy behind a product, specify its functional requirements, and generally manage the launch of features.

Product Owner is a role in Scrum accountable for maximizing the value of a product, primarily by incrementally managing and expressing business and functional expectations for a product to the team.

Product vision is a description of the essence of a product: what are the problems it is solving, for whom, and why now is the right time to build it.

Program increment in Scaled Agile Framework (SAFe) is a timebox during which an Agile Release Train (ART) delivers incremental value in the form of working, tested software and systems. PIs are typically 8–12 weeks long.

Program increment (PI) planning in Scaled Agile Framework (SAFe) is a cadence-based, face-to-face event that serves as the heartbeat of the Agile Release Train (ART) (see Agile Release Train), aligning all the teams on the ART to a shared mission and vision.

Q

Quality is the degree to which a set of inherent characteristics fulfill requirements (fit for purpose).

R

Release planning is a process in Lean manufacturing that has a goal of synchronizing the projected range of potential delivery dates in the future with tasks to be done today between delivery teams.

Release Train Engineer (RTE) in Scaled Agile Framework (SAFe) is a servant leader and coach for the Agile Release Train (ART). The RTE's major responsibilities are to facilitate the ART events and processes and assist the teams in delivering value.

Retrospective is the review and analysis done at the end of every Sprint. The aim is to continuously improve the performance of the Scrum team and adopt better practices.

Roadmap is an artifact that distills the product vision into a high-level plan of features delivered. The roadmap outlines product features that span multiple releases, frequently for one year or even longer.

S

Scaled Agile Framework (SAFe) is a set of organization and workflow patterns intended to guide enterprises in scaling Lean and Agile practices.

Scrum is a framework using an Agile mindset for developing, delivering, and sustaining customer-centric products and services, originally refined in 1995 by Ken Schwaber and Jeff Sutherland from work done by Hirotaka Takeuchi and Ikujiro Nonaka. Named after the SCRUM in rugby, this is the most recognized Agile framework based on team-based delivery within timeboxed iterations, called Sprints (see Sprint).

Scrum events (previously, Scrum Ceremonies) – Meetings in Scrum, such as Sprint planning, Daily Scrum, Sprint Review, or Sprint Retrospective. Each event in Scrum is a formal opportunity to inspect and adapt Scrum artifacts. Events are used in Scrum to create regularity and to minimize the need for meetings not defined in Scrum.

Scrum Master is a role in Scrum responsible for ensuring the team lives Agile values and principles and follows the processes and practices that the team agreed they would use. The responsibilities of this role include resolving impediments (see Impediment) and establishing an environment where the team can be effective.

Scrum of Scrums is a scaled Agile technique that offers a way to connect multiple teams who need to work together to deliver complex solutions. It helps teams develop and deliver complex products through transparency, inspection, and adaptation at scale.

Spike is a product backlog item that has the goal of providing clarity into delivering a user story via a timeboxed investigation and analysis.

Sprint is a short, timeboxed period when a Scrum team works to complete a set amount of work. Sprints are at the heartbeat of Scrum and Agile methodologies.

Sprint backlog is a list of tasks identified by the Scrum team to be completed during the Scrum Sprint.

Sprint planning is a Scrum event that starts the Sprint. During this event, the team defines what can be delivered in the Sprint and how this work will be achieved.

Sprint Review is an event in Scrum that takes place at the end of the Sprint and has a goal of gathering actionable feedback on what the Scrum team has completed. The Scrum team presents the results of their work to key stakeholders (see demo), and progress toward the Product Goal is discussed.

Stakeholders are people and organization units who frequently interface with the Product Owner, Scrum Master, and Scrum team to provide them with inputs and facilitate the creation of the product backlog.

Story points are units of measure for expressing an estimate of the overall effort required to fully implement a product backlog item, for example, a user story.

Subtask is the smallest unit of work to be tracked. Subtasking is a technique for Scrum team members committing to the parent user story or task to break their work down further and align on who will do it and how.

Sustainable pace refers to the pace at which a team works so that it produces a good flow of business value over an extended period of time without getting burned out.

T

Task (as opposed to user story – see user story) is an element of the product backlog that does not produce customer-facing value by itself. It can refer to design work, data analysis, or compliance review.

Team (also referred to as Scrum team or development team) is a group of individuals (typically between five and nine members) working together to deliver the required product increments.

Technical debt is a concept in software development that reflects the implied cost of additional rework caused by choosing an easy solution now instead of using a better approach that would take longer.

Test automation in software development is the use of software separate from the software being tested to control the execution of tests and the comparison of actual outcomes with predicted outcomes.

Test-Driven Development (TDD) is a software development process relying on software requirements being converted to test cases before the software is fully developed and tracking all software development by repeatedly testing the software against all test cases.

U

Unit testing is a software testing method by which individual units of source code – sets of one or more computer program modules together with associated control data, usage procedures, and operating procedures – are tested to determine whether they are fit for use.

User experience (UX) refers to the user experience while interacting with a product, system, or service. It includes user perceptions of utility, ease of use, and efficiency.

User experience design is the process design teams use to create products that provide meaningful and relevant experiences to users.

User story is an informal, natural language description of features of a software system. It is written from the perspective of a user of a system.

V

Vanity metric is a metric that is not informative or actionable.

Velocity measures how much work a team can complete in an iteration. Velocity is often measured in story points (see story point). Velocity may also measure tasks in hours or an equivalent unit. Velocity is used to measure the effort it will take a particular team to deliver future outcomes by extrapolating on the basis of its prior performance.

W

Work in process, or Work in progress (WIP) refers to any work that has not been completed but that has already incurred a capital cost to the organization. Any software that has been developed but not deployed to production can be considered a work in progress. Sometimes, the term "work in progress" is used with the same meaning.

Working software is fully integrated, tested, and ready to be shipped to customers or deployed into production.

X

XP (Extreme Programming) is a software development methodology intended to improve software quality and responsiveness to changing customer requirements by using an iterative and incremental approach. XP includes 12 development practices, such as Small Releases, On-site Customer, Sustainable Pace, Simple Design, Continuous Integration, Unit Testing, Coding Conventions, Refactoring Mercilessly, Test-Driven Development, System Metaphor, Collective Code Ownership, and Pair Programming.

Index

© Mariya Breyter 2022
M. Breyter, *Agile Product and Project Management*,
https://doi.org/10.1007/978-1-4842-8200-7

Printed in the United States
by Baker & Taylor Publisher Services